γινώσκω
Ginóskó

David Kuraya

Ginóskó
by David Kuraya
Copyright © David Kuraya, 2024

First edition
Published by Kuraya Creative Studios

All right reserved.

Dedication

For Curtis Kam, The Wizard of Waikiki

Contents

Opening Acts   1
   Foreword (1) Lance Pierce   2
   Foreword (2) Curtis Kam   4
   Introduction By David Kuraya   6

1: Commercial Card Magic from Maui   11
   Check Yo' Self   12
   Blackjack for Brother John   22
   High Five and a Handshake   29
   Asking the 8 Ball   33
   Nacho Card   38
   MIT Aces (Kuraya & Guastaferro)   44
   All Who WANDer   51
   Pentatonic   56
   Intermission: Schooled!   62

2: Behind The Bar   65
   The First One Under   67
   Post-it Crane   72
   Hot Swizzle Action   74
   Intermission: Coffee Talk   80

3: Coin Operated   83
   Finger Palm to Finger Palm Switch   84
   Beijing For Mere Mortals   89
   Rolling Unnest   104
   Shots Backfired   107

4: Cocktail Parties & Table Hopping   115
   Interruption Or Opportunity?   116
   Marked for the Nearsighted   118
   Winning the Tough Tables   121

5: Stand Up   127
   Beachcomber Opener   128
   What if I Actually Showed You?   131
   Banzai!   136
   Under Pressure   139
   Jimmy's Rings: My Family, My Home   145
   Roses in Spokane   149

6: Armchair Philosophizing **153**
   Painless Practice Through Flowstate   154
   Names: The Real Magic Words   157
   A Cure for the Common Cold Feet   159
   Intermission: Why Would Anyone?   164
   The Ginóskó Philosophy   167

7: Friends & Mentors **181**
   Dr. Ron Pyle   182
   Dr. Kainoa Harbottle   192
   Tom Dobrowolski   198
   Dr. Jason Fleming   202
   Nathan Coe Marsh   206
   Tony Cabral   212
   Lance Pierce   218
   Jack Carpenter   226
   Jade   234
   Ian Rowland   244

8: Warren & Annabelle's **249**
   Camelot   250
   John Shryock   255
   John George   267
   Chris Blackmore   283
   Dana Daniels   296
   Warren Gibson   309

And The Curtain Comes Down... **327**
   Hana Hou!   328
   Thanks & Acknowledgments   330

"My belief is that relationships are the most important experience in all of life."
— *Dr. Ron Pyle*

Opening Acts

*"Pay attention to the people you meet.
They just might change your life down the road."*

— *Sig Anderman
founder & CEO of Ellie Mae*

Foreword (1) Lance Pierce

This is what it's like having a conversation with David Kuraya: I say something and then I wait. Not long, just a brief moment, but in that short time I can tell he's fully absorbing what I said and processing it. He then responds with something thoughtful and usually pretty deep. Then I say something else, hoping to rise to his level, and we do it all over again.

Every time I talk with David, I feel like I learn something. It's often subtle, and I may have to look for it, but I don't think I've ever talked with anyone who was more involved and present than David is. It feels like he hears every syllable I say. Combine that with the fact that he's always respectful and the perfect gentleman (which I've never managed to be), and I have to say that simply being around him is something of a delight.

I've come to think that, in his own way, David may be a little bit of a genius. He has so many talents and learns so fast that it's actually mind-boggling. I've known quite a few magicians in my life. However, very few have progressed as rapidly and as competently as David, not just as a sleight-of-hand practitioner but also as a performer. I know that this hasn't just happened by accident. Far from it! David sought out every magical teacher he could reach and learned from them. He took care to study the best texts, associated himself with top entertainers and learned 'under fire', working in high-pressure environments.

He's the consummate student: hungry, humble, and eager. It's almost as if he knew from the get-go where he wanted to be and aimed right towards it, wasting absolutely no time and leaving others in the dust.

Now he's written a book. Normally, if someone had been into magic for as short a time as David and told me they were writing a book, I would have advised them to wait a while. I'd have suggested they maybe develop their experience, collect the best thoughts and ideas they can — always striving for excellence — so when they *do* finally write their book, they help as many people as possible. There's time. You don't need to write a book today.

But when David told me he had something in the works, my first thought was, "Great! Let's see what you have." Because it's David.

When I read the first draft, I was impressed by David's ideas and direction, particularly his focus on ginóskó: 'the understanding that comes from experience paired with intellectual study'. It's an important part of who David is and how he approaches life. Yes, it's a philosophical thing, and maybe not for everyone, but the value is there if you want it.

In this book are tricks, essays and interviews. Practice the tricks. Absorb the essays. Enjoy the interviews. Then realize that it's not the tricks that are important, or what's directly said in the essays or who's interviewed. Instead, consider the themes that run through the entire book: relating to audiences in a human and personal way; the quest for excellence; a passion for magic we can share with those of like mind; an understanding of magic that can never be described or taught but only experienced.

All these themes, and much more, are embedded in every page of this book — in the way the tricks are scripted, in the essays, and in between the lines of every interview. These things are often ineffable and won't always be immediately obvious to you. You may have to ferret them out a little — but trust me, they are there. There's no better encapsulation of who David is than the book you now hold.

I know David would like you to go out in the world and do great things. If he can be a small part of your journey through this book, he'd be absolutely proud to help. Perhaps you'll read this book and think some sections aren't particularly useful. But I believe the value is always there if you look for it.

— Lance Pierce

Foreword (2) Curtis Kam

Magic has seen a lot of good performers. We've also enjoyed quite a number of writers who could explain what good performers do. When we're really lucky, a good performer is *also* a good explainer. These talents converge only rarely and by accident. It's a problem in every field. In fact, it's often said that someone with natural talent who's never struggled to succeed will find teaching difficult.

This is a book by a strong performer who is also a great teacher, so there's hope. Granted, David isn't Tommy Wonder or Johnny Thompson — at least, not *yet*. Those guys came to us with a lifetime of thoughtful performances behind them and many productive years remaining. While David does perform for people who pay good money to see him, he's still at the start of his journey — or perhaps I should say he's near the *end* of the start. He has already achieved a great deal but I'm confident his greatest achievements still lie ahead.

In this book, you'll read about various aspects of David's work, such as his performances at Warren & Annabelle's, a unique purpose-built restaurant and theatre for magic shows in Lahaina on the island of Maui. Sadly, this amazing venue was lost to wildfires in the period just before this book's publication. David also talks about crazy corporate shows. Maui is a leading resort destination for corporations and celebrities of all sorts, and David has performed for the truly famous, the talented artists *behind* the truly famous and the truly famous-adjacent.

David has performed for huge crowds in odd places and for five VIPs sitting on a sofa, on the beach or in the dark. Heck, David and I once did strolling magic at a *funeral*. (I turned that gig down twice before David repeated something I once told him: "This will be worth it just for the story." This became a sort of mantra for us.)

As I said, your author is also a successful teacher. You'll hear it in his writing. He thinks about magic, what he's learned, and how to teach what he's learned. He talks to working pros and asks good questions. He listens and watches with one eye on his own understanding and the other on yours.

My highest hope for this book is that it's David's first. With any luck, others will come, and I'm happy to welcome you to this journey.

— Curtis Kam

The author (left) with Curtis Kam

Introduction By David Kuraya

Here's why this book is called γινώσκω (ghin-oce'-ko).

It all goes back to my kindergarten years. During recess, one of my classmates fell and scraped his knee on the playground. I had a Band-Aid, so I offered it to him between his sniffles. He didn't know how to use it so I showed him how to peel off the wrapper, remove the tabs and place it on his knee. He stopped crying and ran off. I realized that my classmate would know how to care for himself better in future because I had shown him how to use a Band-Aid.

Decades later, my fascination with sharing ideas and skills remains undimmed. Over the last twelve years, I've directed about 3,000 middle and high school band and chorus students in Hawaii's public schools. I've taught magic classes at Punahou School (Barack Obama's alma mater) as well as teaching Biblical Studies, Economics and American History at a Christian school with fewer than twenty students. No matter where or to whom, I love teaching.

My favorite word related to learning is the Greek word ginóskó (ghin-oce'-ko). Roughly translated, it means 'to know intimately'. It refers to personal knowledge gained through experiences and relationships rather than what you can get from books.

Every craft encourages students to achieve ginóskó and learn valuable lessons from it. All education majors study *theories* of teaching. However, only the *experience* of actually teaching a class exposes them to the joy, stress and responsibility that teaching involves. The strategies we learn as apprentices are especially memorable because they result from *experience* and *relationships*.

With a bit of research, anyone can give a lecture on music theory. However, only an experienced music teacher can adjust a beginner's posture and hand position in a way that will assist their long-term success. An enthusiastic teacher inspires their students to progress from reading notes and rhythms to refining their articulation, dynamics, musical phrasing and expression. Throughout the school year, that child and his band mates work together to learn the art of performance. Eventually, they experience the gratification that comes from 'killing it' in front of a live audience after months of incremental growth. The relationships within the team help each individual to grow and develop.

The experiential and relational development of a teacher or musician mirrors the development of a magician. Far from a solitary pursuit, music and magic are fundamentally social enterprises. We grow not only through self-study but by seeking out mentors, meeting like-minded friends and engaging with real people in performance. The two arts also share similar creative processes. We can use the same principles that apply to powerful music composition to construct magic effects.

Magicians and musicians are craftsmen. However, unlike sculptors or woodworkers, performance artists are, by necessity, leaders. Practitioners in these callings guide their audiences through thoughtfully curated exhibitions of technical skill and emotion. The burden of this sort of leadership rests more heavily on the shoulders of the lone conjurer than the ensemble band member. Like a jazz band conductor, the magician selects the material they'll perform, dictates the performance's tone, tenor and tempo, assigns roles and sets expectations for everyone present. They shepherd the entire group through the experience.

Magic is an intimate art. The audience trusts the magician to lead them to an emotionally coherent interpretation of the logical impossibilities they're witnessing. Seen through this lens, bad magic — like bad music or bad teaching — is essentially a failure of leadership. Ginóskó describes the kind of wisdom one receives from an experienced leader: hard-won and genuine.

Thinking about ginóskó during the study of magic also strengthens one's capacity for improvisation and variation, both in front of the practice mirror and while actually performing. I consider the patter, themes and stories that accompany each effect to be fundamental components of their design. In this book, I haven't included scripts with every magical routine. I have sometimes included my preferred verbiage, which you can use if you want, but I encourage you to develop your own scripts to reflect your personal style and tastes. Your interplay with the audience must be personable, articulate and conversational — quite a tall order! Strong communication engenders trust. In fact, it is one of the most technically effective and most mysterious sleights the magician can master.

This book is a collection of original routines refined through years of experience, experimentation and relationships. I've worked them out over many performances and carefully evaluated the impact they have in order to improve them. In addition, sessions with honest friends and mentors helped me to tighten every one of them. My goal is to help you to build a stronger relationship with your audiences while increasing your own confidence and efficacy.

Ginóskó is a many-faceted truth that marries the technical with the personal. Similarly, I wanted this book to be based on true stories from my life featuring my closest friends and mentors. You'll hear from them personally in the last two chapters. I know their wisdom will encourage you and help you realize your goals as an artist, because they had that impact on me. I'm proud of the tricks I've included in this book and hope you get plenty of value from them. However, I believe the interviews in the final two chapters also contain great value and many pearls of wisdom.

The road to magical growth can be frustrating. As you'll see, I've often felt this way myself. The stories of my personal failures aren't easy to share, but it would be dishonest to talk about experiential knowledge without also sharing the failures and harsh lessons from which it's derived. I hope these stories help you to remember why you become an entertainer and rekindle your perseverance and joy.

Aloha, and welcome to Ginóskó.

— David Kuraya

The author conducting a school band

Ginóskó
Knowledge gained by experience, by an active relationship between the one who knows and the person or thing known.

1: Commercial Card Magic from Maui

"In any performance art, it is the performers who create the magic through whatever medium they have chosen to work in. Just because magicians perform 'magic' doesn't mean their performances are going to be magical. Our magic should be strong and memorable – but we, as performers, need to be even stronger and more memorable."

— *Gary Kurtz*

Check Yo' Self

Effect

The magician hands a card box to a spectator and asks her to take out the cards and shuffle them. She finds the box contains one card with 'JACKET' written on it. Prompted by this strange message, the magician checks his jacket pocket and finds another message, made of cards strung together, reading, 'IN YOUR POCKET'. He finds several more messages about his person, the last of which directs him to check the card box on the table — which now contains a full deck of cards!

Method

This production of a full pack of playing cards is inspired by Chad Long's 'Now Look Here'. To perform this trick, you'll need to construct a few gimmicks using items you can find at any craft store. The gimmicks aren't hard to make and they'll last for years. As you will have gathered, you need to wear a jacket for this routine.

Card Boxes
You need two matching card boxes. The first contains only a single double-backed red card with the word 'JACKET' written on both sides in bold, clear letters as shown. The second contains a full deck of cards.

The Sign Gimmicks

These are 'chains' of cards held together by 0.6-inch binder rings (see illustrations). You need 16 rings in all. You'll also need ten red double-backed playing cards, a thick marker and a tool to cut small holes in the cards. I recommend a mini screwdriver to make the holes as small as possible.

Gimmick 1

Take five red double-backed cards.

Card 1. Leave it as it is.

Card 2. Top: in large letters, horizontally across the card, write IN. On the bottom, write THE.

Card 3. Top: YOUR. Bottom: OTHER.

Card 4. Top: POCKET. Bottom: HAND.

Card 5. Top: draw a large arrow pointing to the card's lower left corner. Bottom: a large arrow pointing directly left.

Arrange the cards vertically in 1-5 order, top sides showing: blank, IN, YOUR, POCKET, arrow. Punch two holes about 2 inches apart along the long sides of each card and use the binder rings as hinges to link them. [See Fig. 1 on next page]

Gimmick 2

Card 1. Leave it as it is.

Card 2. On both top and bottom, write IN.

Card 3. Top: THE. Bottom: YOUR.

Card 4. Top: BOX. Bottom: HAND.

Card 5. Top: a large arrow pointing straight down. Bottom: an arrow pointing right.

As before, arrange the cards vertically in order with the top sides uppermost: unmarked, IN, THE, BOX, arrow. Link them using the binder rings. [See Fig. 2 on next page]

Setup

Accordion-fold Gimmick 1 behind the unmarked card and hold it with the arrow card nearest you, pointing to your left. Hard crimp the upper *left* corner of the front unmarked card so it bends *away* from you. Later, you'll hold this corner to let the packet fall and unfold into a chain.

Put this folded packet upright into your right inner jacket pocket with the unmarked card furthest from your body. You should be able to clip the crimp between your left second and third fingers when you retrieve this packet.

Accordion-fold Gimmick 2 into a packet with the arrow nearest you, pointing down. Hard crimp the upper *right* corner of the front unmarked card so it bends away from you. Place the gimmick in your outer-right trouser pocket with the unmarked card furthest from your body.

Place the full card box in your outer right jacket pocket.

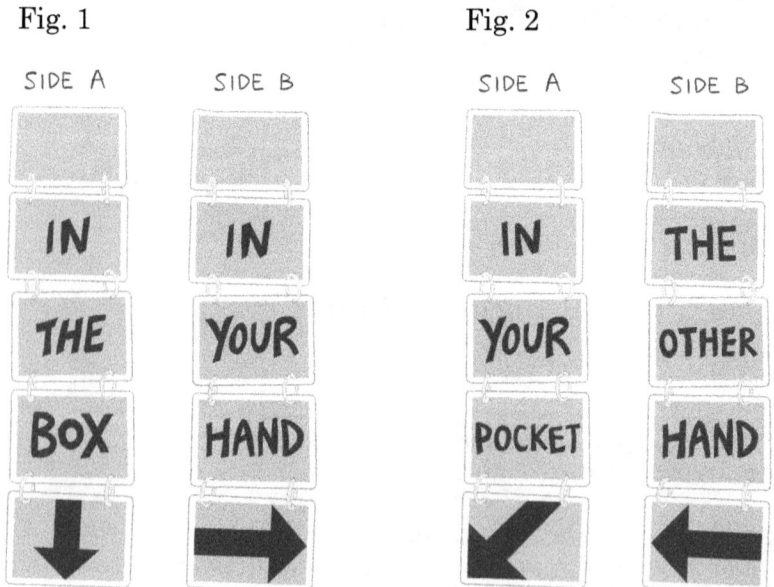

Presentation

Display the card case (which actually contains a single card) to your audience and hand it to the spectator (let's call her Jenny) on your right. Ask her to take the cards out and shuffle them. Continue with your introduction. In the meantime, Jenny discovers there is only one card in the box.

"Jenny, have you thoroughly mixed those cards?"

Jenny lets you know there's only one card in the box.

"Oh! Easy night, I guess."

Take the card in your left hand and the box in your right.

"Wait, there's something written here."

Display the card that says, 'JACKET'.

"In my jacket?"

Pat down your jacket as if you're frisking yourself. Turn your body to your right and open your jacket with your right hand (still holding the empty box). Retrieve Gimmick 1 with your left hand, clipping the crimped corner between your first and second fingers. Your thumb contacts the back upper corner, holding the packet together as shown.

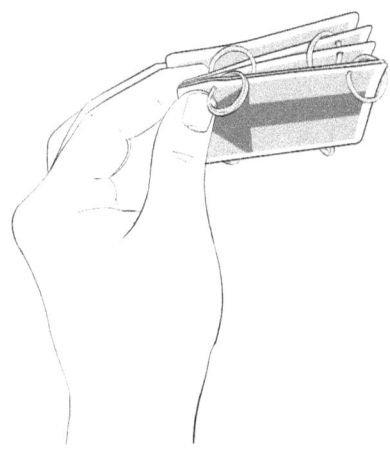

As your left hand enters your pocket, your right hand enters your outer jacket pocket, exchanging the empty box for the full one.

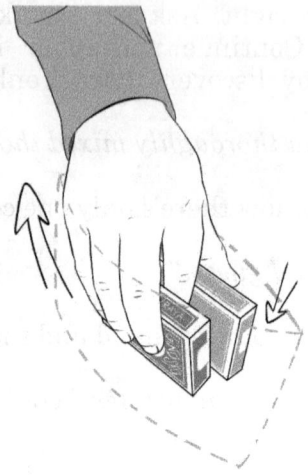

Keeping both your hands in their pockets, pause for a beat and look at the audience with a puzzled expression.

Take out Gimmick 1. Because you clip the crimp between your first and second fingers, you can immediately release everything else with your thumb and let the cards fall down into an open chain. The audience will see the message: 'IN YOUR POCKET'.

As soon as the gimmick begins unraveling, remove the full box from your jacket pocket, bringing it into view. The absurd appearance of Gimmick 1 will take a moment to register, which provides perfect cover for the deck switch. Hold up Gimmick 1, standing square to the audience so its arrow points to your right trouser pocket as shown.

"It's not quite a full deck. Any ideas, Jenny?"

Jenny will inform you that the cards are suggesting you look in your pocket. Look at the front side of Gimmick 1 for the first time.

"Ah! Good call."

Table the full box in front of Jenny and reach into your right trouser pocket to remove Gimmick 2. Let your left hand fall to your side. Allow Gimmick 2 to fall open and reveal the message, 'IN YOUR HAND'. Hopefully, the audience will read it out loud.

"In my... ?"

Lift your left hand again (dropping your right hand to your side), this time showing Side B of Gimmick 1: 'THE OTHER HAND'. [Fig. 8]

Lift Gimmick 2, revealing its second side: 'IN THE BOX.' [Fig. 9] Position yourself so the arrow points directly to the tabled card box.

"In the box?"

Look around for a few beats and then notice the card box.

"That box?! Jenny, pick up the box and give it a shake. How does it feel?"

She will report that it now feels heavier.

At this point you're in a great position because both your hands are full and the audience will have largely forgotten about the card box on the table. As you deliver the above lines and interact with Jenny, fold the gimmicks and place them back into your pockets or performing case.

Have Jenny look in the card box and take out whatever is inside. She discovers that it now contains a full deck of cards, which she takes out. Take the cards from Jenny and spread them, at chest height, faces towards the audience. Let everyone clearly see see that a full deck of cards has somehow materialized in what was an empty box.

"I think we got 'em all! Let's start over, Jenny. Please shuffle the cards."

γινώσκω: Students And Magic Audiences

Over the years, I must have watched thousands of sixth-graders walk into my band class for the first time. Up to that point, their school experience has largely consisted of desks, chalkboards and books. Suddenly, they're faced with music stands and strange instruments without a single desk in sight. I love watching the mix of emotions on their faces, such as surprise, wonder, excitement, anxiety and perhaps a little confusion.

If you think back to your school days, you can probably remember which school subjects you liked or disliked. You could look around your class and quickly spot the athlete, the math whiz, the bookworm and even the slacker.

When a new group of sixth graders enters my band room, they're faced with a new subject in an unfamiliar setting. They are all beginners so it's a level playing field. They wonder "Will this be fun or will I embarrass myself?", "What's this teacher like?" and "Will I be good at this?"

These sixth-graders, with their slightly anxious facial expressions, are similar in some ways to an audience at the start of a magic show. People sometimes have to learn how to react to a magician randomly visiting their table. They might feel excited about seeing magic in a formal close-up setting but also hesitant about participating. How can we get them to relax and enjoy the entertainment despite the unfamiliar situation?

Chad Long's excellent and amusing 'Now Look Here' routine creates a fun conversation between the magician and the cards. The words written on the cards boss the magician around and tell him what to do. Ultimately, the magician takes no credit for the magic even though it happens in his own hands. When I was working on my version, I simply asked myself if I could keep the conversation but find a way to change the participants.

I opted for a deck production to eliminate the selection procedure and any of the usual card trick directions: take one, remember it, show it around and put it back. I used the message cards to shift the power away from the cards themselves and create a larger role for the the spectator. This also provides misdirection for the box switch.

From the get-go, the message cards are the boss. They cause the magic to happen. As with Chad's trick, the magician is just along for the ride.

At the end of this short opener, you've shown the audience that amazing things happen when they cooperate with you. This is a good place from which to start your show (or the school year). It's always worth asking yourself how you can help your audiences feel relaxed and ready to participate.

Credits

Chad Long describes 'Now Look Here' like this: "A card is selected and lost in the deck. The spectator is led through a 'Pasteboard Ping-Pong' game as they look up to your pocket, over to your hand and finally down to the table where they find the selected card." On his 'Now Look Here' DVD, he teaches both his routine and another by Scotty York. Chad's original trick, 'Back and Forth', is in 'The Lost Cheesy Notebooks – Volume One' (1994).

I originally learned this deck switch from Curtis Kam. Shawn Farquhar independently created an identical deck switch. His 'SWITCH' video explains it in detail with multiple applications (www.palmermagic.com).

Blackjack for Brother John

Effect

Here's a blackjack-themed packet trick using just four cards taken from a regular deck. It's strong, visual and easy to follow.

The magician shows four identical Jacks. They suddenly turn into two separate blackjack hands: a pair of aces and a 'natural' (two cards totaling 21). Finally, they turn into a five-card hand made of spot cards that total 21.

Method

"I have a confession: magicians cheat! Is that a surprise to anyone? Steve, let me show you my version of blackjack."

As you deliver these lines, remove the Ace of Spades, Four of Clubs, Jack of Spades and Six of Hearts from the deck. Without showing the faces, arrange them in this order with the six at the face. (The order and suits of the four and six don't actually matter but I'll use this set-up for the purpose of this description.)

"I tried making up my own way to cheat when I was a kid. I took out the black Jacks from every old deck at home to hustle my friends at blackjack: one for my hand, one up the sleeve, one up the other sleeve, and one stuck to gum under the table. I was in middle school."

To show four Jacks, perform Jason Alford's Bander Lift (a modified Diminishing Lift sequence).

Block Push-Off three cards as one and execute a Triple Turnover, showing the Jack. Turn the triple down and take the top card (Ace) with your right hand ("one for my hand").

Performing another Block Push-Off followed by a Double Turnover, using your right-hand fingers beneath the right-hand card to show the Jack a second time. Turn the double down and take the top card (Four) onto the right hand's card, slightly jogged to the left. Gesture toward your left sleeve with the two-card fan ("one up the sleeve").

Using the long edge of the right-hand fan, flip the third card face up to show another Jack. Flip the card face down and move your hands apart for a moment, gesturing at the table ("**one up the other sleeve**"). As you do so, use your left thumb to pull its top card to the left.

Bring your hands together, take the bottom left-hand card onto the right-hand fan and spread to the left. Immediately use the three right-hand cards to flip the remaining Jack face-up into your left hand. Gesture to your right sleeve with it saying, "**and one stuck to gum under the table**". Turn the Jack face down and place it under the entire packet. (In the usual version of the Bander Lift, you place the last card on *top*. Place it on the *bottom* in this case so you can go directly to the next phase.)

At normal performance speed, this display looks as though you showed four Jacks and pointed to the different places in which you used to hide them.

Situation: (from the face) Jack, Ace, Four, Six.

"Of course, this was an awful strategy. You can't make 21 with Jacks alone."

Block Push-Off three cards as one and execute a Triple Turnover, showing the Ace.

"You need an Ace to make 21."

Turn the triple down and deal the top card of the left hand packet onto the table (this is the Six).

"In fact, with two aces, you can split and increase your chances..."

Execute a Double Turnover, displaying the Ace of Spades again. Turn the double down and deal the top card (the four) onto the tabled card.

"...but you need an ace and a Jack for a perfect blackjack! Live and learn."

Openly show the two cards you have left and drop the Ace, followed by the Jack, face down onto the tabled cards. Your audience will think the trick is over. Time to go for the kill.

Situation: (from the face): Six, Four, Ace, Jack.

"A middle schooler flaunting Aces and Jacks all night quickly draws suspicion. I didn't know that professional cheaters use inconspicuous cards like a Four. Plus Six is ten. Another Four is fourteen. Another Six is twenty."

Four spot cards appear, totaling twenty. To do this, take the packet in Dealer's Grip and execute a Gemini Count. Note how the cards are dealt onto the table for the final display. This is the home stretch and the best part!

The Gemini Count

(First display) Starting in left-hand Dealer's Grip, use your left thumb to spread the topmost card slightly to the left so that it pivots on its lower-left corner. At the same time, your left index finger buckles the bottom-most card [Fig. 1]. This exposes the right edge of the two middle cards so your right fingers can take the double from between the top and bottom cards [Fig. 2]. Turn it face up onto the packet. The Double Turnover from the center reveals the four.

Execute Brother John Hamman's Instant Double technique to turn the double face down ('The Secrets of Brother John Hamman', pg. 11).

Table the 'Four' (actually the Ace) to your right.

Fig. 1

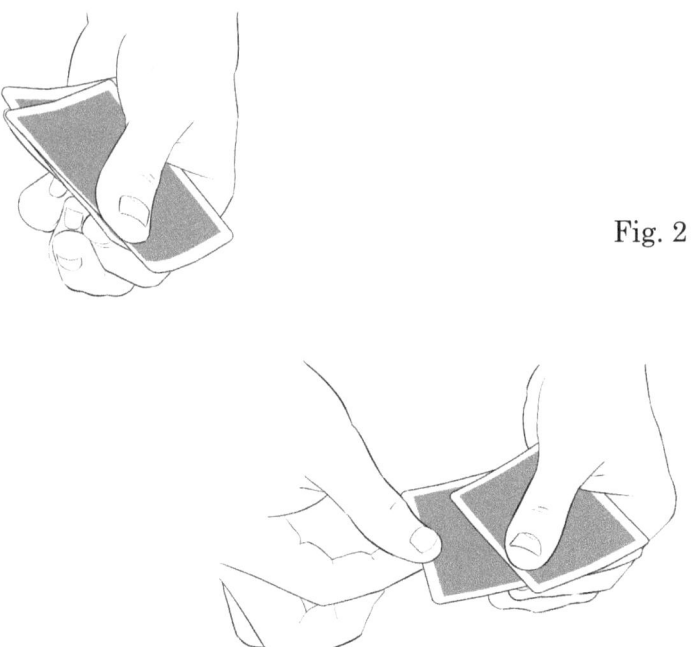

Fig. 2

(Second display) Repeat the same pivot with your thumb, and take the double from the bottom. Turn it face up onto the packet, showing the Six. Turn it down and deal the top card to the left of the first card.

(Third and fourth display) Following the same actions, take the bottom card of the two-card packet and turn it face up onto the last card, showing the Four again. This time, take the face-up card with your palm-down right hand. As you turn your hand palm up to drop the third card (the Four) onto the second card to your left, your left thumb moves underneath the last card and flips it face up, showing the Six. Place the Six face down onto the left pile. You've just shown four, six, four, six (which equals 20).

"But like I said, you still need an Ace to make 21."

Turn over the single card on the right side of the table, revealing the Ace.

"If anyone's interested, there's a game in the lobby after the show. I'm dealing."

If you're worried about the way in which the Gemini Count shows duplicate cards, Kaufman explains that some spectators will see four different cards while others will see two matching pairs. I was skeptical of this assumption when I first read it, but try it out for yourself!

The Bare Bones

Setup from the face: Six of Hearts, Jack of Spades, Four of Clubs, Ace of Spades.

1. Bander Lift (to show four Jacks). Place the Jack under the packet.

2. Triple Turnover, showing an Ace. Turn it down and deal the 'Ace' face down onto the table.

3. Double lift to show the second Ace. Turn it down and deal it face down onto the first 'Ace'.

4. Show the remaining two cards. Place the Ace and then the Jack face down onto the tabled cards.

5. Gemini Count. Deal the first card to the right and the rest into a pile off to your left after you display them.

6. Reveal the Ace by turning over the single card on your right.

γινώσκω: 'I've Seen This One!'

You take out your cards to perform one of your favorite routines. Just as you get started, one of the less endearing spectators exclaims, "I've seen this one!" I expect every close-up magician has heard this tired remark numerous times. What's a good way to deal with this situation? I'd like to offer a couple of suggestions that might help.

The first comes from 'Back To The Future', oddly enough. There's a scene where Marty McFly, having been transported from the present day back to 1955, sees a movie he recognizes on TV. He can't help but exclaim, "I've seen this one!" One of the other characters replies, "What do you mean, you've seen it? It's brand new!"

I think it's worth remembering this response. I've found that it's an effective way to deal with the 'I've seen it' types, plus it tends to get a laugh from everyone else.

Another good tip is to know a few packet tricks that you can perform with a small number of cards taken from a regular deck — such as the routine I've just described. They come in handy whenever you sense you have a 'Marty McFly' to contend with. Some laymen may know a few card tricks performed with a full deck (such as The 21 Card Trick) but most have never seen tricks you can perform with just a few cards. A packet trick like 'Blackjack for Brother John' will get the attention of 'Marty' and then 'Mc-Fry' him!

It's a fact of performing life: spectators will say unhelpful or obnoxious things from time to time. What lines have you collected for these moments?

Credits

The 'Pinochle Trick', 'Gemini Count', 'Instant Double' and 'Triple Turnover Technique' are all creations of Brother John Hamman. See 'The Secrets of Brother John Hamman' by Richard Kaufman.

According to conjuringcredits.com: "The 'Block Push Off and Pull-Down' sowed the seeds for the Buckle Count. Its invention may have been claimed by more than one magician, after which the sleight circulated." Also: "Marlo published the Diminishing Lift Sequence, using secretly reversed cards and Multiple Turnovers to switch cards, creating a better illusion, in Ibidem, No. 21, June 1960, p. 10. Marlo's notation dates it as August 23, 1959."

The Bander Lift is a brilliant creation by Jason Alford which I've included here with his permission. Here are a few words from Jason himself.

"The beauty of the move is that you do it slowly and openly. Because you place the right-hand cards into a reverse spread, when your left thumb pulls the third card to the left, it's logical to put the bottom left-hand card with the right-hand cards because of the way the cards are spread. Done slowly and deliberately, this sequence works beautifully. The only concern is the motivation for separating your hands before taking the third card onto the two right-hand cards."

In the routine just described, gesturing with the Jacks while telling the story provides the motivation for separating your hands.

High Five and a Handshake

How can we create an atmosphere of fun and trust when we meet strangers? To my surprises, I found the answer in Dr. Daley's 'Cavorting Aces'.

This routine is a tool I use to play with the audience. I let myself get a little 'snarky' and poke fun at them. However, it ends on a more friendly note with me high-fiving or shaking hands with everyone as I go on to my next effect.

I like this simple effect because it sets a tone of 'Let's work together!' instead of, 'Hey, watch me!' It also gets the spectators involved immediately without them having to pick a card. I expect some readers will look at this routine and think there's not much to it but it *does* have merit.

Remove the two Jokers and hand them to a spectator we'll calk Steve.

"Steve, I'm going to turn my back. Keep those Jokers face down and insert them together, as a pair, anywhere into the pack."

Turn your back and give Steve a moment to do so.

"Have you done it, Steve? Really? I ask because during my last show some wise guy pocketed the Jokers when I turned my back."

Turn around and look at him suspiciously. Turn to his wife, Misty.

"Did he put them in there, Misty?"

She says he did.

"I'm not sure I trust you either. Steve, do you mind if I check for myself?"

Run through the pack face up until you reach the two Jokers in the center.

"Oh wow, My bad. I have trust issues [pause for a few beats]. What? You just trust that I have trust issues?! You sweet summer child. Look, let's make this easy. Don't worry about me. As long as you trust yourself, you're good. For example, you tell me, is this card a Joker?"

Point to the card on the face. Steve tells you it's not a Joker. Execute a Herrmann Turnover Pass, apparently turning the pack face down.

"Steve, this card on top... is also not a Joker."

Execute a Double Turnover, showing a random card.

"By the way, this guy [point to yourself] is also not a Joker."

Turn the double over again.

"Steve, hold out your hand, palm up, like a table."

Place the pack onto his hand.

"Misty, please put your hand on top of the pack, making a card/hand sandwich with Steve. In this position, the cards are literally out of my hands. You know they are because they

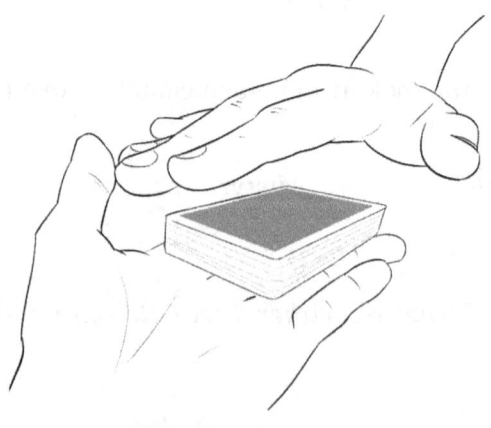

are in yours. And yet one Joker rises to the top to give you a high-five, Misty. The other Joker sinks to the bottom to give you a firm handshake, Steve. Do you believe me?"

They will most likely say that no, they do *not* believe what you have said.

"No?! Fair enough. I was suspicious of you at first, too. Let me prove to you that I'm a man of my word."

Have Misty lift her hand and show that one of the Jokers is now on top. Turn the pack over, showing the other Joker on the bottom.

Give Misty a high-five and give Steve a firm handshake.

"I think we just had a moment, gang. Let's do another one."

γινώσκω: Clues for Cavorting

I often follow this routine with David Williamson's 'Memory Test', which is his version of Eddie Fechter's trick, 'Be Honest, What Is It?'

To do this, just take the two Jokers and apparently place them in your back pocket. Classic Palm them and secretly replace them on top of the face-down pack. You can then get two more cards from the pack in order to perform the Williamson/Fechter routine.

Credits

'High Five and a Handshake' is inspired by Dr. Daley's 'Cavorting Aces' from Stars of Magic, Vol. 7, No. 3 (1950). Larry Jennings, Harvey Rosenthal and Ken Krenzel have all played with the plot.

Stephen Minch provided a history of this trick in his 1990 book 'Close-up Impact'. I am not claiming that I have improved on earlier versions. Sometimes I just enjoy revisiting a plot or trick that I feel is overlooked or neglected. I'd like to place on record my thanks to Tyler Wilson for helping to clarify the plot while punching up the comedy in this quick routine.

The history of the Turnover Pass (also known as The Alexander Herrmann Pass) can be described as speculative at best. Current research suggests that the sleight most likely originated with either Herrmann's brother, Compars, or J.S. Hofzinser. I recommend www.conjuringcredits.com for a comprehensive history.

The author performing at a social event

Asking the 8 Ball

This is a loose variation of Hofzinser's 'Ace Problem'. Shuffled deck, no table needed and tons of interaction. To begin, remove the four eights and hand them to a spectator, whom we'll call Steve, to examine.

"Steve, I sometimes try to read people's minds, but it's more fun to have the cards do the work. Let me show you."

Holding the deck upright, use your right forefinger to pull back the cards at their outer corner and riffle them so Steve can see the indices (a standard Spectator Peek). Ask Steve to call stop. Hold a fourth-finger break below Steve's card (e.g. Six of Spades) and finish riffling through the pack.

Side steal the selection to the top and take a break under it. Ask Steve if he ever owned a 'Magic 8 Ball'. Place the eights face up onto the face-down deck. You now have a break under five cards — the four Eights and the selection.

"You shake it, ask a question and a vague answer like 'Ask again later' appears in a little window."

Shake the deck like an 8 ball, openly lift up at your break and peek at Steve's card. This is my favorite peek in all of card magic.

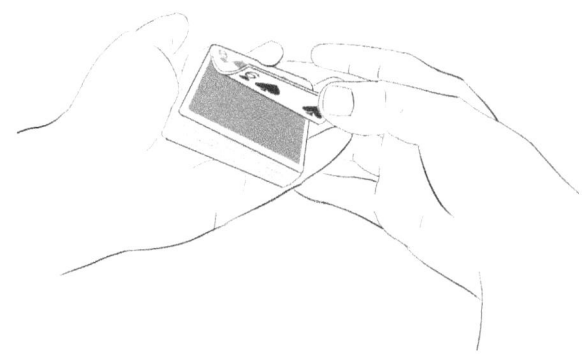

"I want you to do exactly that with the eights, but just before you do... a pop quiz."

As you deliver this line, reposition the Eights so that the Eight matching the selection's suit is face up on top.

"Please name each suit as I show them to you."

Display the Eights as follows. Take the five-card packet and the next face-down card beneath them into right-hand End Grip. You now hold a six-card packet with a thumb break between the two face-down cards.

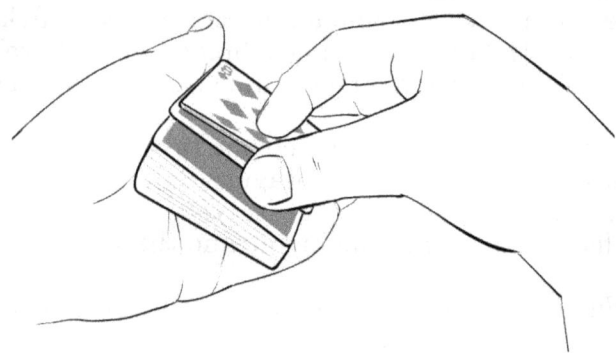

With your left thumb, peel the first Eight back onto the deck. As you peel the second Eight onto it, drop the lowermost face-down card onto the first Eight, keeping a break beneath it. Peel the third Eight onto the deck.

This leaves you with a back-to-back double card (the fourth Eight and the face-down selection), which you drop onto everything. Have Steve name the suits as you display each eight. Place the four-card packet on his hand and have him put his other hand on top. Have him shake the packet of cards like an 8 ball.

"Great job! It's important that you know the suits for this next part because the question I want you to ask the Magic 8 Ball is, 'What is the suit?'"

Steve does so.

"Perfect! When you shake a Magic 8 Ball, a little tile flips over to reveal a message. Let's see if anything happened."

Have Steve lift his hand off the packet and take the cards from him. Fan them to show that the spade is now reversed. Ask him if this is the suit of his selected card. He confirms that it is. Hand the four-card packet back to him.

"That's amazing, but we still don't know where your card is in the deck."

Separate the deck into two halves, the top half in your right hand and the bottom in your left. Casually gesture with the two halves. Bring the halves back together, putting the right-hand packet under the left, cutting the pack.

It's time to get another spectator involved. Hand the pack to Misty face up. Yes, she's here, too.

"Misty, when Steve shakes the Magic 8 Ball again, I want you to ask, 'Where is Steve's card?' Got it? Shake it up, Steve."

Misty asks the question, but nothing happens.

"Steve, did you feel anything? No? Misty, you asked the question so maybe the answer is in your hands."

Have Misty spread through the face-up pack. One card is reversed near the center. Remove it from the spread and look at it without showing it to the audience.

"Wow! I don't think this is Steve's card, Misty, but all the same, I think it answered your question. It's a spade, but it's the Eight of Spades. And if this is here, then there's only one place Steve's card could be."

Use the Eight to gesture toward Steve's hands. Ask Steve to name his selected card. Turn over the face-down card among the Eights, revealing his selection.

"I'm not sure if it was the 8 Ball or our excellent question-askers. All I know is that it wasn't me. Give it up for everyone who's not me!"

γινώσκω: The Hobbs and Pierce Touch

The display sequence in this routine is similar to an ATFUS move. Stephen Hobbs suggested performing a Deep ATFUS instead. It's bold and it gets you exactly where you need to be with even fewer moves. Thank you, Hobbs!

Here is Lance Pierce's description of Deep ATFUS applied to 'Asking the 8 Ball'. In this version of the trick, instead of using a single card under the 5-card packet to hide the matching 8, you'll use the entire upper half of the pack!

Situation: you're at the point in the routine where you hold five cards from above in End Grip — the face-up Eights on top and the face-down selection beneath them. The target Eight (in our example, the Eight of Spades) can be any card in the packet except the rearmost one. For the sake of explanation, let's say it's third from the top.

With your left thumb, peel off the first Eight onto the deck. After showing this Eight, bring your right-hand packet over it and pick up the Eight under the other cards. Having collected the Eight, move your right hand forward an inch or so and give the packet a downward bend over your left forefinger, just as a small flourish.

Bring your right hand back again and peel the second Eight onto the deck. You'll see your target Eight on top of the right-hand packet. This is your cue for the secret move.

Bring the packet over the deck again, apparently to pick up the second Eight. In reality, you move your right hand slightly to your left and secretly lift half the deck beneath it. Without hesitation, move your right hand forward with the half deck beneath the Eights, side-stepped slightly under your right hand. This gives the long edge of the packet the clean razor edge that it's had all along.

Flex the packet and half deck downward over your left forefinger, just as you did before when you were only holding a small packet. This conveys the distinct impression of thinness. Then come back to peel off the Eight of Spades onto the left-hand cards.

After peeling off the Eight of Spades, bring your right hand over it *as if* you are picking it up beneath the packet, but really leave the half-deck on it. Bring the remaining packet forward and flex it downward over your left forefinger as before. Now name the fourth Eight on the face of the packet (without peeling it) and continue with the routine.

This extremely bold move is both deceptive and efficient. The Eight of Spades is reversed in the center of the deck and the selection is reversed in the packet.

My thanks once again to Lance Pierce for this description. You'll find many more beautiful finesses like this in Lance's lecture book 'Elements'. Warning: this book contains so much of Lance's brilliance that after reading it you'll want to name your first child after him.

Credits

Karl Fulves documents Johann Nepomuk Hofzinser's 'Ace Problem' in his article, 'Two Unsolved Card Problems', in 'The Pallbearers Review' Vol. 5 (1969).

ATFUS first appeared in Edward Marlo's 'For Card Men Only' (1949). The Deep ATFUS or Bold ATFUS appeared in Marlo's 'Unexpected Card Book' (1974).

Nacho Card

Here's another nod to Hofzinser's 'Ace Problem'. The magician *refuses* to find the spectator's selection but amazes everyone nonetheless.

Take a shuffled pack in left-hand Dealer Grip and pinky-pulldown the bottom card's non-index corner, crimping it (say the Seven of Spades). Spread through the cards, faces towards you, and remove three Queens, one at a time, setting them face down on the table without showing them. Do *not* remove the Queen whose suit matches the crimped card on the face of the pack (in this example, Spades).

Locate the Queen of Spades and execute the following reversal of the bottom card: gather all the cards below the Queen of Spades in your left hand and then turn this hand over [Fig. 1], carrying its cards face down and over the left end of the right-hand spread. [Fig. 2]

Your left fingers then reach beneath the Queen of Spades to hold it in place as your right hand takes all the cards above the Queen, turns them sideways and places them face down onto the cards in your left hand. [Figs. 3 and 4]. I first learned this technique from Earl Nelson's 'Sleeve Aces'.

Situation check: The Queen of Spades is now reversed on the bottom of the deck. The crimped Seven of Spades is somewhere in the middle. This setup may seem quite involved but it only takes a few moments under the guise of setting aside three cards from a shuffled pack. Gesture to the three tabled cards.

"Steve, none of these are your card. Oh wait, this is far more impressive if you choose a card first!"

Locate the crimp and get a left fourth-finger break above it. Execute Eddie Fechter's Timing Force: invite Steve to say 'Stop' whenever he wants while you cut several small packets of cards onto the table. When he does so, cut all the cards above the break onto the tabled pile.

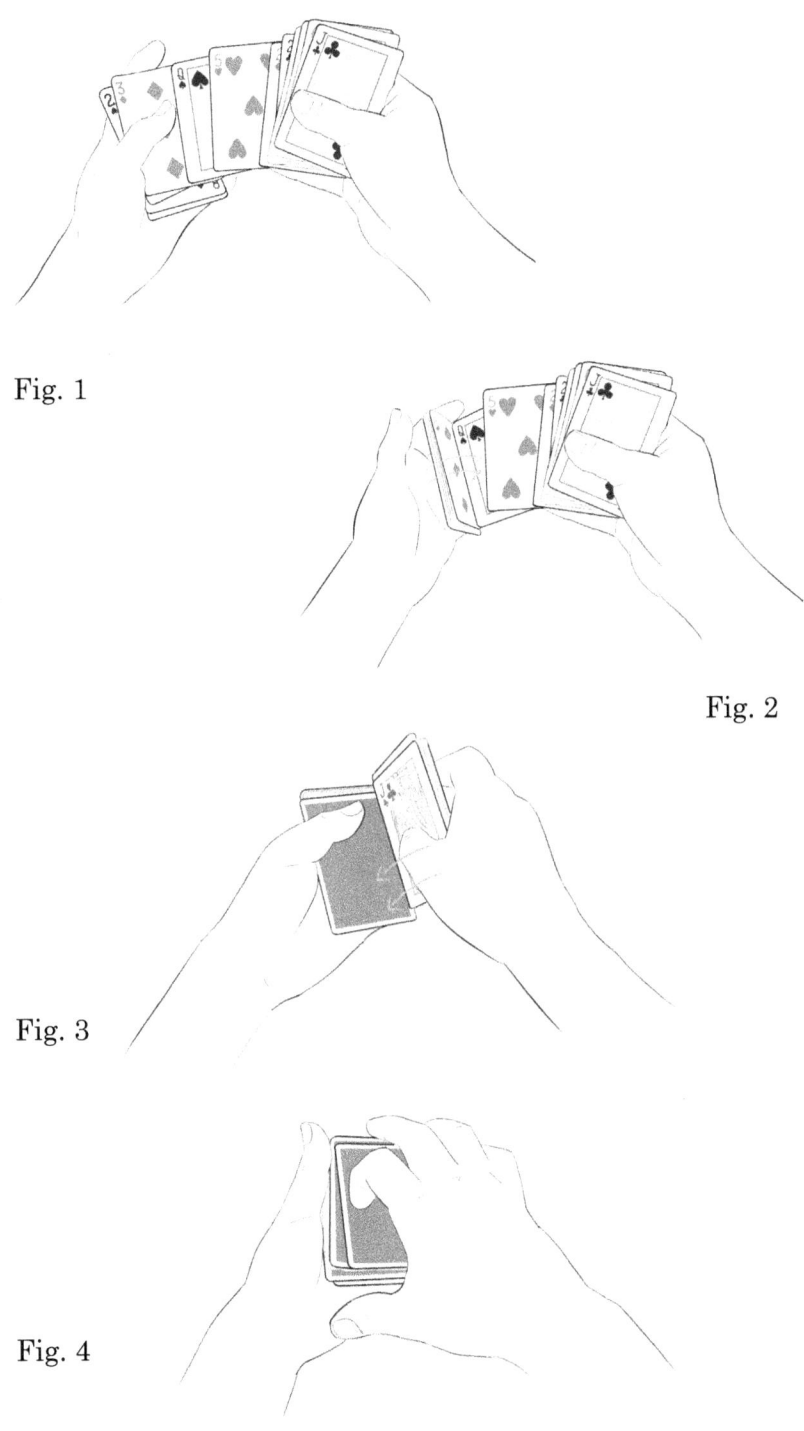

Fig. 1

Fig. 2

Fig. 3

Fig. 4

Take the selection with your right thumb and first finger, removing the crimp from the card as you hand it to Steve. Allow him to show this card to everyone as you reassemble the pack. Make sure the reversed Queen remains on bottom.

Take Steve's card and apparently insert it into the center of the pack but really put it second from the top using Marlo's Tilt/Vernon's Depth Illusion.

Situation: the Queen of Spades is reversed on the bottom. Indifferent card face down on top with the Seven of Spades second from top.

Dramatically cast a shadow over the pack and take the top card with your right hand.

"Believe it or not, this is also not your card. Is it?

Turn the card over. Steve will confirm it isn't his. Adopt an 'applause cue' stance as if you've worked a miracle and insert the card anywhere into the pack. The audience will feel confused and mildly outraged.

"Oh, I see. You're used to magicians _finding_ your card. But I am not most magicians. Tonight, I will amaze you by _not_ finding your card! Let me show you. Steve, please cut off a few cards and flip them face up on top."

Steve cuts to a random card. Ask him if it's his card. He will confirm it is not.

"It could have been... but it isn't! Amazing! Do it again, but cut deeper this time and turn the whole lot over."

Steve cuts to another random card and you again get him to confirm it's not his selection.

"It could have been again – but wait! Are any of these face-up cards yours? [Steve will say no] This is getting stranger by the minute. Ladies and gents, most magicians would have found Steve's card by now. Let's face it. You won't find acts like this anywhere in Vegas. No... you have to fly to the middle of the ocean."

(Obviously, you adapt this patter to refer to wherever you happen to be performing). You've walked your audience through the Balducci Cut Deeper Force. A clump of face-up cards is on top of the face-down pack. The first card of the face-down section is Steve's selection.

Take the face-up cards, turn them face down and place them under the pack. This conveniently puts the reversed Queen in the center of the pack, ready to reveal later.

"Steve, I've successfully failed to find your card. But thanks to all the random cuts you made, this card is now on top of the deck."

Thumb the top card onto the prediction packet.

"You're not going to believe this, but..."

Pick up the packet and execute a Double Turnover. Ask Steve if it's his card. He will yet again say no. Proclaim 'Yes!' triumphantly, as if it's all going superbly well.

"You don't seem impressed. You weren't impressed when I found these three either. But at least when we don't find your card..."

Turn over the packet and finish with John Bannon's Discrepancy City Display. Briefly, execute an Elmsley Count finishing with the face-down card outjogged. Remove the face-down card and display the Queen to the audience, revealing the match.

"...we're consistent!"

Place that Queen face-up under the packet. The reversed card is the third card from the face. Set the packet in front of Steve.

"Ladies and gentlemen, we have reached the climax of this anti-card trick. With all the cards face-up on the table, my sleeves rolled down and me not blindfolded, I will still fail to find Steve's card. Heck, I'll even have him tell me what it was. Steve, what was your card?"

Steve names the Seven of Spades. Spread the deck face up on the table. Run through the deck frantically repeating the name over and over as though you're searching for it. There's a face-down card in the center. Don't acknowledge it. Keep going until the very end.

"Boom! I just failed to find your card 52 times in a row!"

Steve (and perhaps other spectators present) will point to the face-down card.

"Nah, that can't be yours. Yours had a face."

They'll hopefully protest.

"Oh, you mean on the other side?"

Turn the card over to show it's a Queen. At this point, most spectators will guess what's going on and spread the Queen packet to find a face-down card.

"No, no! Don't do it!"

Steve turns it over anyway and reveals his chosen card.

"That's on you."

γινώσκω: A Memory by Jack Parker

After I created 'Nacho Card', Tomas Blomberg reminded me of a similar routine in Jack Parker's '52 Memories' called 'HofCity'. If you're a fan of this card problem, I can't recommend it enough. While Jack's take on the plot and presentation were different, he also used Bannon's Discrepancy City Display and exploited the reversed card that remains after the display. His routine involves two spectators and gets the deck out of the way much sooner. You may also enjoy his interpretation!

I must thank Tyler Wilson once again for helping me tweak the presentation to maintain focus on the premise — *not* finding the card.

Credits

Earl Nelson published his routine for 'Sleeve Aces' in 'Variations', p. 53 (1979) and again in 'Variations Revisited', p. 67 (2003).

Eddie Fechter published 'A Fechter Force' in 'Card Cavalcade' (1972). John Bannon's 'Discrepancy City Display' first appeared in 'Impossibilia' (1990).

The 'Cut Deeper Force' is usually credited to Ed Balducci (Ireland's Yearbooks 1968). It's based on Lynn Searles' 'The So Simple Force' in 'The Jinx Summer Extra', p. 135 (1936).

'Tilt' either belongs to Edward Marlo or Dai Vernon. I recommend reading these sources and reaching your own conclusion: 'Tilt' by Edward Marlo (1962), Dai Vernon's 'Vernon on Cards' in 'The Pallbearers Review — Close-up Folio No. 10' (1977), 'How Deep Is This Illusion?' 'Sticks & Stones No. 10' (1977).

More details on the Hofzinser 'Ace Problem' are highlighted in 'Asking the 8 Ball'.

MIT Aces (Kuraya & Guastaferro)

> *"When we look at a painting or sculpture, it never physically changes. Magic, however, evolves and can grow stronger over time. Even when an effect has reached its final version on the page, we can bring it to life in new ways each time we perform. In this respect, we are always en route. Looking at magic through this lens, we can unveil new ways to make even the simplest of effects soar."*
>
> *— John Guastaferro, 'En Route'*

I've never met John Guastaferro in person, but I'm a long-time fan of his card magic and ideas. His 'One Degree' concept has helped many magicians polish their magic and his 'Palm Reader Plus' routine has been a fixture in my strolling repertoire for years. John published 'Blackjack for Brother John' when he was editor of Genii Magazine's 'Magicana' column — my first published piece in a magic magazine! Along with all of his accomplishments in the magic world, John is also a virtuoso guitarist.

John Guastaferro

John and I belong to an online group of magicians who regularly brainstorm card magic ideas. Some years ago, I submitted an unfinished idea for a routine in which, while trying to find a selection, the magician accidentally finds the four aces instead. John took this idea and created 'MIT Aces'. I've simply added my script to it.

On another occasion, John and I worked together on variations of Eric Mead's 'Signed Stunner'. We came up with different versions but we both used a rolled up playing card as a makeshift magic wand. My version, 'All Who WANDer', is the next item in this book. John's version, 'Mystery Wand', is in his new book, 'The Nth Degree'.

Effect

The magician fails to find a selected card four times in a row, instead finding the four Aces. He places the Aces under the spectator's hand and they change into the spectator's selection. Take special note of the four-for-one switch toward the end, which I think you'll find exceptionally clean and streamlined.

Method

Start with four Aces on top of the deck. Although it's not essential, it helps to have two mates on the bottom of the deck (such as the two red nines). Have a card selected and noted. Take back the card and control it second from the bottom. (I usually have the selection put back in a spread and cull it to the desired position.)

Give the deck a few false shuffles and cuts as you say:

"Ladies and gents, I don't know if you've heard about 'card sharps' and expert card cheats? They practice for years until they can take a shuffled deck, like this, and then deal themselves all the best cards, like Aces and so on. I used to do all that stuff but I stopped because it felt dishonest. So these days I just do magic. For example, instantly finding... Steve's chosen card!"

Turn over the top card (an Ace).

"Wait a minute. Steve, was your card an Ace?"

Steve says his card was *not* an Ace. Set the Ace aside.

"Ha ha, I guess old habits die hard. So, yes, I used to do all that flashy card cheat stuff, but no more! These days, it's just magic tricks. Like finding Steve's card."

After more false cuts/shuffles, produce the next two Aces in any way you wish and set them aside on the table. Have fun with the freedom you have here, but appear more and more frustrated each time an Ace appears.

"Are you sure it wasn't an Ace? I'm starting to think that either you're lying or it's those old habits again."

For the last Ace, double undercut it to the face and produce it by turning the deck face up or using John's Ballet Cut ('One Degree', 2010).

Hold the deck face up in Mechanic's Grip, displaying the Ace. Raise the deck up towards yourself, also known as 'necktie-ing the deck', to momentarily hide the face from the audience. Stud turnover a double [Fig. 1] and take it in your right hand as your left continues holding the deck upright.

You will now perform two actions. First, with your left hand get a pinky break below the selection by pushing then pulling back the card at the face (a good opportunity to glimpse the selection). Next, use your left thumb to secretly pull the card from behind the Ace onto the face of the deck during a casual flicking gesture. [Fig. 2].

"I have a confession…"

Begin lowering your left hand as your right replaces the Ace on the face of the deck. [Fig. 3]

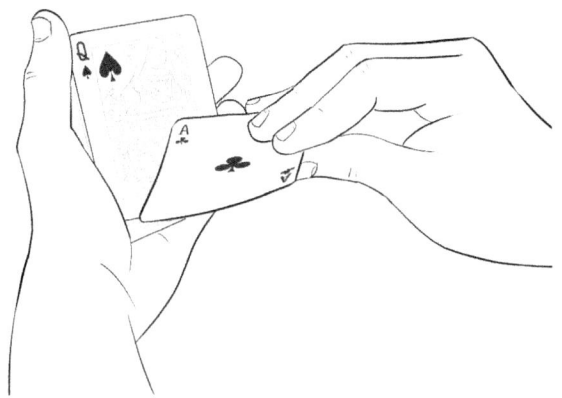

Fig. 1

Fig. 2

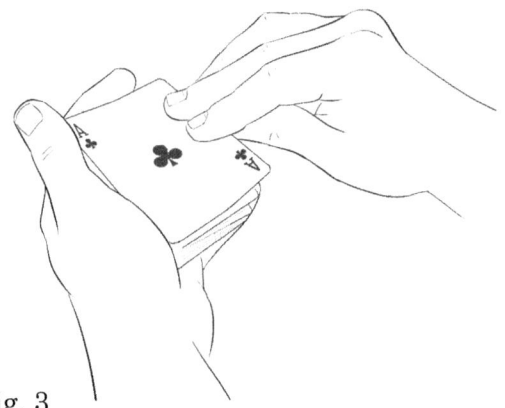

Fig. 3

Situation: you're holding the deck face up in your hand. You have a break under the three face cards (from the top down: a face-up Ace, a reversed indifferent card, and the face-up selection).

"... I love the Aces! I can't stop finding them! I've tried rehab, twelve steps... everything! Steve, please <u>help</u> me!"

Have some fun acting as if you desperately need Steve's help with your 'addiction' and see how he responds to your plea!

Pick up the three tabled Aces and stagger them next to the Ace on the face of the deck. The right hand takes all six cards, still in a staggered spread [Fig. 4]. Lever the packet face down [Fig. 5].

Square the cards with your right hand [Fig. 6], then lift off just one card in overhand grip as if it's four [Fig. 7]. A face-up card will show on the deck as a convincer, which is why it's not a bad idea to use two mates.

Have the spectator cover this single card which he believes to be the four Aces.

"Keep them away from me! Out of sight, out of mind, out of the deck."

Turn the deck face down, set it on the table, and cut it.

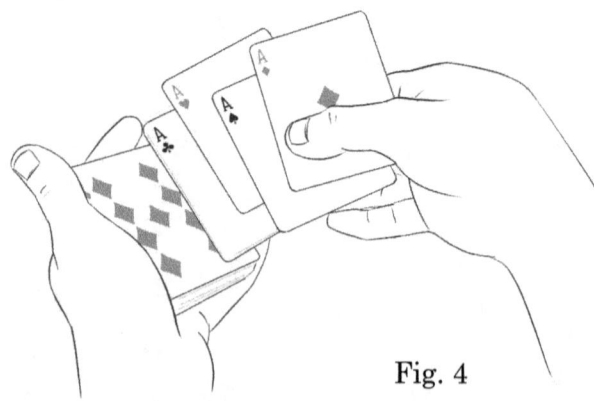

Fig. 4

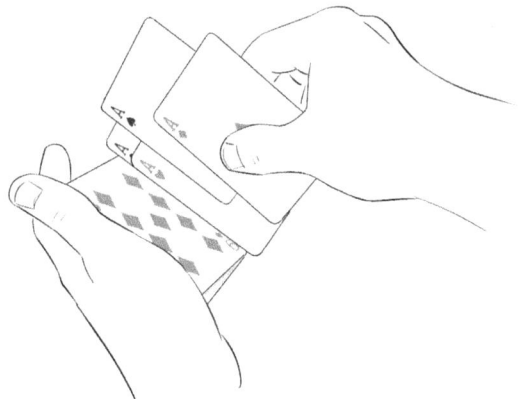

Fig. 5

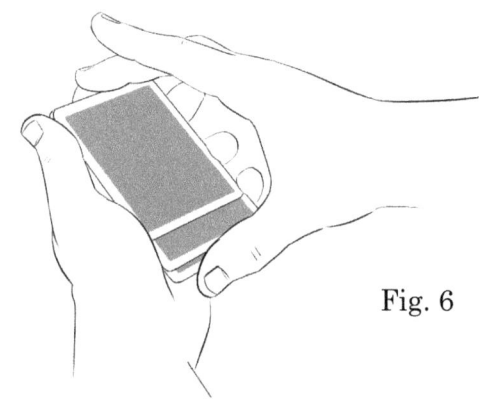

Fig. 6

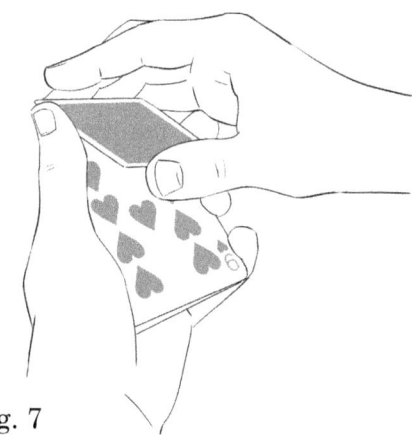

Fig. 7

"Okay, we've got all that stuff about card cheats and finding Aces out of the way. Back to the <u>magic</u>. Steve, I shall now <u>magically</u> make your card turn over in the middle of the pack without touching it. The cards are out of my hands. What was your card?" [Steve names it.] "Watch. One, two... three!"

Table spread the cards, reveal the face up Aces and look aghast, angry and dismayed. Your old addiction to finding Aces has flared up again! Steve's hand still covers what everyone thinks are the four Aces.

"Wait... there's still something under your hand? Is it four cards? Oh... it's just <u>one</u> now? Is it the... Two of Diamonds?"

Steve confirms that it's his selected card.

"Yes! We did it! Maybe there's still hope for me. Thank you, Steve. I could kiss you, but there's more magic to do."

γινώσκω: One Degree

I mentioned John Guastaferro's 'One Degree' concept. He explains it as follows. "It's about making small, intentional improvements to create powerful outcomes, particularly in the areas of: (1) elevating the impact of your magic; (2) connecting with your audience; and (3) hitting the targets you set for yourself. While the typical approach of any young magician might be to make massive changes to achieve massive results, I believe the extraordinary is closer than we think. Just one degree away." (One Degree, 2010).

This notion is similar to the 'marginal gains' approach to peak athletics performance pioneered by Sir David Brailsford. This is worth reading about online even if you have no interest in athletics.

What 'One Degree' adjustment can you make to a trick that you do all the time to make it more fun, amazing, memorable or clear?

All Who WANDer

The Ambitious Card is a classic of magic but I retired it from my strolling set a few years ago. I was tired of it and my audiences could tell. However, I reconsidered when, after tinkering with Eric Mead's 'Signed Stunner', I came up with a presentation that I like. In short, a kid and an impromptu magic wand upstage the magician. You'll need a pack of cards and a wand. For those of us on a teacher's salary, a Sharpie will do.

From a shuffled deck, have a kid choose a card and sign it. Have this selection replaced and control it to second from top of the deck. The kid's name is Steve.

"Steve, I'm going to tell you the real secret of magic. It's the magic wand."

Remove a wand (or Sharpie) from your pocket.

"Some magicians learn sleight of hand or even use trick cards. I only need to take this magic wand and tap the deck twice. When I do that, your card comes to me."

Execute a double turnover to show that the chosen card has risen to the top.

"Doesn't that look easy? It only takes two taps! But you didn't know what was going to happen, so I'll do it again."

Turn the double over, and insert the top card into the center of the pack. Tap the deck twice and turn over the top card to show that it's the chosen card.

"Amazing, right? It's so amazing that your parents forgot to clap! [The audience offers some applause.] No, no, I'll earn it."

This minor humorous moment gives you an off-beat to execute a Top Change. Ask Steven's Dad to lift up about half the cards. Place what everyone thinks is Steve's card (but you've actually top changed it for an indifferent card) onto the half-deck in your left hand. Ask Dad to drop the cards he's holding back on top. Hand Steve's Mom the magic wand and invite her to to tap the deck *twice* and turn over the top card. When she does so, everyone can see that Steve's chosen card has risen to the top a third time. Turn it face down again.

"Steve, the adults are taking all the credit, but to be honest, anyone can do it. In fact, in a moment you will make your card come to you. We will even use your magic wand!"

As you talk to Steve, apparently shuffle the selection into the deck. Holding the pack ready for an Overhand Shuffle, cut off the bottom stock of the pack and shuffle the cards singly back onto the left hand's packet, injogging the first card. After completing the shuffle, lift up on the injog with your right thumb and cut the pack. The chosen card is now back on top.

With just a little bit of suitable prompting from you, Steve will point out that there's a problem with the plan you just suggested: he doesn't have a magic wand.

"What? You don't carry one? Dad, did you bring yours? No? Don't worry, I'll make you one."

Execute a Triple Turnover, showing an indifferent card (let's say the Five of Hearts).

"If I roll this Five of Hearts into a wand for you, it should still work. I learned this on Pinterest."

Turn the triple over. Take the top card and set the pack down. It seems you're holding the indifferent card, in this example the Five of Hearts, but it's actually Steve's signed selection. Roll the card lengthwise, long edge to long edge, to create a long tube with the back facing out as shown.

Give this 'wand' to Steve and have him firmly grip the end so that it doesn't unroll prematurely and reveal that it is the signed selection. Pick up the pack and get a fourth finger break under the top two cards.

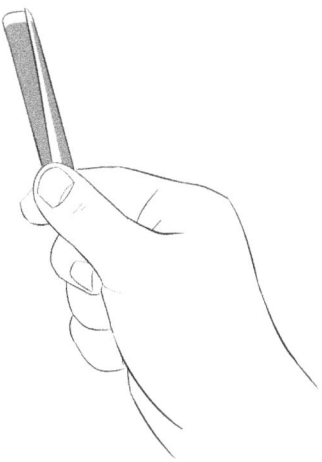

Still holding your break, turn over the top card onto the pack. Immediately pick up the two cards above the break as one in End Grip. Push over the next face-down card on the pack with your left thumb. Use the long edge of the right hand's cards to turn it over onto the deck as shown below. Take this card under the right hand's packet. Apparently, you've turned over the top two cards of the pack.

"Steve, your card isn't on top yet."

Turn the three-card packet in your hand face down and insert it anywhere into the center of the pack. The Five of Hearts (the card they think is rolled up in Steve's hand as his 'wand') is now face up in the middle of the pack.

"Let's do some magic, Steve. Sit up tall! You're gonna find your signed card. Go to town! Tap the deck a few times, and your card will rise to the top. Your whole family will go nuts for you."

Steve will start tapping the deck excitedly.

"Dude! I said two times, remember? Two taps and your card comes to the top. Haven't you paid attention this whole time!? If you tap it too many times, it doesn't work."

Show that top card is *not* Steve's chosen card. Turn it face down, raise the deck upright and spread the cards, showing the faces to the audience. As you do, everyone will see there is one card reversed in the center.

"I don't even know where your card... whoa! What's up with this one?"

Turn the card over, showing that it is *not* the chosen card but the Five of Hearts — which everyone thinks Steve has been using as a 'wand'.

"Wait...if this is the DIY Magic Wand Five of Hearts, what are you holding?"

Steve unrolls the magic wand, revealing the signed selection.

"What?! Now you're just showing off! Does he do this all the time, Mom and Dad?"

γινώσκω: Wand Tips

I love performing 'All Who WANDer' for families because it involves everyone and it makes the child the star of the show. John Guastaferro's version, in his forthcoming book, 'Nth Degree', uses two Chapstick caps to hold the 'wand' card together to make it even more realistic. This is a wonderful idea!

Credits

Eric Mead's 'Signed Stunner' first appeared in 'The Magical Arts Journal' (November 1986, Vol. 1, No. 4). It was the inspiration for this fun routine. 'The Ambitious Card' was known as 'The Eye Popper' throughout the 1930s and 1940s. Gustav Alberti from France is credited for the 'ambitious' presentation, in 'Recueil de Tour de Physique Amusante' (1877). It was translated into English in Professor Hoffmann's 'Drawing-room Conjuring' as 'The Ambitious Card' (1885, p. 46). See conjuringcredits.com for a comprehensive history.

Pentatonic

Dai Vernon's 'The Trick That Cannot Be Explained' (TTTCBE) is my favorite effect to share with people who linger after a show or in informal situations.

One of the reasons I love TTTCBE is that it's based on *improvisation*, which is of course also important in music. A magician presenting TTTCBE is quite similar to a jazz musician improvising around a melody. In both cases, the performer has to constantly be aware of what's happening, respond in an appropriate way, build their performance from known elements and bring the things to a satisfying conclusion. These strategies are like notes or melodic 'licks' for a jazz soloist — at your disposal but, in each case, only used as and when appropriate.

In music, we sometimes use what's called the pentatonic scale — one that only has five notes instead of the more customary eight. Similarly, with this version of TTTCBE you are never more than five steps away from leading the spectator to the target card. I think this matters because with any performance of TTTCBE, the longer it goes on, the less impact it has.

So, as I say to my band students at the beginning of class, "Let's play!"

Step 1. Table Three Cards. Remove three cards of equal value, such as three Jacks, and table them face down. Ask Steve, your spectator, to shuffle the rest of the deck. When he's satisfied, have him turn over the top card. If this just happens to be the fourth Jack, go to Step 5.

Assuming this is not the case, point to the top card and ask Steve if it was his chosen card. He will appear confused and tell you that he hasn't chosen a card yet.

"Oh, right. That's normally how this sort of thing works. I won't have you pick a card this time. I've already chosen three for you."

Ribbon spread the pack face up on the table. Ask Steve if it looks mixed enough and let him shuffle again if he wants to. This quick spread gives you a chance to see where the fourth Jack is. All you need to know is whether it's near the top, middle or bottom. You now follow one of three paths.

Step 2a. Near The Top. Scoop up the cards and hand them to Steve face down. Tell him to deal them one at a time into a face-up pile. When you feel Steve is quite near the Jack, invite him to stop dealing at any time. If the last card he deals is the Jack, go to Step 5.

If Steve deals past the Jack, don't worry. You're now working with a small bank of cards, so your odds of hitting the Jack in the next phase are good. Go to Step 3.

If Steve stops before dealing the Jack, point to the value of the card he stopped at and have him deal that many more cards. You will probably only have to do this once to get the fourth Jack in play. Go to Step 3.

Step 2b. Near the Bottom. Give Steve the *face up* deck, invite him to deal cards one at a time and when he's near the Jack tell him to stop whenever he wants. If the Jack is either the last card dealt or the card on top of the remaining packet, go to Step 5.

If Steve deals past the Jack, move on to Step 3.

If Steve stops dealing before he gets to the Jack, have him look at the value of card he stopped at and deal that many more cards (exactly as in Step 2a). Move on to Step 3.

(continued >)

Step 2c. Near the Middle. With the cards ribbon spread in front of Steve, invite him to open his hand as wide as he can and drop it onto the spread of cards, subtly gesturing towards the center of the spread. Steve does so. Ask him to push all the cards under his hands forward.

On rare occasions, the Jack you're trying to get to will be at either end of the gap Steve created in the spread (like the Four of Diamonds and Three of Spades in the illustration). In this case, immediately ask Steve to take those two cards under the table and go to Step 4. However, on most occasions, the Jack will be among the group of cards Steve pushed forward.

Step 3. Cut Card. Spread out the face-up pile of cards that Steve dealt or pushed forward, putting the rest of the deck away. Invite Steve to slide any one of the cards towards himself. If he happens to choose the Jack, go to Step 5.

If not, say that the card Steve just touched (e.g. the Two of Hearts) is what they call in casinos a 'Cut' card, meaning it's used to mark a position in the pack. Scoop up the remaining cards and then cut the Jack to the back of the packet. Drop everything face down onto the face-up Two of Hearts as in the illustration.

Invite Steve to give the packet a cut and complete the cut. Pick up the packet and spread it, showing the Two of Hearts in the center. It will, of course, be between two other cards, one of which is the Jack. Tell Steve that he placed the Cut card between two other unknown cards. Have him take these two cards out of the spread. You have narrowed Steve's options down to two possible cards in just three apparently random steps. Not bad!

Step 4. Dani With A Twist. Invite Steve to pick up the two cards and mix them under the table. Tell him to wait until he feels ready and then slap either one of the cards face up onto the table. This procedure comes from the work of Dani DaOrtiz.

Take all the other cards off the table except the three face-down cards (the three Jacks) that you placed aside at the start. You will now be able to finish the routine in one of two ways.

Conclusion A: Steve slaps the Jack onto the table.

"The Jack of Spades! Remember, you shuffled and cut the cards and made a whole bunch of random choices. I feel like you did the trick for me. And now, the Jack is the last man standing. [Notice the three face-down cards] Well... except for these three cards that I placed aside at the start."

Proceed to step 5.

Conclusion B: Steve slaps the indifferent card onto the table. Immediately ribbon spread the rest of the deck face up.

"Wow, that was dramatic! You shuffled, cut and eliminated all of these cards. I felt like the spectator this time. There are just a few more mystery cards left. These three that I set aside before you made any choices [turn over the three Jacks] and the one you're holding under the table — the only card that no one has seen yet, and even you don't know what it is!"

Step 5. Coda. Take a little while to build up the dramatic tension and then reveal the perfect match... all Jacks!

Credits

Dai Vernon's original concept for 'The Trick that Cannot Be Explained' first appeared in 'More Inner Secrets of Card Magic' (1960). Conjuringcredits.com aptly describes the effect this way: "...the performer confidently improvises his way through the procedural portion of a magic trick — without the audience recognizing this fact — to arrive at a desired outcome. There are many approaches to this concept."

I first saw Dani's under-the-table solution to a two-card equivoque on his DVD, 'Reloaded'.

The Conjuringcredits.com entry for 'The Psychological Stop Trick' says 'This concept was in use among mid-19th century European conjurers. It was described in R.P.'s 'Ein Spiel Karten', 1853, p. 43 of the Pieper translation, under the title 'The Non Plus Ultra'. Johann Hofzinser was also using the idea around the same time, and near the same place, which he published as 'The Sympathetic Numbers' in 'Kartenkünste', 1910, p. 23 of the Sharpe translation."

The ruse of trying to force a card by estimating when a spectator is likely to call 'stop' appears in 'The Encyclopedia of Card Tricks' (1936/1937) by Glenn G. Gravatt and Jean Hugard. A similar approach called 'Psychic Stop!' appears in 'Expert Card Technique' by Frederick Braue and Jean Hugard (1940).

Intermission: Schooled!

In 2007, I was a sophomore music major at Whitworth University. Though I had only been studying sleight of hand for about a year, I thought I was getting fairly good. I studied Ellusionist videos and any magic lessons I could find on YouTube — which at the time was just two years old. I loved learning slick moves and the guys in the videos convinced me I'd look cool if I bought their magical miracles.

One afternoon, a poster appeared on our campus walls announcing a forthcoming magic show by Derek Hughes. I wrote his name on my wrist, rushed back to my dorm and logged in to (wait for it) MySpace. I messaged Derek to ask if he'd like to meet up during his visit to our school. I was pleasantly surprised when he accepted within minutes.

On the day, we met at The Ramada Inn and sessioned for about three hours. With youthful eagerness, I showed him every flashy move and card revelation I'd learned. Derek was kind enough to watch patiently. Once I'd finished, he proceeded to show me the most polished close-up magic I'd ever seen. Every line either clarified the effect, moved the narrative forward or made me laugh. Everything he did and said had a purpose. I immediately felt embarrassed about all the lame moves I'd made him sit through.

Instead of talking to me about tricks, Derek introduced me to the importance of *scripting*. He explained that he always scripted his shows from start to finish. Although he naturally ad libbed with the audience now and again, he generally stuck to his script and therefore never lost his place on stage.

Derek explained that an audience can always sense whether or not a performer is comfortable and prepared (and good scripting makes a tremendous difference). He also told me that the show must feel 'alive' at all times — not just a perfunctory trot through familiar steps. These were priceless lessons for a kid who only knew bits of finger-flinging he'd learned from YouTube.

That evening, during his show, I watched Derek give a stellar performance. The students loved his original brand of comedy. They were astonished and delighted when he tore up a newspaper and restored it, caused a signed card to end up in an 'impossible' location and swallowed sharp needles. I could see how everything he'd told me translated into a funny, amazing and memorable performance.

It's easy to brush off beginners. I'm ashamed to admit I've done it myself once or twice. But every magician was a beginner at one time. Someone lifted us up by encouraging our passion and wide-eyed enthusiasm. Someone showed us there's more to entertaining an audience than just 'doing a trick' or trying to impress people with deft sleights. Someone disciplined us to put down the cards and try writing a script once in a while. These gems of advice pay big dividends if the student is willing to listen and learn.

What's the best way to honor the people who've patiently walked alongside us as teachers and mentors? My friend, Tom Dobrowolski, suggested one good way to honor them: "Pass it on."

The author's performance engaging every spectator... almost

2: Behind The Bar

"Suddenly it dawned on me, like finding religion, <u>you are the magic</u>. The props just come along for the ride. If you're a strong enough performer, it doesn't matter what you do. You're selling 'you.' That was the greatest discovery I ever made."

– Albert Goshman

The author performing at the Maui Coffee Attic

The author sessioning with the legendary Doc Eason

The First One Under

My mother often tells the story of when she watched 'The Wizard of Oz' on her family's first color television. The film started in black and white and, after an iconic song and a tornado, Dorothy found herself in The Land of Oz. When Dorothy tentatively opened her cottage door, everyone's jaw dropped with hers when the TV lit up in vivid Technicolor.

Something similar happened to me when I started studying magic. At one point in the early 2000s, all I had to learn from were a few rather melodramatic magic websites. Then I came across my first 'proper' magic DVD: Doc Eason's 'Bar Magic' (Vol. 1). I watched as Doc made his audience cry with laughter, gasp in delighted amazement and shriek with stunned disbelief. At one point, he even got people singing!

This was my arriving-in-Oz moment. I watched that DVD countless times, promising myself that if I ever had a bar show of my own, I would perform Doc's legendary 'Card Under The Glass' routine. I kept my promise in 2015 when I landed a twice-a-week bar gig at the Maui Coffee Attic.

After months of experimentation, I decided to use the card box instead of a glass. Some argue that the glass is stronger because the card appears in plain sight. However, I prefer the box because you can create suspense and anticipation leading up to the moment when you push the box aside to reveal the card. That said, you could perform the routine I'm about to describe with either the box or a glass.

Magicians sometimes avoid the 'Card Under...' plot because they fear getting caught — which is an understandable concern. My solution was to build my confidence with a first phase that *guarantees* I won't get caught, no matter how observant the audience may be. The success of this first phase gives me the confidence to make the card appear a second time, a third time... and maybe even an eighth time!

I hope you enjoy 'The First One Under.'

Remove the cards from the box to have them shuffled. Set the box to your right and have a card chosen by the spectator seated immediately in front of you. As you may have guessed by this stage, his name is Steve.

Ask Steve to show his card up and down the bar as you turn your back and secretly reverse a card. You do this using the same move I've previously described in 'Nacho Card', which is based on Earl Nelson's 'Sleeve Aces'.

To wit: spread through the face up pack until you find a three near the center. Gather all the cards below the three in your left hand [Fig. 1]. Turn these face down and over the left end of the right-hand spread [Fig. 2]. Your left fingers can touch the back of the three and hold it in place while your right hand takes away the rest of the face-up cards and flips them face down onto the left-hand cards [Fig. 3] You're left with a face-down deck with the face-up three on the bottom [Fig. 4].

Begin an overhand shuffle, turning slightly to your right so the audience won't notice the reversed card on the bottom. Ask Steve to call stop whenever he likes. Have him place his selection onto the left-hand packet and toss the remainder of the pack onto it. The reversed three is above his selection in the center of the pack.

"Steve, I'm going to hold the cards at my very fingertips. Not my fingertips... my very fingertips. If I shake the pack, one card reverses itself. Did you see it happen?"

Ribbon Spread the cards face up onto the bar. The audience will immediately notice two things: (1) a reversed card in the center and (2) their face-up selection next to it. In other words, it'll look like you missed it by one. Let this picture sink in for a few beats, and then slide the face-down card (the three) out of the pack.

Ask Steve if he still remembers the name of his card. All your attention is on Steve and all the audience's attention will be on the mysterious face-down card. Simply cut Steve's face-up chosen card to the back of the face-up pack and turn the pack face down.

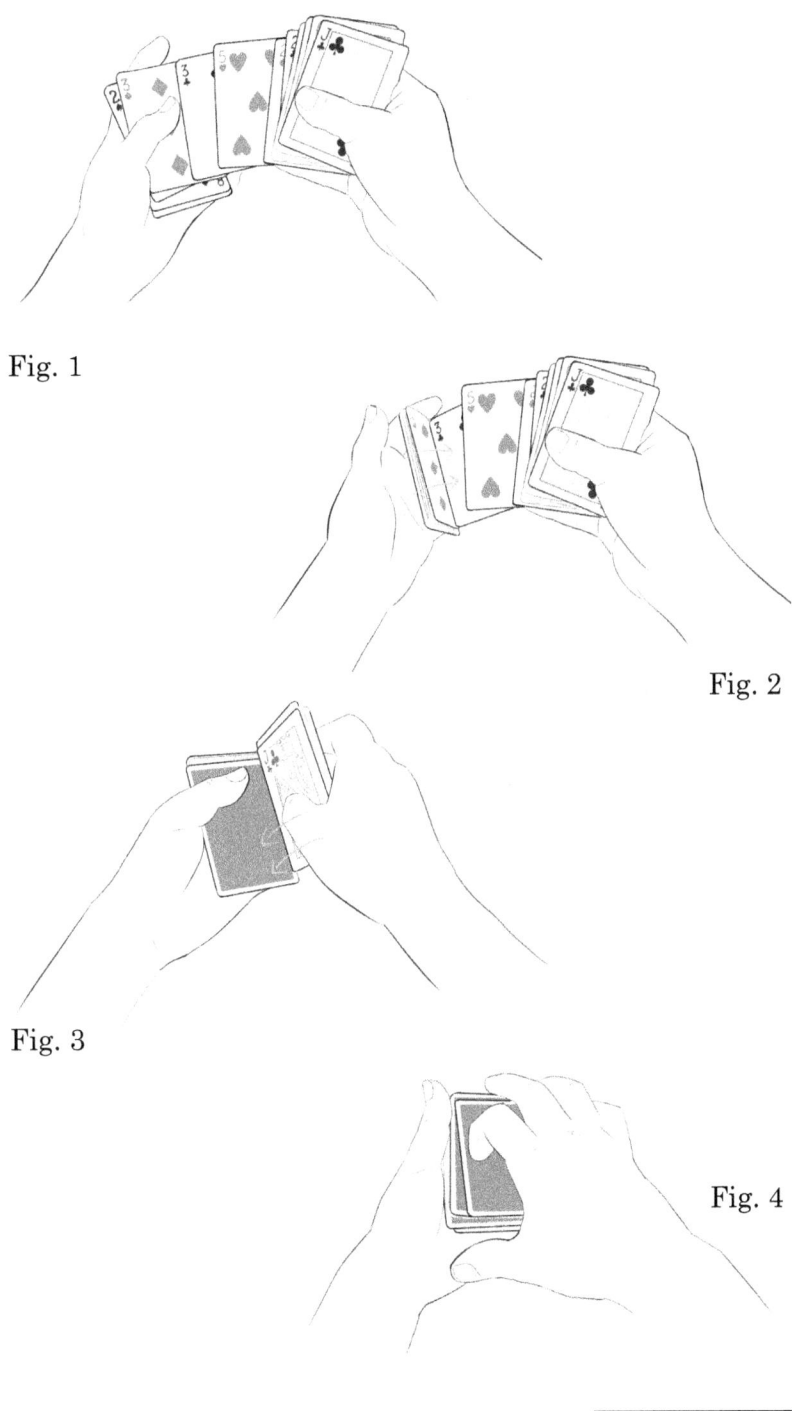

Fig. 1

Fig. 2

Fig. 3

Fig. 4

With the selection on top, take the pack into right-hand End Grip in preparation for a One-Hand Top Palm.

Ask Steve what his card was. Let's say he says the Five of Spades. Pick up the tabled card with your left hand and look at it yourself. Smile, slide it toward Steve and invite him to turn it over. You want to convey an intriguing sense of confidence, as if the face-down card is, impossibly, going to turn out to be Steve's selection.

Up to this point, the audience has been wondering what you'll say when you discover that you missed the card. Now, they're doubting themselves. They're wondering if you have already somehow switched the card or whether you have a duplicate… or what? All the focus is on Steve turning over the face-down card that you seem to feel very confident about. This gives you all the time in the world to do a One-Hand Top Palm.

The moment Steve flips over the card, revealing the three, load the palmed selection under the card box by releasing it onto the table and sliding the box onto it with your right hand.

"Wait, you said three, right?"

Look along the bar.

"I never miss a card. Five of Spades? Really?"

Everyone confirms that the chosen card was the Five of Spades.

"There's an explanation for this. This three is an indicator card. It indicates one of two things. Either it indicates that I screwed up [this gets a laugh] or that your card is three… three feet away… under the card box."

Slowly move your eyes over to the card box. On a good night, the audience will start reacting before you even turn it over.

γινώσκω: A Worker's Warm Up

As with music or exercise, a warm up serves to get you physically and mentally prepared for more difficult or challenging work. It's also good for building confidence. After you perform 'The First One Under', the audience realizes that you were miles ahead of them from the start. I believe this tends to boost both their respect for you as well as their attention and interest in whatever you're going to do next. This makes it a lot easier for you to entertain them in a loud bar setting, so the sooner you achieve this reaction, the better.

This is the beginning of a much longer routine, but I believe you can fill in the rest with your own ideas. I hope it will get you started on a classic of bar magic, 'Card Under Box' (or glass if you prefer).

Credits

I'd like to dedicate 'First One Under' to Doc Eason: Over The Rainbow, Under The Box.

According to Doc, 'The Card Under Drink' was performed by Al 'Heba Haba' Andrucci as early as the 1930s. Andrucci's student, Bob Sheets, was known for performing it too. Published routines didn't appear until much later, with 'Card Under Glass' in 'The Complete Works of Derek Dingle' (1982) being the earliest write-up. J.C. Wagner published his routine a few years later in 'The Commercial Magic of J.C. Wagner' (1987).

There's no shortage of items magicians throughout history have used to surprise spectators this way — hats, napkins and drink coasters being just a few. Edward Marlo's 'Rub-Away Mag' is a 'Card Under Magazine' found in 'Off The Top' (1945).

Post-it Crane

This brief moment of weirdness is for slow nights where Steve and one or two other people are sitting around the bar. To prepare, fold a square Post-it note into a paper crane and crumple it into a ball. (There are dozens of origami crane or 'flapping bird' tutorials online.) Place this in your right trouser pocket. If you're working behind a bar and want to save your pocket space, you can find some other place to stash it that's out of sight and easy to grab behind the bar. You'll also need the rest of the Post-it pad.

Take out the pad of Post-it notes and peel off one note.

"Steve, have you ever tried origami? Let's make an animal. I'll make the first fold."

Make a fold in the note and pass it to Steve to make any random second fold. Keep passing the Post-it note back and forth with Steve, adding random folds, until it becomes an abstract folded figure or, more likely, just a crumpled ball of paper. I'll refer to this as the crumpled ball from now on.

"Beautiful! It's a probiotic. Lactobacillus Acidophilus, if I'm not mistaken."

Place the crumpled ball on top of the Post-it pad. Reach into your right pocket and finger palm the crane as you say:

"You don't see it? Maybe I just have a strange imagination. Let's try something more concrete. What's a more familiar origami figure that you can visualize?"

With a little luck, plus perhaps some subtle prompting from you, Steve will refer to a crane or 'flapping bird'.

"Good suggestion! I can make that. Here, peel off a Post-it."

Pick up the crumpled ball with your thumb and first finger. With your other hand, push the Post-it pad towards Steve. As you do this, you *apparently* discard the crumpled ball to one side. In reality, you roll it into thumb palm and toss the finger-palmed crane to the side, still on the bar but outside the area between you and Steve where everyone's interest is (or should be) focused.

There's no heat on this switch at all. The crumpled ball seems unimportant at this point and Steve is focused on peeling off a fresh Post-it note. Keep your eyes on the pad of Post-it notes as you execute this move, remembering that the audience tends to look wherever *you* look. You can quietly ditch the crumpled ball behind the counter, on the floor (if it won't be seen) or in your pocket.

Steve removes a Post-it note and hands it to you. Instead of folding it into a crane, roll it into a wand.

"No, it's not a straw. It's not recreational, either. This is a magic wand."

Wave your 'magic wand' over what Steve assumes is the crumpled ball from earlier on. Have him *carefully* unfold it. Straighten out the wrinkles and reveal that the crumpled ball has magically transformed into a crane. Wish Steve and everyone else happiness and good luck.

If Steve didn't suggest or ask for a crane / flapping bird, reveal it anyway and say it's whatever they asked for.

"Ta dah! There you are: a hippo."

Steve objects that it looks like a crane.

"Hey, hey! No hippo shaming at this bar, please."

γινώσκω: Magic Decluttering

Take a look in your 'everything' drawer. Is there a piece of magic you can create with something in there?

Hot Swizzle Action

As you show the audience an ungimmicked miniature cocktail shaker, olives magically appear and vanish. Finally, a piece of fruit appears from nowhere.

You need a small cocktail shaker and a metal swizzle stick to act as your 'magic wand'. You also need two matching cocktail olives and any fruit that will fit into the shaker such as a small orange. You can perform this routine walk-around or behind the bar from your pockets.

The Secret Move

Here's the main move used throughout the routine. Start with one olive in the closed cocktail shaker and one finger-palmed in your right hand near your little finger. The wand (swizzle stick) is in your right hand. [Fig. 1]

Pick up the cocktail shaker from the table with your left hand as you place the wand down with your right. Your right hand comes over to the *top* of the cocktail shaker; your left hand is on the *bottom* portion. This is the ready-position for pulling off the top of the shaker. [Fig. 2]

Pull off the top portion of the shaker with your right hand, which has the hidden olive in low Finger Palm. Bring your hands side by side. [Fig. 3] As you do this, rotate *both* your hands so that your thumbs move up and over towards the audience. This will cause the olive inside the shaker cup to spill out onto the table. [Fig. 4]

As you spill the olive from the cup portion of the shaker onto the table, allow the hidden olive in your right hand to roll into the top portion of the shaker, unseen by the audience.

Replace the lid of the shaker onto the cup portion. The hidden olive is now loaded. You're ready to proceed with the next vanish.

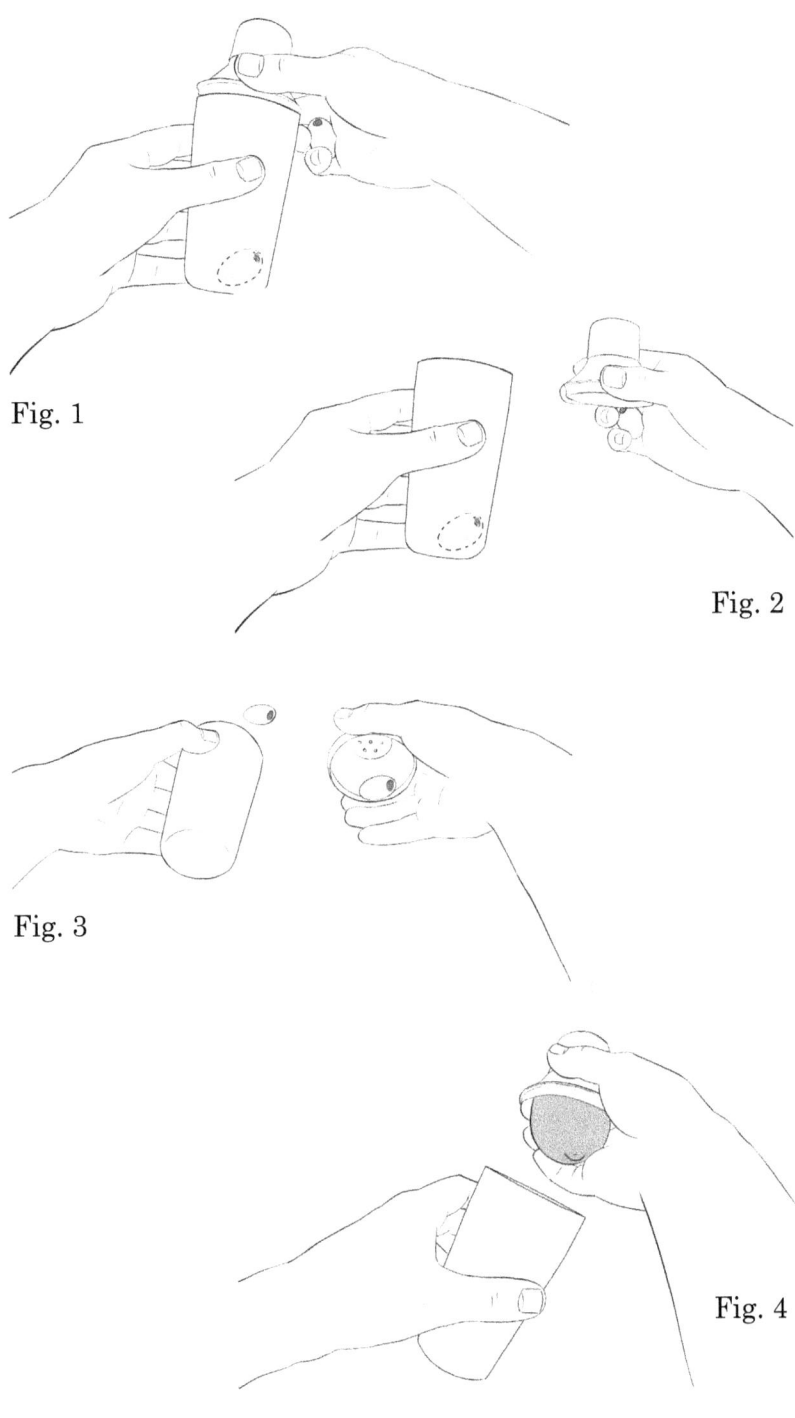

Fig. 1

Fig. 2

Fig. 3

Fig. 4

Routine & Presentation

Begin with an olive finger-palmed in your right hand. The swizzle stick is in your left trouser pocket. A second olive and a small orange is in your right trouser pocket. In your back right pocket is a screwdriver, about the same size as the swizzle stick.

Introduce the cocktail shaker to the table.

"Here's a mini, er, what do you call it... keg? Right, Steve?"

Steve informs you that it's called a shaker.

"Ah. Sorry, I'm not much of a drinker. My friends have a great time with the stuff, but I never got into it. I don't even know what a screwdriver is."

Steve tells you it's the name for orange juice and vodka.

"Orange? That doesn't make any sense."

Let Steve or any of the spectators examine the mini shaker. As you take it back, secretly load an olive into it. You're one ahead. Reach into your pocket, finger-palm the second olive, and come out of the left pocket displaying the swizzle stick that will serve as your 'wand'.

"What is this supposed to do?"

Grab the swizzle stick with your right hand and squint at it as if you're reading from it.

"Swizzle stick? What the heck is a swizzle? Is this swizzling? [Perform a weird gyrating action with the stick] Did that do anything? Any ideas?"

Steve explains what 'swizzling' means. Try to imitate the action. Look into the shaker and discover the olive.

"Oh, <u>that's</u> what this thing does! Where's the closest bartending school? I'm a natural. Hey, what if I swizzle way over here?"

Move to the other end of the bar and swizzle. Perform a standard ball vanish with the olive, using the swizzle stick as a wand, ending with the olive hidden in your right hand.

"Woah! Well, olives cannot be created or destroyed, right? I'm sure it didn't get far."

Perform the Secret Move to reveal an olive in the shaker while loading one into the top portion and closing up the shaker again.

"There it is. Everything's beginning to make sense. Well, the screwdriver thing still doesn't make sense. Steve, you try! Take the swizzle stick and prepare to swizzle. I'll just put the olive away."

Put the olive in your pocket and come out with the small orange palmed.

"You have our undivided attention. Go right ahead."

Steve proceeds to swizzle like a pro.

"Wow! I felt something. Did you guys feel something? Let's see what happened."

Perform the Secret Move, this time dumping out the olive and loading the orange, using the same technique to cover the orange with the top of the mixer.

"Nice one, Steve! I hope you're warmed up. You'll have to swizzle a lot to make a screwdriver with that olive. What did you say was in that drink again? Oh yeah, vodka and…"

Hold the shaker a few feet above the bar and dump out the orange. As the audience reacts, exchange the swizzle stick for the screwdriver tool in your back pocket.

"This still doesn't make sense."

Hold up the orange in your left hand.

"Why is this thing called a screwdriver?"

Lift your right hand, in which you now hold an actual screwdriver. Let everyone see how surprised you are that the swizzle stick has transformed into a real screwdriver. Stare at the screwdriver and the orange for a few beats.

"Oh! I get it now."

Stab the screwdriver into the orange and pour the juice into the shaker.

"Who wants a keg of screwdrivers? Gesundheit!"

γινώσκω: by Tyler Wilson

The main point of this script is to let the audience see that weirdness happens around you, the magician, when you're handling objects that you say are unfamiliar to you. The 'weird' events don't seem so weird to you because you claim to know very little about alcohol or drinking so you don't know any different. You can enjoy the ironic situation of the audience knowing something that you don't: namely, that these bar tools are *not* supposed to work like this. The fun part is that at no point in the routine do you have to overtly explain this to the audience.

Magicians often try to figure out who they are on stage — what's referred to as their 'performing persona'. In this case, we decided to write a routine about who the magician is *not*. See if thinking about who you *are* and are *not* could help you write your next act.

Credits

This routine was devised by Dr. Jason Fleming, Tyler Wilson and the author.

The 'Secret Move' taught in this routine comes from Jay Sankey's 'Magus Capsule' (2004), a teaching DVD that came with 'a spun aluminum, satin-finish capsule with built-in chop cup feature'.

This routine is largely the work of Jason Fleming. Several years ago, as a Christmas gift, he gave a few friends the original script for the routine plus a mini shaker and a swizzle stick. Tyler Wilson played with the script and had the wacky idea of referring to a 'screwdriver' (vodka and orange juice) during the routine and producing an actual screwdriver at the climax. I simply put together Jason's clever routine and prop with aspects of Tyler's script. The result is the routine you've just read.

Intermission: Coffee Talk

Meeting Derek Hughes taught me to script my magic shows and to focus on the audience as much as the routines and sleights. By the end of my college career, I had performed at campuses throughout the Inland Northwest and developed a network for corporate shows. I had also been the opening act for stand-up comedians touring through Spokane. I remember thinking, "I must be getting pretty good by now."

But I was about to be put in my place again.

In the fall of 2010, I moved to Honolulu to continue studying music at the University of Hawai'i. I felt miserable. My friends in Washington, who had become like brothers and sisters to me, were all of a sudden an ocean away. I was depressed and lacked the motivation to study properly.

I moved into an upstairs room at a YMCA on University Avenue. The street noise kept me up late and woke me up early. The neighbors were quiet but the roaches came in every size.

One morning, I came down the stairs wearing a black T-shirt with club, heart, spade and diamond symbols across the front. Tony, the manager of the Y, greeted me as he always did and then pointed to my shirt. "Are you a magician or something?" he asked. I said I was. He told me that I ought to meet his friend and former English teacher, Brad Kerwin, who was often known simply as 'Dr. K.'. He gave me Brad's number, which I called as soon as I was done with class.

Talking to Brad on the phone felt like catching up with an old friend. He was kind, funny and excited to meet up. He invited me to the next meeting of a regular magic session he held at a place called Coffee Talk in Kaimuki.

The following Monday, I stuffed as many magic toys as I could into a backpack and caught a ride with Tony to Coffee Talk. I couldn't wait to show off my skills. As I walked in, I

Brad Kerwin, also known as 'Dr. K.'

Curtis Kam, the author and Brad Kerwin

noticed a small side room in which several guys were shuffling cards, reading books and palming coins. Just as I arrived, they made a phone call to sing 'Happy Birthday' to a friend on the mainland by the name of Kainoa Harbottle. I later learned that this group included Brad Kerwin, Jason Fleming, Kekoa Erickson, Bulla, Richard Hucko and Curtis Kam.

I quietly watched these guys enjoying their magic session. After a few hours, I realized that there wasn't a single trick, sleight or method I'd seen before. The truth of the matter was that I had nothing to bring to the table. Before I got there, I had arrogantly assumed I'd be able to impress these magicians I'd never met before. I was wrong and in a single evening I was humbled again. However, everyone I met was accepting and I soon found a new community of brothers.

On many Mondays, after we'd spent hours together at Coffee Talk we would session until two or three in the morning at Kahala Zippy's. I'd get up at 8 AM on Tuesday, drink half a pot of coffee and go to class. To be honest, I can't remember much from those Tuesday morning classes.

"While we can never fully comprehend our limits, to see our ignorance is itself a kind of wisdom."

— Daniel D. Doriani

3: Coin Operated

"In music, striking the right note at the wrong time results in a sour note. The ear as well the eye are capable of suspicion and detection. We must forever strive for perfect harmony in our execution."

— *Roger Klause*

Finger Palm to Finger Palm Switch

Before we dive into the next routine, try this exercise with two coins. This is Curtis Kam's Finger Palm to Finger Palm Switch.

Place Coin A in right-hand finger palm. Hold Coin B at the fingertips of the thumb, first, and second fingers of the same hand.

You're going to exchange these two coins.

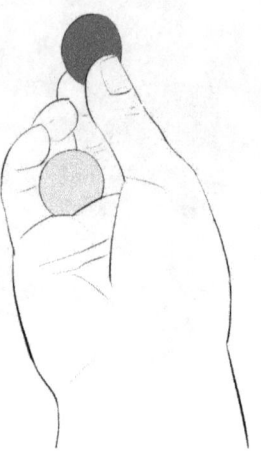

From this position, move your fourth and fifth fingers toward the base of your thumb. Note that you are not trying to touch your thumb with these fingers. You're dislodging Coin A from Finger Palm so its uppermost edge swings down and contacts the lower part of your thumb.

Your thumb applies slight counterpressure to hold the coin in place by its edge.

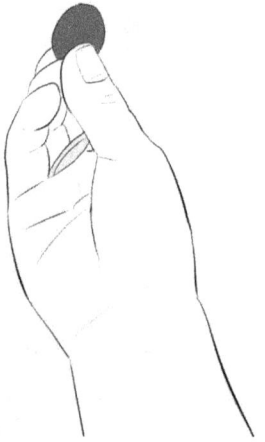

Keeping the coin pinned, lift your fourth and fifth fingers away and toward Coin B until this coin is entirely concealed from the audience by all four fingers.

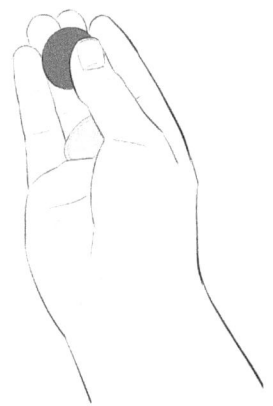

Release Coin B from your fingertips, and it will slide into the gap between the fingers and the pinned Coin A. Don't worry about the sound at this stage. Just familiarize yourself with the actions.

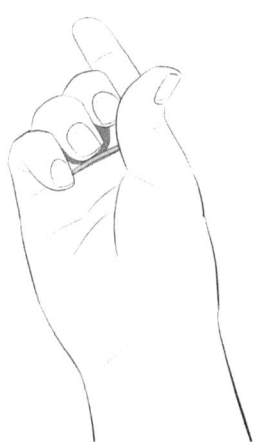

Curl your fingers around the edge of Coin B until your fingertips can lightly touch the upper side of Coin A, which you still hold with your thumb.

Now move your thumb under this coin and push it to your fingertips, keeping Coin B in Finger Palm.

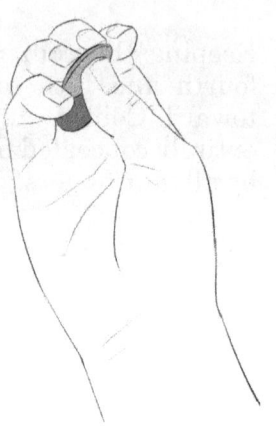

You're now back to the starting position with the coins reversed.

Practice this with one coin at your fingertips and one coin palmed until you can do it smoothly and quickly with minimal wrist movement. Eventually, add another coin in the palm and hold two coins fanned at the fingertips. Once you've mastered that, execute the sleight exchanging three for three.

Tacking the coins together with putty is another way to practice and slowly add coins.

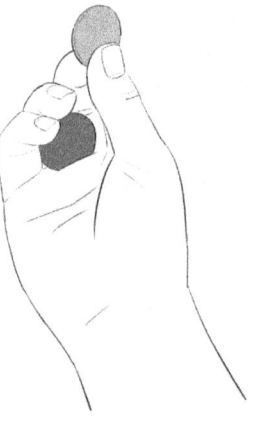

γινώσκω: From The Wizard of Waikiki

A few words from Curtis: "I don't mean to suggest that this is a truly visual change at the fingertips. The audience does see the coins drop out of sight for a second. However, experience shows that it's perceived as a change, and looks like a change, despite the fact that to you, it feels like you're juggling live bees." ('By All Means', Kam, pp. 22-23)

Aren't you glad we started with just two bees?

Credits

See Curtis Kam's 'Palms of Steel 2: Fists of Fury' to find out more about what Curtis calls 'the gory details'. He first described this move in his 'By All Means' lecture notes (2007).

Curtis Kam performing 'Beijing Coins Across' and making it look easy

The author, after much practice and frustration, performing 'Bejing For Mere Mortals'

Beijing For Mere Mortals

'Beijing Coins Across' is one of Curtis Kam's signature creations with ungimmicked coins. Three silver dollars appear at his fingertips, and even though his hands never seem to touch, the coins travel one at a time from his left hand to the right. Just as the last coin makes the journey, they all transform into Chinese coins!

The Chinese coins change back to silver coins one at a time at the fingertips, but then they all change back to Chinese coins in the blink of an eye. Exasperated, the magician tries to put the Chinese coins away, but they all come back and, you guessed it, change one more time.

A Different Approach

The day I decided to learn Curtis' routine, I remember jumping on eBay and impulse-buying three silver Peace dollars and matching Chinese coins. When they arrived, I quickly realized that my hands were neither large enough nor strong enough to work with six dollar-sized coins simultaneously. I also discovered that while the sleights Curtis used worked in his hands, many of them looked unnatural in mine.

I've made a few adjustments to the routine using half-crowns or half-dollars. I've also simplified a few of the moves to make them look more natural for my hands. I think many 'non-palms-of-steel' magicians like myself will find the strategies below a bit more manageable.

The explanation is broken down into bite-sized steps. I recommend learning them one day at a time. When you perform coin magic, it's essential to know each step of your routine extremely well so you don't find yourself pausing awkwardly while holding a fistful of palmed coins. Master each step before moving on, so your mind is always one step ahead. With Curtis' kind permission, I'm happy to bring you 'Beijing for Mere Mortals'.

Props and Setup

You need three identical silver coins and another set of three identical coins that contrast strongly with the first three. All six coins need to be the same size. After trying various coins, I now use soft Barber half dollars and Chinese replica coins. I find that because these coins have smoother surfaces than most regular coins, they move more silently against each other.

Producing Three Silver Coins

Use any production sequence you like. The one that follows is simple and mostly works out of Finger Palm. If you have your own method, feel free to skip ahead.

One. Begin with the Chinese coins in your right trouser pocket and the silver coins in Finger Palm in your left hand. When you're ready to perform, allow your hands to meet momentarily. Reach into your left hand with your right thumb, slide out a single silver coin, and secretly move it directly into right-hand Finger Palm. [Fig. 1]

Produce the first coin from your right hand in any way that you like. In most cases, I produce the coin from a spectator's elbow or shoulder. After displaying the coin, allow it to fall openly onto your fingers, preparing to Finger Palm it again.

Clean-Up. Keeping the visible coin in Finger Palm, turn your right hand palm down over your palm-down left fingers and tap your right hand's finger palmed coin against your left first fingernail. As you do this, push another coin out of left-hand Finger Palm to your fingertips [Fig. 2]. Done smoothly, when your hands separate, it will appear that you've simply passed a coin from your right hand to your left — a Fingertip Shuttle Pass.

Two. Produce the second coin (actually the first coin again) however you wish. One magical way is to wave the visible coin in your left hand over the right's closed fist. Open your hand, revealing the coin. [Fig. 3]

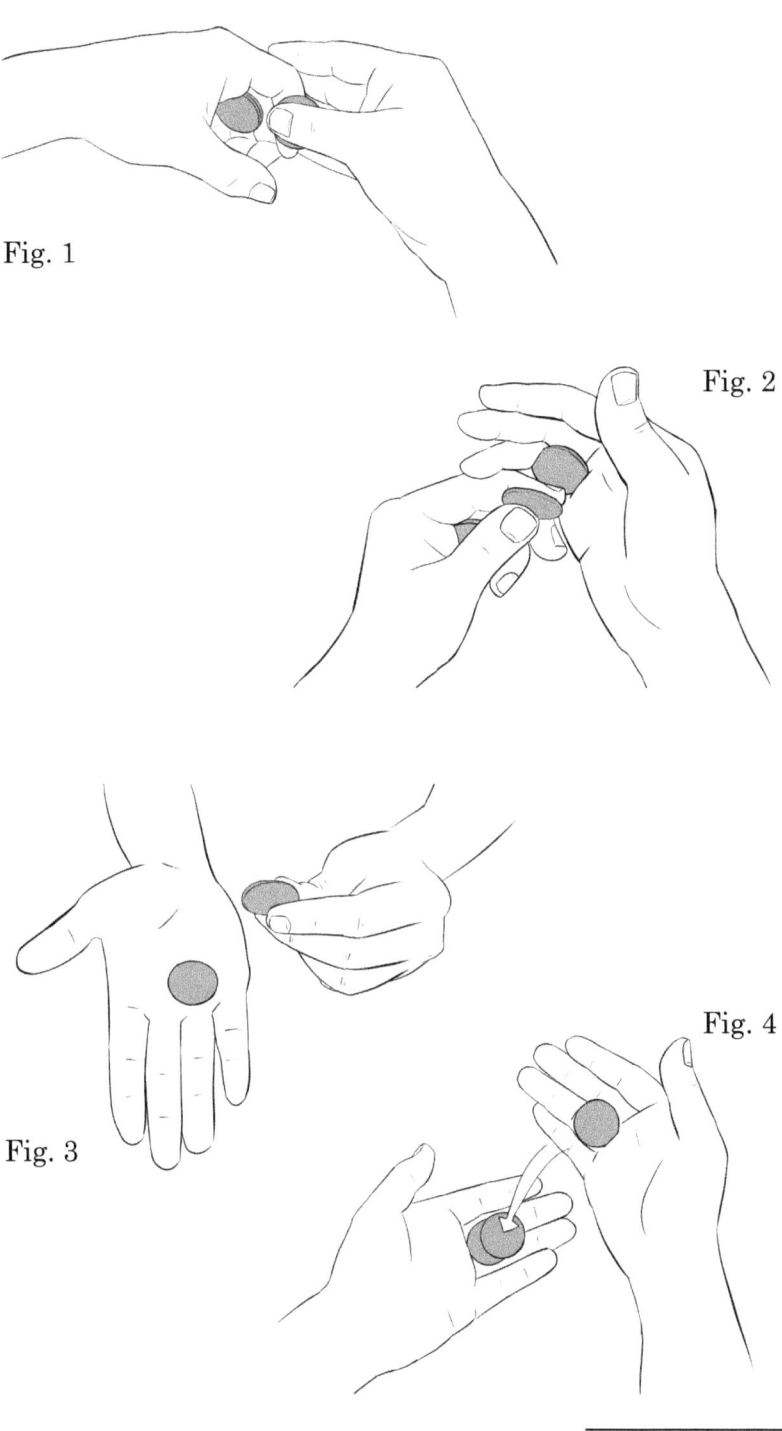

Fig. 1

Fig. 2

Fig. 3

Fig. 4

Clean up. Drop the left-hand coin onto the right-hand one. You now *seem* to toss both coins back into your left hand, the right turning palm down while the left hand turns palm up to receive them. In reality, your right hand turns down and releases only one coin, retaining the other in Finger Palm. The falling coin drops onto the left-hand finger palmed coin and you display both as if they just landed there. [Fig. 4].

The audience will hear two 'clinks' and it will seem as if you've dropped both coins from your right hand to your left. Display both coins in a fan at your left fingertips.

Situation: your left hand holds two spread coins. One coin remains Finger Palmed in your right.

Three. Transfer the two-coin fan to the fingertips of your right-hand [Fig. 5]. Immediately reach in front of your body with your left hand as if about to produce a third coin. After a few attempts, reveal that the third coin has already appeared with the coins in your right hand [Fig. 6].

To do this, curl your right-hand fingers until the fanned coins nearly touch the Finger-Palmed coin. Your thumb and index finger hold the two fanned coins in place as your third finger contacts the finger-palmed coin and pins it against the fan of coins [Fig. 7]. Uncurl your fingers. You've added the third coin to the fan at the fingertips. This should happen quickly and silently as your left hand provides misdirection.

Intermission. At this point, let your audience examine the coins. As they're doing so, reach into your trouser pocket and Finger Palm the Chinese coins. When you're ready to move on, take back the silver coins.

First Coin Across. With the Chinese coins Finger Palmed in your right hand, take the silver coins at your right-hand fingertips, holding them in a fan just as before.

Open your left hand palm up and drop the lowermost silver coin of the fan onto your fingertips. Drop the next coin onto the palm [Fig. 8]. The last silver coin in the right hand taps the two coins, "One, two..."

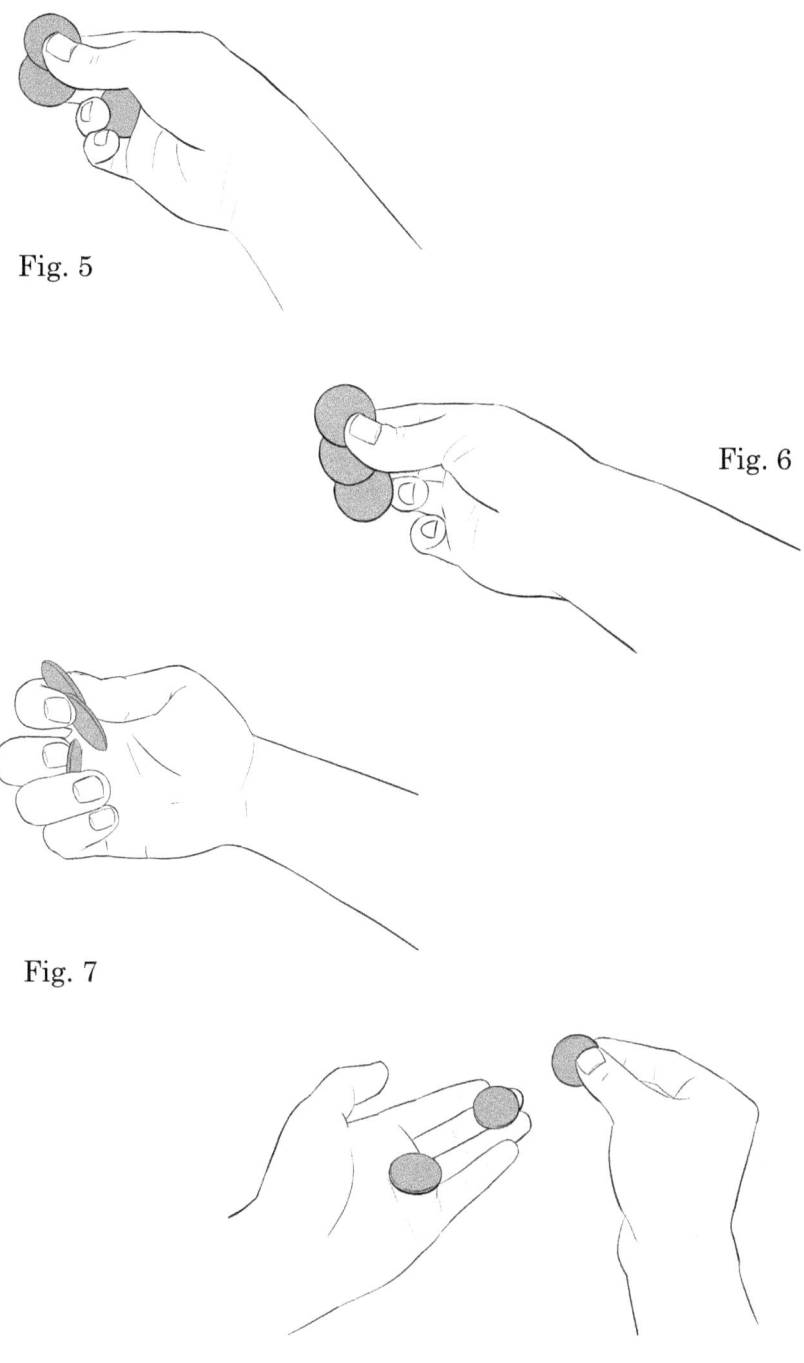

Fig. 5

Fig. 6

Fig. 7

Fig. 8

On the count of 'three', you perform two actions at the same time.

Lightly toss the coin at your left fingertips onto the coin on the left palm so it 'clinks'. [Fig. 9]. At the same time, your right hand pulls its coin out of sight into fingertip rest.

Close your left hand over its coins into a loose fist. Your right hand silently adds the silver coin onto the stack of Chinese coins in Finger Palm. It will look as if you've placed all three coins into your left hand.

After a magical gesture with both fists, show that a silver coin has crossed to your right hand by pushing it out of fingertip rest. Open your left hand to show that two remain. With your left thumb, push one of the silver coins in your left hand up to fingertips again, ready for the next phase.

Second Coin Across. Close your left hand over the two coins again. As you do, turn your hand palm down and move the coin at your fingertips into heel clip position [Fig. 10].

In one smooth motion, your right thumb pulls its silver coin into Finger Palm as this hand takes the left hand's coin out of heel clip [Fig. 11]. Just as this coin is stolen, turn your left hand palm up and point to your left arm. The standard line here is, "The coin traveled up my sleeve, across my chest, and down the other sleeve." Gesture with your right-hand coin as you explain, covering the steal.

Make another magical gesture with both hands and allow the visible silver coin to fall onto the Finger-Palmed coins. The audience hears that a second coin's arrived. Open your left hand, showing one coin. As they look at the single coin, push the two silver coins in your right hand up to your fingertips. Pushing the two silver coins up from the five-coin stack will take some practice.

Third Coin Across. Here comes the surprise. Holding the left-hand coin at your fingertips, begin rotating it rapidly like a key. As you speed up, pull it into Finger Palm [Fig. 12]. "The last coin vanishes from here and goes in the opposite direction…"

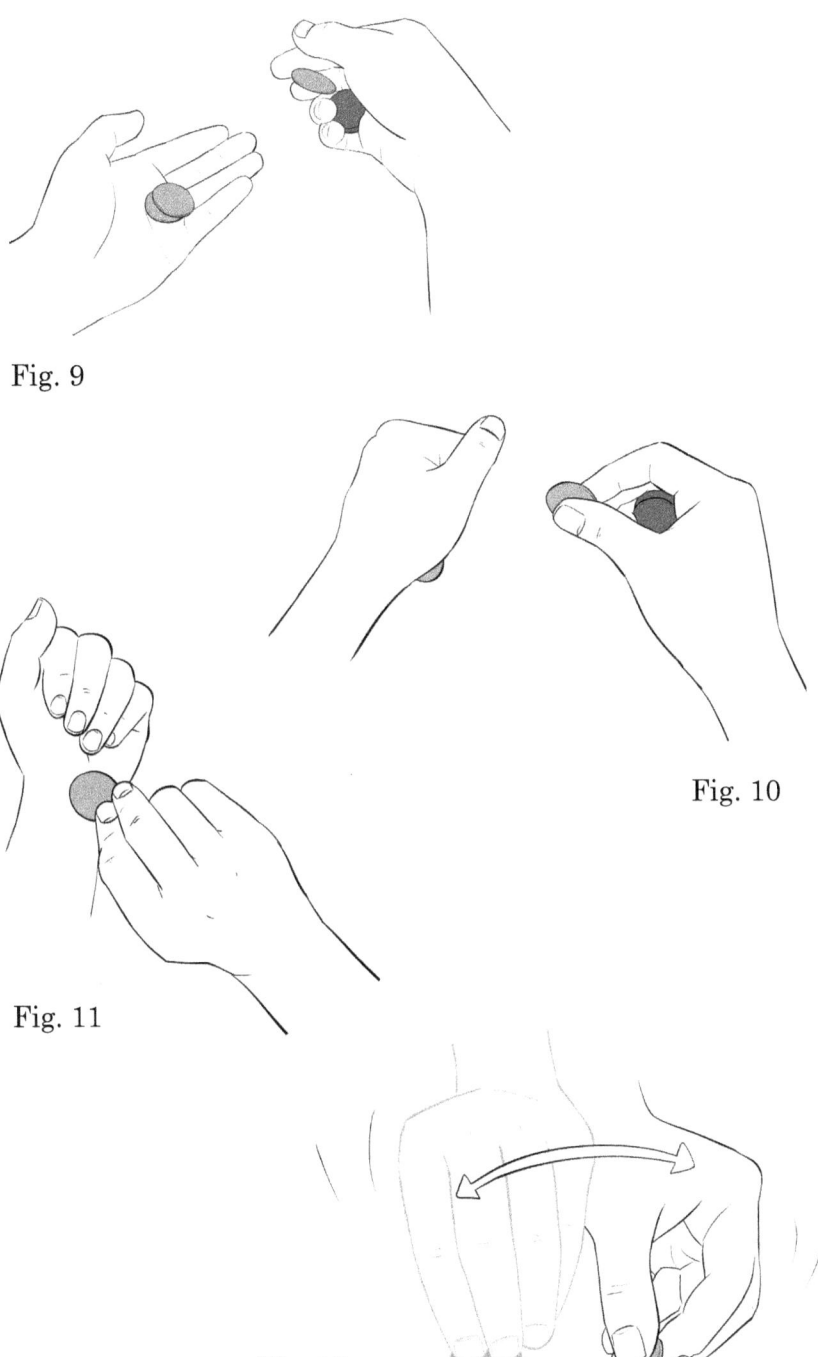

Fig. 9

Fig. 10

Fig. 11

Fig. 12

The moment it's out of sight, open your hand in an upward tossing motion [Fig. 13].

"...it flies around the world and past China."

Follow the invisible flying coin with your eyes. With practice, this one-handed vanish is quite surprising. As the invisible coin reaches your right hand, execute the Finger Palm to Finger Palm switch (described in the previous section). In this case, drop the two visible silver coins into Finger Palm and exchange them for the three Chinese coins [Fig. 14].

"When they come back...they have a Chinese accent."

Situation: three Chinese coins visible at the right-hand fingertips, two silver coins in right-hand Finger Palm, one silver coin in left-hand Finger Palm. Whew! You might need a water break at this point.

Intermission. Here's a simple way to clean up and put the coins into position for the next phase. "They really look like Chinese coins. They have a hole through the center. They even sound Chinese." Lower your right hand, allow the Chinese coins fan to close into a stack, and curl them into a Thumb Palm [Fig. 15].

Toss both silver coins into your left hand. Done casually as you speak to the audience, it will appear that you've tossed the three Chinese coins into your left hand. Holding the silver coins in a loose fist, jingle them near a spectator's ear. "Do those sound Chinese to you? [She says yes] Wow, I didn't know you speak Chinese."

Bring your hands together and tap the edges of the Thumb-Palmed Chinese coins against the silver ones [Fig. 16], then bring the Chinese coins back into view by placing them in a fan at your left fingertips . It should appear that you simply took the Chinese coins out of your left fist.

Move the Chinese coins openly between your hands. Finish with the fan of Chinese coins in your right hand and the silver coins Finger Palmed in your left.

Fig. 13

Fig. 14

Fig. 15

Fig. 16

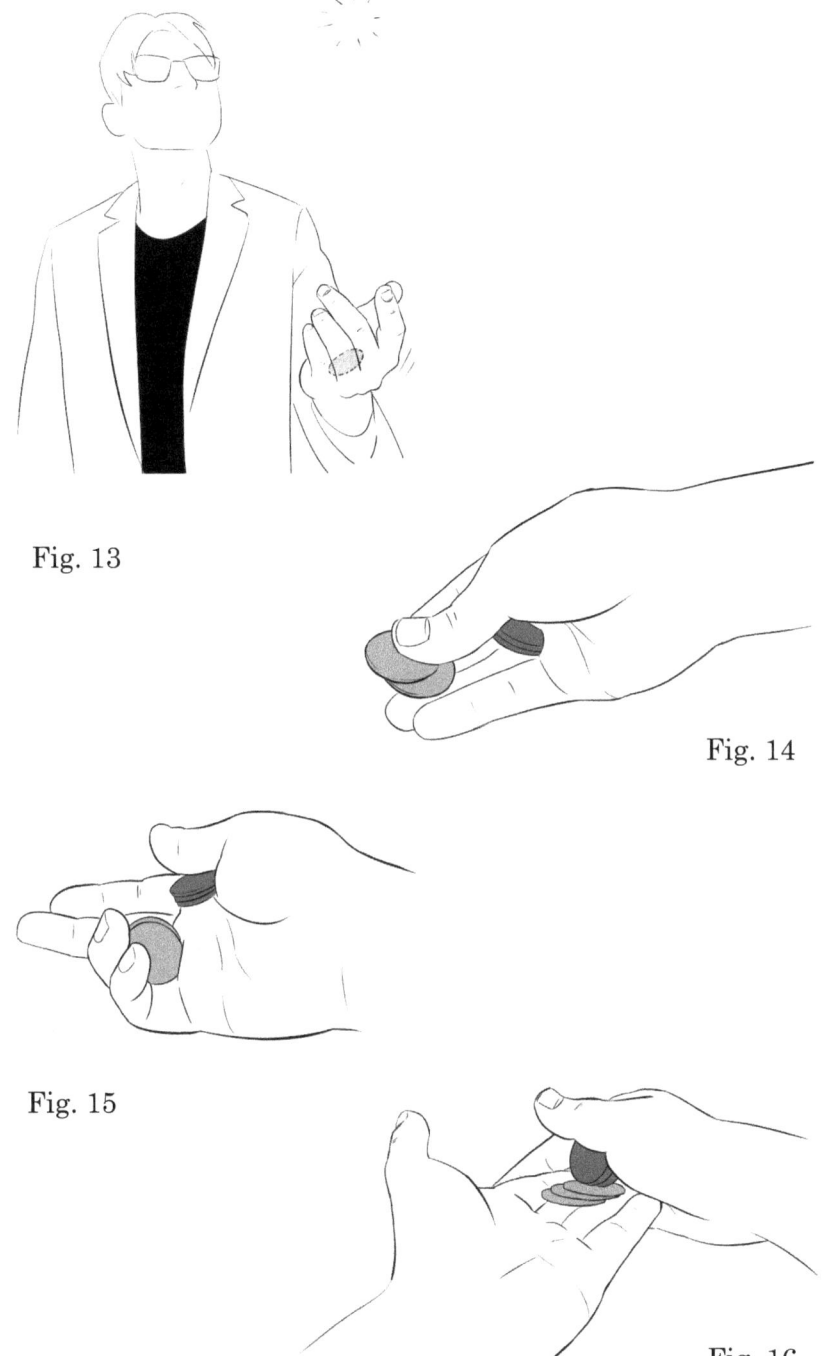

97

Finger-Tip Wild Coin. You now cause the Chinese coins to visually transform back into silver coins one at a time.

First Change. Bring your left hand to the top coin of the fan of Chinese coins *as if* you're going to take it. Instead, push a silver coin out of Finger Palm behind and above the top coin of the fan. At the same time, your right hand fingers steal the bottom coin of the fan into Finger Palm [Fig. 17 and 18]. (This steal of the bottom coin is used in several versions of 'Three Fly'.) With practice, it will appear as though the coin instantly changed as you took it with your left hand. Hand the silver coin to a spectator to examine.

Second Change. As your left hand leaves the spectator's hand, immediately execute the same change as you come back to meet your right hand and apparently take the top coin. The right fingers again steal the bottom Chinese coin and add it to the coin in Finger Palm. Don't hand out the silver coin this time.

Situation: in your left hand, one silver coin is at your fingertips and one in Finger Palm. In your right, one Chinese coin is held at the fingertips and two are stacked in Finger Palm. The spectator holds one silver coin.

Third Change. Place the silver coin in your left hand behind the visible Chinese coin in your right. Immediately tilt your right hand palm up until the fan of contrasting coins is parallel to the floor. At the same time, push out the third silver coin in your left hand and place it on top of the silver coin in the right.

Steal the Chinese coin into Finger Palm as your right hand comes away with the two silver coins [Fig. 19 and 20].

Fig. 17

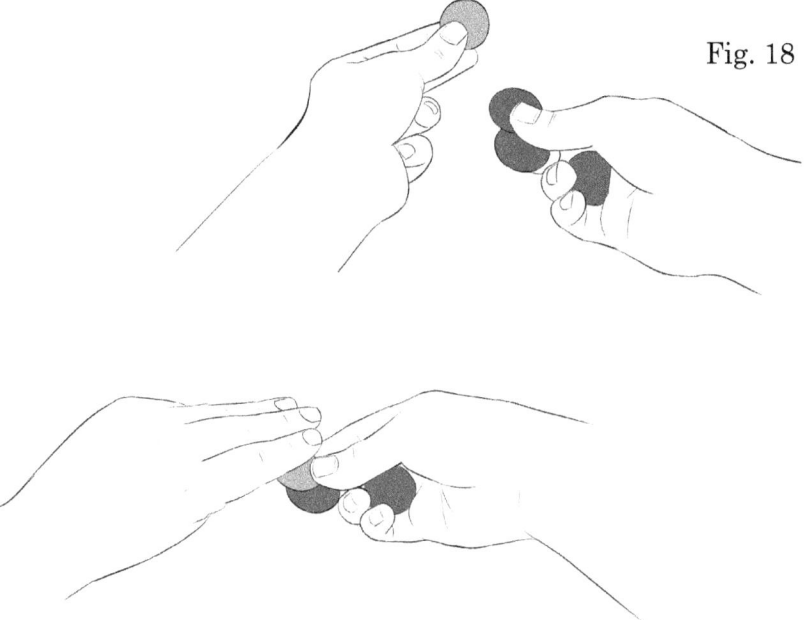

Fig. 18

Fig. 19

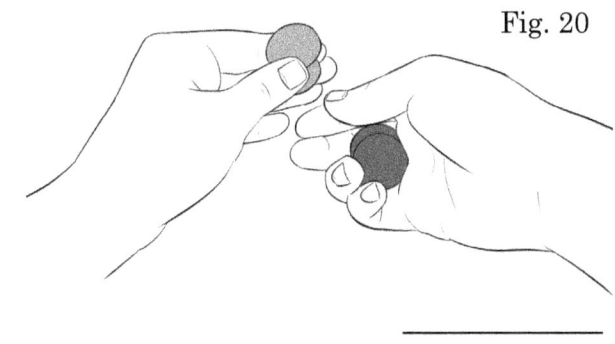

Fig. 20

I like to turn both coins over so the audience is now looking at the other side before taking one in each hand. [Fig. 21]

With practice, it will appear as though the Chinese coin turns silver as you rotate the coins. This change isn't in Curtis' original routine. Take the silver coin from the spectator and form a fan of silver coins at your left fingertips.

Flash Change. Next, transfer the stack of Chinese coins from Finger Palm to Thumb Palm in your right hand. To do this, curl in your right fingers, causing the stack to turn over and move into the fork of your thumb, where you grip it. This is covered by pointing to your wristwatch with your right index finger as you make the adjustment, saying, "Just a moment ago…"

Approach the fan of coins with your right hand and execute Sol Stone's Tumble Change [Fig. 22].

"…these were Chinese coins." Briefly, your right hand scoops the fan of coins into Finger Palm as your left hand takes the coins out of Thumb Palm, spreading them before your right hand moves away. For the fine details on this striking transformation, see 'Coin Magic' (Kaufman, pg 99) or 'Palms of Steel 2: Fists of Fury'.

False Ending. Begin putting the Chinese coins into different pockets, as if to finish your performance, but secretly retain one in left-hand Finger Palm.

"The hardest part of this trick is getting the coins to stop!" Produce the Chinese coin from your right elbow, and do a coin roll with it before taking it with your right hand (which is still holding out three coins). Now, do a retention pass into your left hand, and immediately produce a second coin (actually the same coin) from your left elbow.

This time, pivot the Chinese coin into Down's Palm or a deep edge grip as you let all three silver coins in your right hand drop out of Finger Palm into your left Fig. 23]. It will appear as though you added the first Chinese coin to the second with a 'clink' sound to prove it.

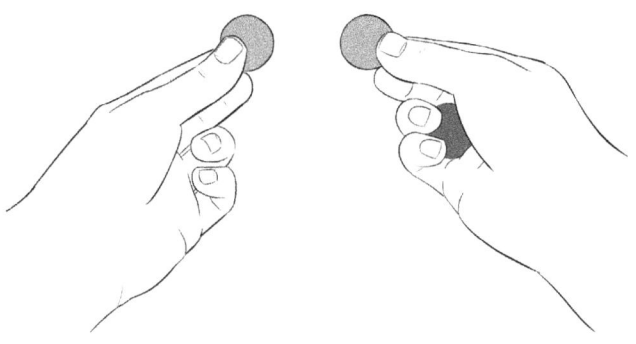

Fig. 21

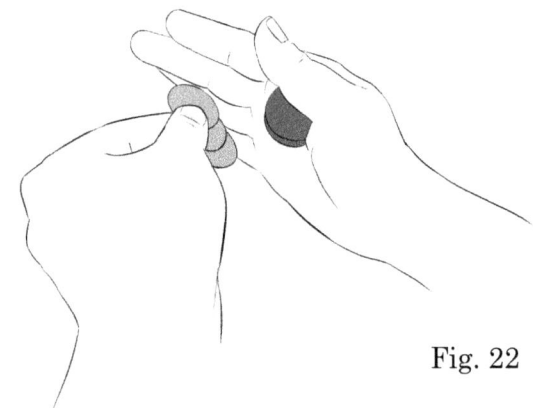

Fig. 22

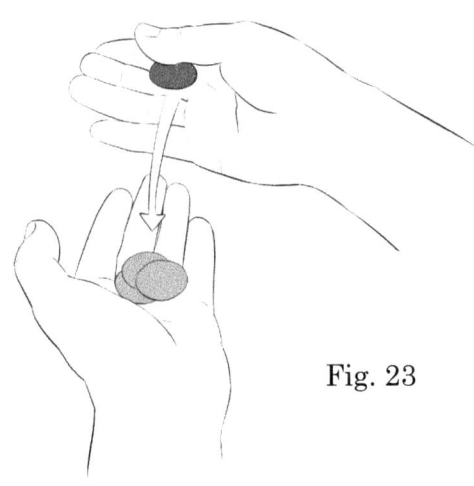

Fig. 23

Produce the same Chinese coin a third time however you wish. Execute a coin roll with the right hand. As you do, lever up the three silver coins with your left thumb in preparation for a modified (and simpler) Finger Palm to Finger Palm switch [Fig. 24]. Allow the coin to roll off your right little finger into the gap between the silver coins and the left fingers.

Immediately Finger Palm the Chinese coin and push up the silver coins, showing that they have turned into silver coins... again!

γινώσκω: A Drop in the Bucket

I'll never forget the grind of practicing sonatas and concertos for trumpet during my music performance degree. Understanding the composer's intentions, working out each nuance, and developing the necessary chops is a slow and grueling process that my father calls 'a daily drop in the bucket'. I remember frustrating days of scarcely noticeable progress even after hours of practice and repetition.

Sometimes, a piece is your worst enemy for months. Then one day you start your practice routine and suddenly realize that the concerto itself seems to accept your efforts. It begins to sing through you.

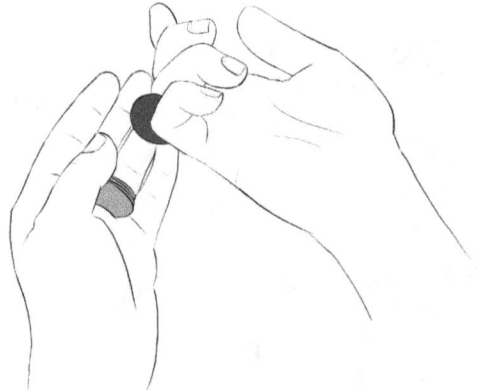

Fig. 24

After more hours in the woodshed, you and the piece step onto a dark recital stage together and hope for the best. When the house lights come back on, you and the piece are friends for life having enjoyed glory (or trauma) together.

Of all the magic I've learned, no other piece reminds me of that process as much as 'Beijing For Mere Mortals'. Put in the time and work, and Curtis' concerto with coins will sing through you, too.

Credits

David Roth's Shuttle Pass is found in Richard Kaufman's 'Coin Magic' (1981), but variations of the utility move were used by magicians long before with different objects. Reginald Scot ('The Discoverie of Witchcraft', 1584) recorded similar maneuvers applied to coins and balls.

Another utility move with many variations is the Utility Switch described by this name in J.B. Bobo's 'Modern Coin Magic' (1952).

The Click Pass used for the first coin across belongs to Juan Tamariz from 'Monedas, Monedas... (y monedas)' (1969).

The Heel Clip and The Heel Clip Steal entered many magicians' vocabulary though Geoffery Latta and Scott Weiser in Richard Kaufman's 'Coin Magic' (1981). But an earlier move, The Steal by Cardini, used similar mechanics. It's in Arthur H. Buckley's 'Principles and Deceptions' (1948). Larry Jennings was the first to apply the move to get one ahead, while apparently showing the same coin, in a trick called 'Hold Tight' in 'Richard's Almanac', Volume 1 (1985).

Sol Stone's Tumble Switch/Change first appeared in 'Coin Magic' (1981). I recommend studying the 'Palms of Steel 2: Fists of Fury' DVD to see Curtis Kam use it to exchange three for three.

Rolling Unnest

Here's a new sleight I created for getting one ahead with a shell coin. We will use this to get one ahead several times in the next routine.

You'll need four silver coins and a matching shell. Display the coins in a fan at your right fingertips. The uppermost coin is on the near side of the spread; the lowermost coin is nearest the audience. The second coin from the top is the nested coin and shell. The mouth of the shell faces you.

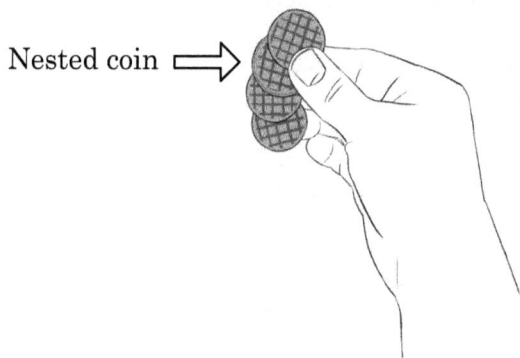

Nested coin

Flash both sides of the coins by briefly tilting your hand palm up. With your third finger, pull the bottom-most coin into finger palm (a move often used in Three-Fly routines).

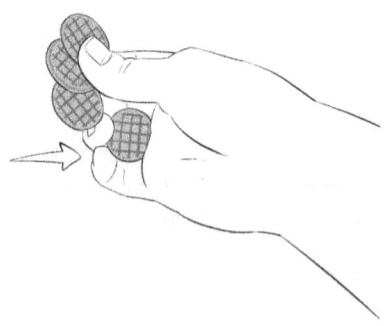

As you turn your hand palm down, place three coins (and the shell) across your left fingers.

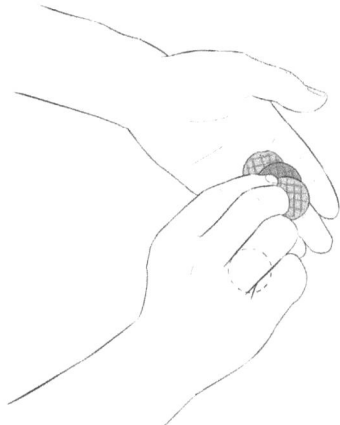

As soon as the coins touch your palm-up left hand, your right thumb lifts the shell and rolls it and the coin above it toward your fingertips.

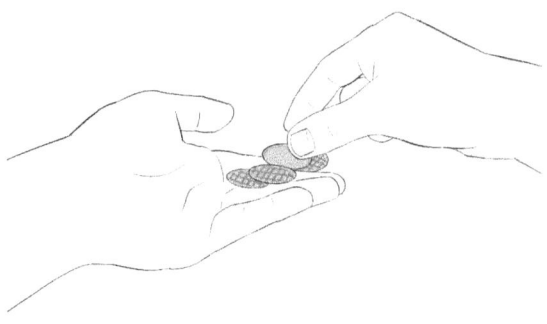

Use your left first finger as a track to help you roll the coins, spreading them evenly. Continuing with this rhythm, I sometimes pick up the coin above the shell and briefly display it to the audience.

When you execute this move, get your right fingers out of the way as soon as possible, using only your thumb to perform the rolling action. This will make the procedure look open, fair, and not too 'cozy'. Display them across your open left hand to the spectators on your left.

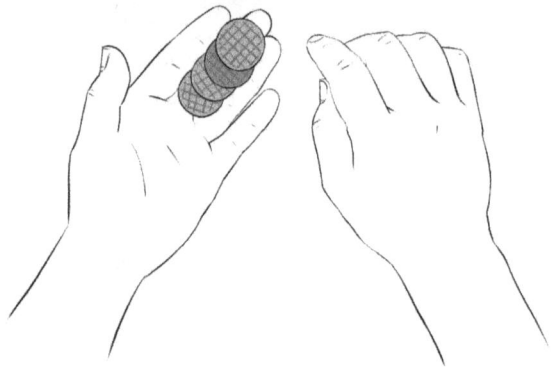

Situation: you're showing an apparent spread of four coins on your left hand. From the bottom: two coins, an empty shell, and the third coin. One coin remains in right-hand finger palm.

That's all there is to it! Rolling Unnest is simply a way to get one ahead, but it's an accessible starting point if you're new to expanded shell work. It features in the routine that follows, 'Shots Backfired', which has a very simple plot. If you're an advanced coin magician, feel free to use this next routine as an opportunity to add your own favorite sleights and strategies!

Shots Backfired

Four coins travel from your left hand to a glass on your right one at a time, 'clinking' as they go. The fourth coin takes on a life of its own and jumps to the glass and then back to your hand three times before finally arriving silently in the glass with the others.

You'll need four coins, a matching shell, a small rocks glass and Steve sitting on your left.

Remove what seem to be four coins (actually four + shell) from a coin purse and hold them in a fan in your left hand in preparation for the Rolling Unnest.

"Before I go any further, we have to agree on one thing. Steve, how many coins do you see here? [He says there are four] Perfect. Some people ask me why four? As a music teacher, it's about as high as I can count."

Execute The Rolling Unnest, leaving four coins (actually three and a shell) displayed on your open left hand and one concealed in right-hand Finger Palm.

"If there is one area where I've clocked my ten thousand hours, it's counting to four. Watch. [Close both hands into fists] One, two, three... [produce the coin in your right hand] ... four."

Music nerds are free to use a 4/4 conducting pattern if they wish. Open your left hand, displaying only three coins.

"Not exactly the reaction I hoped for but, to be fair, you didn't know what would happen. You didn't know that one coin was going to travel magically from one hand to the other. That's why I brought the glass. So you can see and hear when the magic happens."

Drop the first coin into the glass. Pick up the remaining three coins (you actually have three + shell) as a fan with your right hand.

Have the people on your right confirm you only have three coins. Perform another Rolling Unnest to show three to the people on your left.

"Steve, you look like you could be a music teacher. What do you do for a living?"

He's probably not a music teacher. Roll with it.

"I'm delegating maestro duties to you anyway. When you're ready, please count off the magic. 120 beats per minute or March tempo, please."

Classic Palm the coin in your right hand as you pick up the glass by the rim. Close your left hand, allowing the shell to nest with the coin beneath it. Once Steve starts counting, drop the palmed coin into the glass and display two coins at your left-hand fingertips.

"Excellent job, Steve. Well on your way to clocking ten thousand reps. Only nine... nine-thousand... to go. I don't know, I've never had to count that far."

Place both coins on the fingers of your palm-up right-hand, with the nested shell and coin on top. Display them briefly to the people on your right. You now execute a variation of Professor Hoffman's shell unnest.

With your left hand, pick up the nested coin and shell between your first and third fingers on opposite edges. Your second finger is on top and your thumb supports the coin from below. Slightly lower your thumb so the coin comes slightly out of the shell, temporarily balanced on the ball of your thumb [Fig. 1] just before you slide the coin against the rim of the shell, creating a two-coin fan.

Display the fan as you finger palm the remaining coin, concealing it in your right hand. [Fig. 2] It will appear as if you simply took the two coins from your right hand into your left. Display the coins to the people on your left. Although this may sound complicated, it only takes a moment.

"The third coin's a charm, Steve. Once again!"

Get Steve to do the counting as he did before — one, two, three, four. Allow the coin and shell to nest in your left fist. Classic Palm the coin in your right hand as you take the glass by the rim again. Perform a tossing motion with your left hand, but instead of dropping the coin out of right-hand Classic Palm, drop your right hand with a little bit of force to create a 'clink'. When you show just one coin remaining in your left hand, Steve (and the rest of your audience) will conclude that the third coin has made the journey.

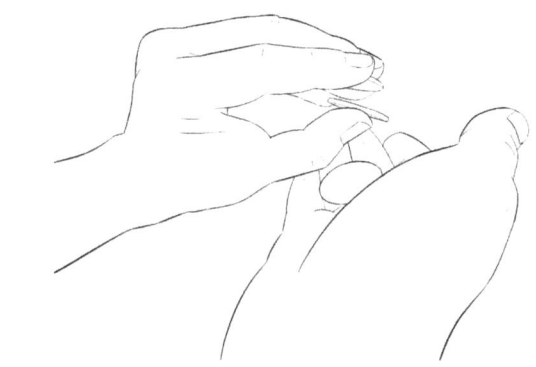

Fig. 1

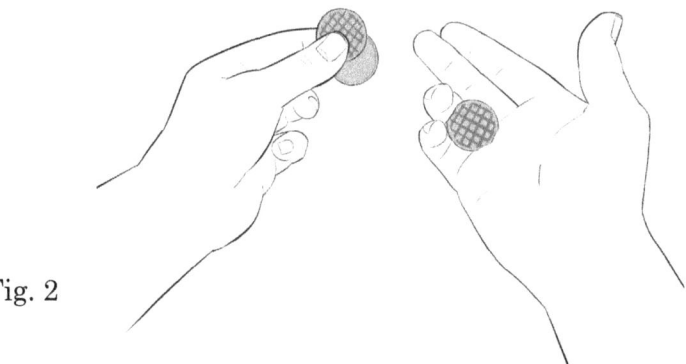

Fig. 2

"Some of you may wonder what this trick looked like before I could count to four."

Display the coin in your left hand and execute your preferred version of the Shuttle Pass to your right hand. Simply drop the coin into the glass.

"I agree, it wasn't too impressive. Let's rewind."

Make a tossing motion from the glass to your left hand, and show the coin has returned to it.

"Maybe it's more impressive in slow motion?"

Simply take the shell off the coin and turn your wrist, hiding the solid coin. [Fig. 3] Dramatically carry the shell to the glass and nest it gently onto the top coin inside.

"I didn't think so. Let's rewind."

Make a tossing motion from the glass to the left hand again, and show the coin has returned.

"Some of you may wonder how many coins I have at this point."

Spill the 'three' coins out of the glass being very careful not to unnest the shell.

"Remember, I can only count to four. Steve, these people still do not trust me. Hold out your hands like an open book, please. I'm going to send the last one to the glass under test conditions."

Stack the coins singly onto Steve's hands, making sure that the shelled coin is at the very top. [Fig. 4] Have Steve confirm that he can see four coins. Square up the stack, remove the shell from the top and have Steve close his hands over the coins like a book. Have him place his closed hands over the glass. [Fig. 5].

"Watch. One... two... three... four!"

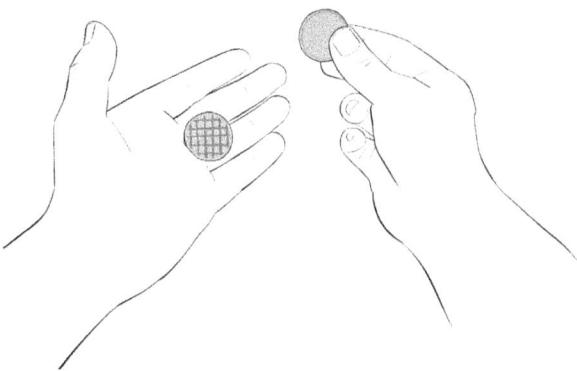

Fig. 3

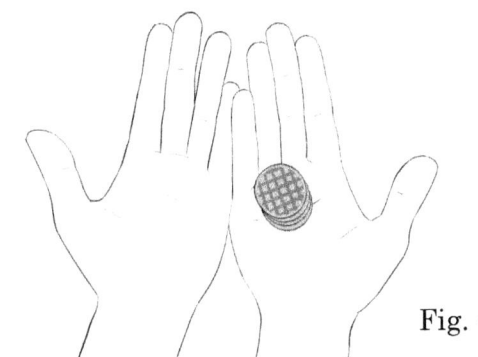

Fig. 4

Fig. 5

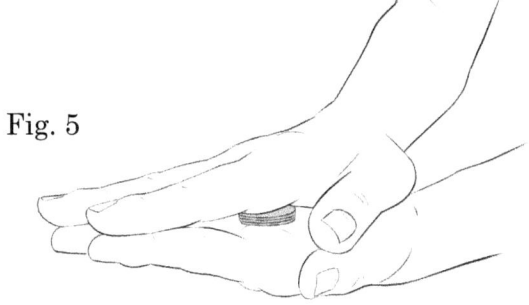

Display the shell in left-hand Spellbound position, and execute a Spidergrip Vanish. On the count of 'three', snatch the shell out of your left hand and immediately Classic Palm it, simulating a one-handed vanish on 'four'. As soon as your right hand takes the coin, close your left into a tight fist, making it seem suspicious.

"*Listen...*"

Bring your left hand up to your ear and slowly open it. Enjoy this subtle sucker moment. Appear confused when there's no clink. Allow the shell to fall into Finger Palm.

Have Steve lift his hands. Take the glass and inspect it for a moment. Place the glass onto the shell, concealing it perfectly. Look over at Steve's closed hands.

"Steve, this goes wrong once in a while. And I love when it does. I think the last coin got trapped halfway. Open your hands and count the coins into the glass. [He finds there are four]. I think we can all agree Maestro Steve's four-count is better than mine, ladies and gentlemen. Give him a hand! Bravissimo!"

γινώσκω: Fire the Narrator!

When performing a trick like Coins Across, the laziest patter option is to simply describe what's happening. "Three here, one left on this side." This is boring!

When I thought about how to script this effect, I used my teaching job to make things a little more personal, fun and engaging. When you script a routine, ask yourself what you could say that might add more fun and interest. Be a performer, not just a narrator!

Credits

Magicians have made coins travel from one place to another for centuries. The plot (using covered glass) was popularized by Bob Kline in 1947 with his 'Copentro' prop, although Jack Hughes created and sold a similar prop ten years prior (See 'The Jack Hughes World of Magic', Vol. 1, 1981). Other precursors include 'The Coin of Mercury' in the May 1900 issue of 'Mahatma' (Vol. 3 No. 11) and Professor Hoffman's 'The Glass and Goblet Cover' in 'Modern Magic' (1876).

Edward Victor performed a coins to glass routine called 'A Silver Collection' at Maskelyne's Theater. The method (totally sleight of hand) is in 'Magic of the Hands' (1937).

The unshell sleight that begins with the grip described appears in Professor Hoffman's 'More Magic' (1890).

The 'Spider' or 'Spidergrip' vanish is mentioned in 'The Conjuring Archive': "Often misattributed to Ed Marlo, this vanish was first put into print by Walter B. Gibson, under the title 'The Misdirection Drop' in 'The Sphinx', Vol. 17 No. 12, Feb. 1919, p. 239. John Moehring discovered this citation. The Gibson vanish is done from French Drop position, as the vanish is commonly done. Marlo's similar Spider Vanish ('Coining Magic', 1957, p. 8) starts with the coin resting in finger-palm position, but uses the same misdirective psychology and actions of Gibson's vanish."

114

4: Cocktail Parties & Table Hopping

"One of my goals with every group I perform for is to leave them at least one energy level higher than I found them. If I accomplish that, I know I'm doing something right."

— *Tyler Wilson*

Interruption Or Opportunity?

Even when I arrive hours early, I often find myself starting late at corporate events that require table-to-table magic. When company members arrive, they usually take their time getting settled. They grab a drink, talk shop and take a few sunset selfies before dinner. It's not uncommon for a half hour or more to pass before they find a table.

Even though it's my job to liven up the event, I hate having to interrupt people who are already engaged and clearly enjoying each other's company. On the other hand, it's a bad look if the event coordinator sees the talent they hired standing around. So, what's the best way to handle this sort of situation?

Here's the best solution I've found so far. Start by targeting a group. To approach them with the right attitude, imagine they are old friends that you haven't seen in ages and can't wait to catch up with. (My friend Jade taught me this little mind trick... more from her later in this book!)

Next, follow this three-step approach:

1. Break into their circle and welcome them to the event.

2. Quickly introduce yourself and your role.

3. Perform just one quick trick but make it clear you'll be back with more later.

Even if the groups *asks* you for more, tell them you're saving 'the good stuff' for the main show that you'll perform at their table later in the evening.

I've found this approach doesn't seem intrusive and also gets people anticipating the magic you're going to show them later, so it's a win-win. It also makes it a lot easier to approach tables once the event is under way: you know the names of the guests (well, at least a few of them), they are expecting you and they already know a little about your personality, your role at the event and the quality of your work. Instead of people thinking of you as an unwelcome (and unrequested) interruption, they see you as an element of entertainment that has been added to their evening. You're a plus, not a minus. To put it in software terms, you're not a bug, you're a feature!

If you do strolling gigs, you probably have a set of what you might call internal checklists. As you approach each table, you know you need to get their attention, introduce yourself and perform a series of tricks — all in one brief visit. You check off each table and move on to the next group. It's quite possible that, after you've visited a table, you never speak to that group for the rest of the evening.

There's nothing wrong with this. Sometimes, you need to entertain hundreds of people in a relatively short amount of time. You need to move it! But I hope the simple strategy I've described allows you to take on a more meaningful role at your events and helps you to use 'cocktail hour' to create lasting memories. Have fun out there!

The author entertaining at the table

Marked for the Nearsighted

This is a cocktail hour 'quick trick' themed around marked cards. Secretly memorize the first and third cards from the top of the deck (e.g. Three of Diamonds / Queen of Spades).

Give the deck an overhand shuffle, starting by tossing half the deck and injogging the next card. Explain that you have some marked cards and special glasses that help you to see the secret markings. Lift up at the injog and keep a thumb break as you take the deck with your right hand.

Dribble the cards into your left hand and stop when you reach the break, apparently stopping at a random card. Examine the back of the card on top of the left-hand packet.

"Even in this light, I can tell by the markings that this card is the Three of Diamonds."

With your left thumb, push the Three to the right. Use the long edge of the right-hand packet to turn the card face up onto the left-hand packet, showing the Three of Diamonds. Turn this card face down and insert it anywhere into the right-hand packet. Place the left packet on the right packet.

Say that you'll do it again and also explain how the secret markings work. Holding the pack in Dealer's Grip, have your audience look at the back of the top card of the pack. Make up anything that sounds plausible about subtle dots or markings.

"I can tell that this card is the Queen of Spades."

Show the card to your audience but don't look at it yourself. They'll say it's not the Queen.

"Really? Hold on, there must be a smudge on my glasses."

Execute a Top Change as your left hand (still holding the deck) removes your glasses. Hold your glasses to the light, and then look at the card.

Look at the face of the card yourself but don't show it yet. Act perplexed.

"I'm seeing the Queen. What did you see?"

Your audience tells you whichever indifferent card they saw e.g. Nine of Spades.

"Here look through these glasses. How many fingers am I holding up? [Two.] What color is my tie? [Red.] What card is this?"

Show them the card. They'll be surprised to see that it's the Queen of Spades. Perform another Top Change as you take back your glasses and put them on.

"You might need some glasses, too. Too much screen time, I think."

Casually flash the Nine of Spades again as you say this.

γινώσκω: No Glasses?

Arizona card expert Steve Ehlers had a fun idea for magicians who don't wear glasses. Buy a funny-looking pair of glasses from a novelty shop and have the spectator put them on so they can 'see' the marks.

Credits

Lance Pierce created the clean, open and innocent-looking procedure for 'reading' the first card. Adjusting your glasses as a way to cover the Top Change is also recommended by Roberto Giobbi in 'Card College – Volume 1' (1995).

Winning the Tough Tables

If you do table-hopping gigs, I'm sure you will have encountered situations where one half of a couple (usually female) is keen and interested to see your magic whereas the other half (usually male) is clearly far less interested. He may look as if he'd much rather be *anywhere* else.

I've often encountered this situation at hospital holiday parties. There are usually female doctors, nurses and staff present who are excited to be having fun with their colleagues outside of work hours. Also present are husbands and boyfriends who had to be reluctantly persuaded to come along. They aren't having much fun to begin with. When a well dressed, charming dude comes along (that's you, the magician), invading their space and winning applause, they feel even more uncomfortable.

I'd like to share a simple routine that has helped me in these situations. You need one jumbo card, a pack of cards and two matching sponge balls. Place the jumbo card in your inner left breast pocket and the sponge balls in your right pants pocket.

Approach the table and stand between the couple that matches the description above. We'll call them Sally and Steve. Sally is on your right and Steve on your left. After some quick introductions and a short trick, address Sally.

"Sally, has Steve ever read your mind?" [It doesn't matter if she says yes or no.] "Good! You two are perfect for this. Sally, take a card and remember it. Do not let anyone else at the table see it."

Take the card back and control it to the top of the pack. Palm the selection in your right hand and position yourself shoulder to shoulder with Sally for a moment.

"Steve, you're the star, not me. In a moment, Sally is going to look you in the eye. When she does, I need you to look into her mind and reveal the card she is merely thinking of."

Reach behind Sally's head with your right hand and show Steve the card. The left hand gestures at Steve as you deliver these lines.

"Sally, whatever you do, do not break eye contact. Got it?"

However you time showing the chosen card to Steve, make sure you do it while you're giving Sally her instructions. This prevents her from seeing what you're doing.

Make sure they both know what you want them to do.

"Ladies and gents, this is a very intimate moment for Sally and Steve. Try not to laugh as it might put them off. Are you two ready? On your marks, get set... go."

Take a few steps away from the table and pocket the selection. Steve will successfully name Sally's card leaving her suitably impressed and amazed. Rejoin the conversation before Steve says too much or gives the game away.

"Maybe he just got lucky. Let's try again. Steve, no peeking!"

Turn to Sally and force the card that matches your jumbo card (e.g. Ace of Hearts). Show your hands empty. Allow Sally to take the pack and lose her chosen card anywhere in the middle.

At this point, you have just promised everyone that Steve will demonstrate his impressive mindreading skills again. However, Steve can see that you have nothing in your hands and you don't have control of the cards. While he may be getting into the spirit of the trick, he'll have to trust you that you're on his side.

"Alright, Steve, you know what to do. Look Sally in the eyes and read her mind! Remember, mindreading is difficult. Sometimes the information only comes to you a bit at a time, like peering through fog."

Take a step back behind Sally, remove the jumbo card from your jacket and let Steve see it. Once he's seen it, put it away. It's then up to Steve to act his part as best he can. If all goes well, he will slowly but surely read Sally's mind — once again leaving her suitably amazed and puzzled by what's going on.

"Did he get it again?! Unbelievable. Alright Steve, next year you and I are working this party together!"

Shake Steve warmly by the hand. You get extra credit if you can get the rest of the table to act amazed and surprised along with you.

There are two phases here. During the first phase, you get Steve in on the game. During the second phase he gets the chance to 'ham it up' because he understands what to do.

I strongly suggest you do *not* end your set with this routine. If you do, then as soon as you walk away it is highly likely that someone will unhelpfully spoil the fun by telling Sally what happened. She may feel embarrassed that the magician, her partner and the whole table played a prank on her. Trust me, it's no fun getting dirty looks from Sally the rest of the night. This is why the next part, with the two sponge balls, is essential.

"That was fun, but I think it's time to bring out the serious stuff. As a sleight-of-hand magician, I love creating magic with everyday things. This is why I'd like to show you... this."

Remove a sponge ball from your pocket.

"Don't you have one, Steve? We'll see about that. The idea is to take the ball into the left hand and lightly blow on the back of the knuckles... and it vanishes. But it's okay, I'll do it again with Steve's."

Execute your favorite retention pass or vanish and produce the ball from Steve's elbow or shoulder. Hand it to Steve for examination. Start chatting with someone new at the table (Misty) and steal a second ball from the pocket.

"Misty, have you ever crossed your eyes and it looks like something is splitting in half?"

Take the ball back from Steve and 'split' it into two via your favorite method. Place both balls on the table for a moment.

"Sally, I'll show you how to do this one more time and then it's your turn. Steve, please hold onto this one tightly. They tend to roll away."

Do a false transfer into your left hand. With your dirty right hand, pick up the tabled ball and combine it with the concealed one. Place both in Steve's left hand. He thinks it's a single ball.

"Sally, hold the other one in your right hand (tightly!) just like Steve. Big smile!"

Place the nothing in your left hand into Sally's right hand and say, "Big smile!". This prevents Sally from speaking up about her empty hand (thanks for the line, Kainoa). The instant stooge is complete.

"Sally, hold up your fist and simply blow on the back of your knuckles like I did. Open slowly."

The ball has vanished! This tends to get a good reaction from the table. Before the reaction dies down, say:

"Wait! The ball must have gone somewhere. Steve, any guesses?"

Have him open his hands. The table (and Steve) will freak out. Let Sally enjoy the feeling of being a magician!

"Sally, now you're just showing off. Steve, you two should put an act together!"

Congratulations! You have just instant-stooged and fooled both Steve and Sally within five or six minutes!

Alternate Ending

If you doubt you'll have time for the sponge balls, here's an alternative ending. After the jumbo card phase, simply stand there holding the jumbo card and wait for Sally to look back at you. You can even shout, "That was amazing!" to get her attention. This lets her in on the joke.

"He needed help, Sally. Thanks for playing along."

γινώσκω: Boo!

In the first routine, we won Steve over by empowering him to ham it up and perform the magic. We also instant-stooged everyone at the table. In the second routine, the 'victim' from the first routine (Sally) gets to fool everyone else! Any tension that existed is now gone.

This is a lot of mileage to from a shuffled deck and two sponge balls. There are no technical sleights to worry about. Make small talk between your lines and focus mainly on Steve and Sally rather than the tricks.

At Warren & Annabelle's nightclub, there are a few coded expressions for different situations. My favorite is the term 'boo crowd'. This refers to one of those rare crowds that is so hot and ready to 'party' that simply walking out and shouting 'Boo!' will get a huge laugh or round of applause.

Boo crowds are a blast. Who doesn't love bringing the house down? Nevertheless, every performer would probably agree that few things are as rewarding and gratifying as winning over a *tough* crowd.

When we give customers who feel out of place a chance to shine, they relax and the atmosphere around the table improves. Everyone feels comfortable and can get into the spirit of the party or event. As entertainers, could we hope to achieve anything more?

5: Stand Up

*"A magician on stage is a combination of many things:
of voice quality; of personal appearance; of personality;
of a particular degree of vitality, sincerity, poise;
and warmth — to only mention the obvious."*

— *Alton Sharpe*

Beachcomber Opener

The Invisible Deck (Ultra Mental Deck) is my favorite trick for experimenting with different presentations. It plays well in almost any setting. Start with the pack and a cocktail umbrella in your left inner breast pocket.

"Aloha, everyone! Thank you for being here. I just came from my pre-show beach walk ritual. The awesome sound of the ocean pumps me up. The sand between my toes calms my nerves. I guess it's not your typical dress rehearsal."

[Cue ocean sounds]

"So let's warm up island-style. Imagine that we're all walking along Keawakapu Beach on Maui. The sun is setting, and the water is warm. Suddenly, Steve here notices something in the sand."

Pick up an imaginary something.

"Steve, can you guess what it is? [Riff with Steve] Actually, it's a pack of cards. You're at a <u>magic show</u>, Steve. That was your clue. Take a look at those cards and examine them."

"Aloha, everyone!" The author on stage.

Hand Steve the imaginary something.

"Is it a full deck? [He says yes.] Wow, fast counting. We'll call you 'Rain Man' for the rest of the night. Reach into the pack and hand me any card. [Steve does so] I'll show it to the rest of our power-walking posse here."

"Marcia, the sun is setting over the horizon, but can you see what color that card is? Red or black? [Red.] Jaime, what suit is it? A diamond or heart? [Diamond.] Terry, what number or value do you see on the card? [Eight.]"

"The Eight of Diamonds, Rain Man! I'll hand that Eight of Diamonds back to you. Finders keepers, right? But when you put it back in the deck, please put it back the wrong way round, deeply frustrating the OCD members of our audience. That was fun! What shall we do now?"

Reach into your pocket and pick up both the deck of cards and the cocktail umbrella. As your hand comes out, drop the deck down your left coat sleeve so that you are left only holding the umbrella.

"I know a great place for Mai Tais.

All right, maybe a sunset walk on the beach in Hawai'i isn't good enough for some of you. Maybe that's why you're at a magic show in Hawai'i. Rain Man, please toss the imaginary pack to me."

While talking, drop your left arm to your side, allowing the deck to secretly fall into your left fingers in readiness for a magical 'production'. Toss the cocktail umbrella into the air, leap backwards and bring your hands together in front of you, causing the pack to appear at your fingertips.

"Ladies and gents, let's find out if our imaginary journey has prepared us for the show. Steve, what was the card that you put back into the pack?"

He tells you it was the Eight of Diamonds. Spread the cards from hand to hand, with the 'even' side facing you. When you get to the Eight of Diamonds, upjog it and continue spreading, showing that there is one card — and only one card — reversed in the deck. Remove the Eight of Diamonds and set the rest of the cards aside.

"It's a red one... it's a diamond... it's the Eight of Diamonds! [Musical cue] This is going to be a great show. You just keep that up, [Tuesday] night crowd!"

γινώσκω: A Strong Opener

I cannot overstate the importance of having a strong opener. The first three pieces in this section are openers that I hope will help you to win the audience's attention. They will establish that you're likable (or at least interesting) and get the audience looking forward to a night of amazing magic.

Credits

The Invisible Deck, originally Joe Berg's Ultra Mental Deck, dates back to the 1930s. There's much debate over who first came up with the idea of presenting the trick as an invisible or imaginary pack of cards, but most sources give the credit to Eddie Fields.

The deck appears by magic!

What if I Actually Showed You?

[By Curtis Kam]

By the end of this book, you'll have heard David ask, "What if?" more than once. He does this a lot. And it may seem like the type of vague advice you get from motivational speakers, like 'be your best self and brightest you'. Personally, I think it's best to illustrate abstract notions like 'What if?' with an example, so here's a story.

One night, David called me and wanted to talk about stand-up effects. There's a trick he's always wanted to do, after reading about it in Barrie Richardson's 'Theater of the Mind'. It's the Water Glass Suspension.

I first discovered this trick in a magic shop. You had a small plastic glass full of water. You then stuck a plastic magic wand into it. Summoning as much suspense as possible, you raised the wand and the glass of water came up with it, as if the water was sticking to the wand. Next, you released your grip on the wand and it, with the glass still hanging from it, magically remained stuck to your fingers.

I had my doubts as to whether this trick was still worth performing, so David and I considered the pros and cons.

Cons: It's difficult to take the effect seriously. The effect is vague. Is the glass somehow levitating? Did the water freeze? Did time stop in the glass? Also, it involves water, which is always messy, and often hazardous, on stage.

Pros: Barrie Richardson liked it and he made it meaningful to an audience. It's not cards or coins and it's not overdone. Whatever the effect is, it's simple and visual from all angles.

We both liked how Barrie Richardson got an audience member to fill the glass. It was reasonably close to having the glass examined and it didn't slow things down. We also liked how Richardson used the effect as an analogy for the audience and their success.

David saw this effect as a closer, which is how Richardson used it. But I asked what if it was an opener instead? Instead of just one person filling the glass with water, suppose you opened your show by running through the audience, asking them to pour water from their glasses into yours? We liked the idea of starting shows with a flurry of activity, especially an activity involving the audience.

Talking about the audience contributing water to this effect led to an interesting analogy. David and I started discussing the ways in which each audience contributes to the show they are watching. After asking a lot more 'What if?' questions, we came up with an opener that I still use today in both stage and parlor performances. David, who was looking for a closer at the time of these discussions, didn't end up using the effect we devised.

Here's the effect we hatched.

You'll need a plastic tumbler, gaffed as described by Barrie Richardson in "Suspension of Disbelief" ('Theater of the Mind', 1999) The Walmart tumbler I found is twice as tall as the one Barrie used and a bit narrower. Instead of the wooden spoon, I use a plastic rod gaffed in the same way. From a little distance, it looks like a plastic straw.

Stick the 'straw' in your top pocket and put the gaffed tumbler into a small bucket. If your audience doesn't have glasses of water, have three small bottles of water in your other hand.

Start with some happy, chaotic music, and run onstage with as much manic energy as you can muster.

Leave the bucket center stage and go out into the crowd, handing out the water bottles and asking each recipient to take the top off. Hand one out to the right, to the left and the center. Come back to center stage, make a broad, obvious gesture to cut the music (the more abruptly the better).

"Thank you, Ladies and Gentlemen (or however you choose to address the crowd) tonight..."

Stop yourself mid-sentence, gesture for the music to restart, grab the tumbler and go out to the person on your right. Have him fill the tumbler about one third full. Return to the stage and look at the water in the glass. Stop the music.

"Did you hear what I just said? I thanked you, as I've done a million times. But I realize I've never said what I'm thanking you <u>for</u>. First, I'm thanking you for being here. Without you, there could still be <u>tricks</u> but there wouldn't be <u>magic</u>. For your laughter and applause, your choices and ideas, the weird things you say and everything else you brought into the room with you tonight, thank you. But there's more."

Gesture to start the music again, run out and get another third of the glass filled. Return to the stage.

"The other thing you bring to the show is your eagle eyes and clever minds. We need that. We make mysteries and there's no point if no one's trying to figure them out. So definitely thank you for that. And another thing…"

Curtis Kam performing

133

Start the music and run into the audience one last time, having the third person fill the glass to the proper level for the trick. Return to the stage and stop the music.

"Most importantly, you bring your imagination. Your hopes and dreams. Your expectations of what magic, if it happened right here, might look like."

Remove the gaffed straw from your pocket and stir the water, gradually slowing to a stop as you deliver the following lines.

"As for me, I add very little. I mix your laughter and applause (look over to Spectator #1) with a pinch of cold hard logic (looking at #2) and a spoonful of wild imagination (looking at #3). And sometimes, if I get it just right, that's enough for you to see... magic."

At some point during the above speech, you slowly take your supporting hand away, leaving the glass floating in the air at the end of the straw. There will be applause here and I suggest you take it.

David and I talked quite a bit about this. The natural applause cue in most levitations and suspensions is the first moment that the effect becomes evident. Some performers suppress this applause, hoping that this will increase the response at the end. In our experience, that's not how it works. At least, not with this trick. So we take the applause now, and then play with the effect a little before the inevitable return to normality.

I like to isolate the glass in the air and move around it so I end up with my back facing the audience and the glass near my face. I take out my phone and take a 'selfie' with the audience.

Gazing intently at the glass as it 'floats', I allow it to return to my hand, remove the straw, pick up the bucket and pour all the water into it. This is how Barrie ends his routine and it's a great applause cue. My last line is the same as my first. I simply say, "So, thank you."

γινώσκω: selfie

A last word about the selfie gag. It started as just a goofy 'What if?' but it turned out to serve an important purpose. You've just done something impossible, and frankly, impressive. With any luck, you've built up suspense and made your audience care. The selfie gag says that, as surprising and impossible as the magic was, it was all done in fun. It says that you, the most amazing guy in the room at that moment, just want them to have a good time.

Banzai!

My first regular stand-up gig was in an Irish Pub on Maui called 'Mulligan's on the Blue'. It's a rather rowdy and poorly lit venue in which to perform, making it challenging to keep the audience's attention. There's another problem too: the showroom offers a perfect view of the Hawaiian sunset. This makes it a lovely restaurant setting, of course, but it's not very helpful when your show starts at 6:30 PM — the hour of the '#sunsetselfie'.

I tried various ways to solve these problems. One was to use several versions of the Vanishing Bottle effect, all of which I eventually referred to simply as 'Banzai'. As well as obviously being well suited to the bar environment, it helped the audience get to know me, and, most importantly, got everyone cheering together and listening.

A few of the old lines I've included here will be familiar to magicians who've performed the Vanishing Bottle. Still, I hope you'll enjoy how this routine gives the audience a role in my act and establishes a catchphrase that helps me to mark magical highlights throughout my show.

You need a suitable vanishing bottle prop. I use the 'Refilled' prop sold by Henry Harrius. This is a very convincing clear latex replica of an *empty* bottle of Corona beer. You also need a paper lunch bag and a *full* bottle of Corona. Place both bottles in the bag and place everything in your performing case.

"Ladies and gentlemen, tonight is all about the art of magic. Sleight of hand and misdirection. The hard stuff! We begin with an empty bag."

Remove the bag from your case and place it on your performing table with a loud *thud*. This gets a laugh (Thanks to Chris Blackmore for this gag).

"Okay, almost empty."

Remove the 'Refilled' prop and display it to the audience.

"In the Hawaiian Japanese community, we have a magic word for gatherings like these. The word is 'Banzai'! We raise our glasses and shout it to wish each other a long and happy life. When I shout Banzai, you shout it back. Are you ready?"

The audience say they're ready. Place the gimmicked bottle into the bag.

"Sleight of hand and misdirection. Shinro Shimpu: Banzai!"

The audience shout, "Banzai!"

"Bottle... gone!"

Turn the bag over, weakly implying that the bottle has disappeared. This will elicit a few groans.

"Wait! That's the easy part. The hard part is making it come back. Banzai! [The audience shout Banzai] It's back. Sleight of hand!"

Remove the latex bottle and display it again.

"Emphasis on the 'slight', I guess. The problem, of course, is that I forgot the misdirection part."

Place the fake bottle back into the bag. At this moment, I cue an audio clip of someone saying, "What's that over there?!" I point to the back of the room excitedly and see if anyone looks.

"Hah! Gotcha!"

Reach into the bag and produce the full, genuine bottle of Corona. Immediately crush the paper bag with the latex gimmick inside.

"Banzai! [Banzai!] You guys are gonna be fun. Just keep that up, Tuesday night crowd! We're going to have a great night!"

γινώσκω: Splitting the Tips

This routine is very simple but I encourage you to try it if you suspect you might have a tough crowd. It's a great way to get everyone listening and participating immediately. In most cases, you'll find the audience can't help but yell 'Banzai!' whenever they feel inclined to applaud throughout the rest of the show.

If you're not a Japanese magician from Hawai'i, you can easily adapt the patter to suit yourself. Just say that you have a Japanese buddy who performs Banzais in Hawai'i. You bought my book. We're buddies now. (Banzais are a traditional form of 'toast' performed at Hawaiian weddings. You can read some very entertaining descriptions online!)

The author performing at Mulligan's

Under Pressure

This is my favorite piece to perform. It's angle-proof, easy to do, fills ten minutes and sets up quickly. Working from your pockets, you can perform it for 12 people or as many as 300.

As you may have guessed, this item is named after the Queen/David Bowie song that features at the start and end of the routine.

Under Pressure is a wild adventure during which a lost card leads to a hopeless situation while a bill vanishes and reappears at the wrong time. Cards end up on the floor, loops opened at the beginning of the show are resolved and amazing stuff happens even though the magician doesn't really seem to do anything.

You'll need a deck of cards, a thumb tip, a coin envelope, a dollar bill, a lemon and a knife.

Preparing the Lemon and Bill

Take a dollar bill and tear off a corner. Roll the bill tightly so that the torn portion is on the inside. This way, when you unroll the bill, the missing corner will be revealed last of all. Keep the corner.

Get your lemon and remove the pip. Using a chopstick or pencil, bore a hole into the lemon about the length of your rolled bill. Insert the bill into the opening like a drill bit, but leave the very end sticking out and crush it against the top of the lemon. With just a little bit of repositioning, you can get the tip of the bill to look like the lemon pip. This ruse has always survived close examination by the audience — even when the lemon is being passed around the room.

Some will argue that a higher denomination bill gets a stronger response. This may be so, but I've found that asking for a dollar gets the bill in my hands quicker. I don't like devoting too much time to getting the bill.

Preparing the Envelope

Take any pack of cards and place the force card of your choice on the very bottom. Take a duplicate of that card and fold it into quarters. Place a thumb tip and the folded card into a coin envelope.

Organizing the Props

Place the lemon in an accessible place. Put the loaded coin envelope and the pack of cards into an inner coat pocket or an accessible place in your case. The torn corner goes in your right trouser pocket. It will stay there until you're ready to switch it in.

Earlier in the show, I have a routine where the lemon is passed around the audience a few times so individuals can make random choices. Whatever reason or excuse you come up with, I highly recommend starting this routine with the lemon already in the audience.

Here's a fun way to introduce it earlier in the act:

"Let's begin with a mental experiment. In this bag, I have a familiar fruit. Sir, can you guess what it is? [The spectator guesses 'watermelon' or anything else] Wow! Yes! This one looks a lot like a lemon, though."

Remove the lemon from the bag and toss it to him.

"People sometimes accuse me of using a plant in my show. Guilty as charged."

While not a *great* reason to have a random lemon involved in your show, it's a reason nonetheless.

Intro: Borrowing the Bill

And now a heartfelt moment.

"At this point in the show, I'd like to ask you all a favor as a public school teacher. As an educator of your children, America... [long, dramatic pause] can I have some money?"

This gets a laugh for two reasons. One, because American teachers are typically underpaid. Two, because I usually perform my Bank Night routine, in which I *win* $100, immediately before this one.

"Okay, I know I just won the hundred, so how about a buck? Does anybody have a single I can borrow?"

Steve passes up a bill. As you ask for the money, reach in your pockets and finger palm the torn corner.

"Thanks, Steve. Did you happen to note the serial number? No? Here you can have this corner. There might be a quiz later."

Tear off the matching corner of the bill and pin this piece onto the bill with your thumb. In the action of handing Steve the corner, execute a shuttle pass. Your left hand turns palm down, keeping the torn corner with the bill, while your right hand turns palm up, bringing the palmed corner into view. It will look as if you've passed the corner from your left hand to your right to give the torn corner to Steve. You do this as you walk out to Steve or ask someone in the front row to pass the torn corner back to him.

Remove the coin envelope from your case. Invite Steve to nominate someone in the audience whom he thinks looks trustworthy. Gesture to the whole audience. Steve points to a random person (Amy).

"Great. By the way, who are you here with tonight? [My wife.] Ah... most people choose their wife. Do you know this person you pointed to? [No.] I see. We'll go with an absolute stranger! I see how it is."

This often gets a huge laugh. Begin folding the dollar into a small packet. Fold the switched corner into it to clean up.

"Amy, Steve would like to trust you with this dollar. I'll secure it in this envelope so you'll be able to find it later. Please lick this envelope and seal it... I'll just get it started for you."

Place the bill into the thumb tip and immediately steal it out in the action of bringing the envelope to your lips to lick it. Hold the envelope up for Amy to lick it shut. She'll refuse, of course, so close it for her and have her take it.

"Amy, can you feel the bill in the envelope? [Yes.] Good, please keep it somewhere safe."

What Amy can feel in the envelope is actually a folded card. She doesn't know this. Reach into your pocket and exchange the thumb tip for the cards.

Under Pressure

"Ladies and Gentlemen, at this time, I'd like to show you the most dangerous, difficult and disgusting card trick I know. Can you stomach it, Friday night crowd?"

The audience will yell out 'Yeah!' and express their ability to stomach whatever follows. I cue 'Under Pressure' by Queen and David Bowie to start playing.

Pick up the cards and point to someone (Greg) in the front row. Execute a Hindu Shuffle Force, forcing the bottom card of the pack (Ace of Hearts). Show the selection to the audience and close the pack, losing the Ace in the center.

Look at the audience and repeat what you just said:

"Most dangerous, difficult, and disgusting."

As you say this, holding the pack face down, Mercury Fold the bottom card (an indifferent card). Place the whole pack so you can grip it with your teeth, loading the folded card into your mouth. (If you prefer, or if you just find it easier, you can have an indifferent card pre-folded and riding under the pack from the beginning).

Show your hands empty, then pull out a card from the center of the pack. Make sure it's *not* the Ace of Hearts before showing it to the audience. You talk to Greg with the deck of cards still between your teeth.

"Wa-dish-yo-cah? [No.] No?"

Show your hands empty again and remove a second card.

"Dish-wan? [No.]"

Start pushing cards out of your mouth onto the floor until there's only one left sticking out of your mouth. Take it out and show it to Greg and the audience. He will tell you it's not his chosen card. Toss it on the ground.

"Nach-yo-cah? Den wah am I still tokee lah dish?!"

Push the folded card out of your mouth. Remove it with your empty hands and unfold it.

"The world's hardest card trick... your card, the Seven of Spades! [No.] What?"

Toss this card on the ground, too. It seems as if every card in the deck is now on the floor. Enjoy a long and painful pause. Fade out the music.

"It seems we've reached a teachable moment."

Offer a nervous laugh and enjoy another long pause.

"Well, you know what they say. When life gives you, uh..." [wait for someone to say 'lemons'] *yeah! Lemons! Where's the lemon?"*

Someone will hold it up.

"Pass that up! I just happen to have a knife."

Just before you cut into the lemon, say:

"And remember, every one of you touched and examined this lemon. Steve, do you still remember your card?" [Yes.]

Cut and separate the lemon, revealing the bill sticking out of the center.

"Wait a second...that's not a playing card."

Remove the rolled-up bill and start unrolling the bill.

"But it would be crazy if it were missing a..."

Finish unrolling the bill, revealing that the corner is missing. People will start to freak out.

"Steve, take that bill. There are two things I need to know. Does your corner match perfectly? [Yes!] Does the serial number match too? [Yes!] Yes! The same bill!"

I have a music cue here. After taking your applause, fade out the music again.

"Greg, I have to know, or I won't be able to sleep tonight. What was your card? [The Ace of Hearts] Of course it was. Steve, I'm sorry. I'll tell you what: I'll mail it to you. After the show, I'll get your address. I'll put it in an envelope and everything. Wait! <u>The envelope</u>! Amy! Do you still have it?"

Take the envelope from Amy, tear it open and pour out a folded playing card. Unfold it and look at it.

"The Ace of Hearts? I'm not sure how, but we got it!"

Bring the music back in one more time, and take your applause.

Jimmy's Rings: My Family, My Home

In this section I want to share the script I use to introduce my Linking Rings routine. It's a true story.

"The 1970s were a great time not to be a magician but a musician in Hawai'i. My father played trumpet in a Japanese Big Band called the New Shirakaba Orchestra. They gigged nightly under Honolulu's city lights, playing the music of the old country. One vignette in their show featured a magician named Jimmy Yoshida.

Unbeknownst to my father, when Jimmy or 'Tengu' (as he was known professionally) wasn't performing with them, he was shaping the global magic community by connecting magic from the East and West from Hawai'i. His signature piece was a trick with silver rings. More on this later.

40 years later, a trumpet-playing magician (point to myself) got off the bus at Zuke's Magic Shop in Kalihi. It's the kind of place you can miss if you're walking too fast. It's built into some guy's garage and they're only open on Saturdays.

I was on a treasure hunt for silver rings, like the ones Jimmy used. Eventually, among dusty shelves of old books, I found an old, tarnished set of silver rings. I bought them for 43 dollars. As I left, I heard the man behind the counter say, "Eh, that kid just bought Jimmy's rings."

These are the same rings that Jimmy used all those years ago, when he performed with my father and The Shirakaba Orchestra. Isn't it strange how life sometimes works out this way? I'm sure many of you have strange stories like this of your own.

I studied the silver rings with my mentor (George Wang) for three years before getting permission from his teacher in Japan (Hidekazu Kimoto) to perform it. I'm one of three people in the United States who knows this routine. Ladies and gentlemen, this is my inheritance. This is my family. This is my home." [Music starts]

The Pros and Cons of Storytelling

The story I've just shared is true and, yes, it's long. There's a potential problem here: most people don't go to magic shows to hear long stories. If you're not careful, stories will bore your audience and you'll lose their attention.

On the other hand, history tells us that stories are powerful. Throughout the ages, people have used stories to entertain and to form cultural identities. How can we use them in a magic show *without* losing the audience? Here are a few thoughts I've had.

Timing and Trust

First of all, get the timing right. Don't just consider the story you want to share. Think about *when* and *where* might be the best time to share it. If you can't find a good place in your act, perhaps you shouldn't tell the story.

In my act, I tell the story of 'Jimmy's Rings' immediately after my 'Under Pressure' routine. The audience have just enjoyed a baffling and rather zany piece of magic with cards, envelopes, a lemon, music, gags, callbacks and tons of interaction. They're ready to sit back, relax and enjoy some quiet, beautiful, elegant magic.

It's also important to cultivate your audience's trust. Before I get to my rings routine, my audience has been fooled and, hopefully, entertained by several other routines. They have started to trust me and to believe that whatever I've got lined up for them will be engaging and worthwhile.

I've seen many young musicians and athletes dread going to practice or rehearsal because it's often more of a sermon than a meaningful skill-building session. Young athletes and musicians don't enjoy fifty minutes of lecture and ten minutes of practice. They joined to *play*.

Bands and sports teams need warm-ups, skill-building, active feedback, repetition and team-building exercises. So long as coaches and teachers acknowledge these needs first, the band or team will be far more attentive when a longer heart-to-heart talk becomes necessary. Likewise, if you're selling a magic show, audiences need you to engage them with *magic* first. If you can't deliver on what they paid for, they probably won't be interested in you or your stories.

Relatable

If you do feature stories in your act, make them ones that people can relate to and understand. Even if you love physics, a story about Bernoulli's Principle slapped onto a complex card trick might be a hard sell. On the other hand, a story that begins with a quirky science teacher is an experience many can relate to.

In the case of 'Jimmy's Rings', I start by talking about live entertainment in Hawai'i. After all, the audience is at my live show (usually in Hawai'i), so this is one topic everyone can relate to. Then I focus on relatable ideas such as family, strange coincidences and diligence.

If the trick is complex, assess whether you need a story at all. If you do, keep it short and sweet. Conversely, if the story is long, keep the trick simple. My story is about complex connections in my life so the trick is simple: rings that link and unlink. This simplicity allows the audience to create their own connections with the story and the magic without me narrating.

Modular Construction

I tell the story of Jimmy's Rings to explain *why* I'm going to perform the Linking Rings. But notice how I can stop at the end of almost any paragraph and cut to the performance. As I tell the story, I gauge whether the audience is feeling bored. If not, I continue with the next part of the story. If yes, I cut the story short and go straight to the performance. This flexibility means I never feel as if I have to rush through the story. It's a bit like a Riffle Force: they can call 'stop' at any time but the result is mostly the same. The only thing they'll lose is a bit of information about me.

Getting to Know You

You might ask why I don't just write a shorter story? Remember, the main goal of each piece in Ginóskó is to build a stronger relationship with the audience and increase their engagement. There are many ways to do this, but when I start telling the story of Jimmy's Rings I only want them to get to know me better. As I share more about myself (within reason, of course), the higher the chance someone might personally connect with something I say, which is another reason to keep ideas and themes relatable.

This story may seem self-centered or egotistical, but it's the only time in my act where I talk about myself at length. People often approach me after a show, eager to share their stories. For example, they might tell me how they labored to achieve a personal goal or about a strange coincidence similar to mine. Others have said they wish they could meet my Dad! Their own memories and relationships connect with mine so they leave with a more meaningful experience than just binge-watching a few tricks.

The author performing 'Jimmy's Rings'

Roses in Spokane

My early stand-up shows were cluttered messes of random routines. I'd plow through them and say goodnight when I ran out of tricks. Over time, my act gained a bit more structure but I still struggled to find the right closer.

One day, I was reading Curtis Kam's book, 'Stage Coach'. On the last page, I read something that made me realize I'd been asking the wrong question about my closer:

> *"It's the few lines you deliver at the end of your show that can make a bunch of random tricks seem like an act. It's a little closing speech, a goodnight toast to the audience in which you tell them that they saw magic and had a good time only because they are clever and imaginative people. This gives you something really to thank them for, which is important. Far too many magicians blurt out 'thank you' at the end of every trick, and neither they nor the audience has any idea what anyone is being thanked for. This ends the show on you and your persona. It will work only if it seems sincere, so mean it or learn to fake it." (Kam, 29)*

After reading these words, rather than wondering which trick I should end my act with, I began wondering what my act could communicate other than vague thanks. How could I thank my audiences *and* show them I mean it? 'Roses in Spokane' is the routine I eventually came up with.

There's no magic in this piece, but you'll have to learn how to fold a napkin rose. Until recently, I used red napkins found in the party section of most stores. Nowadays, I use the type of tissue paper used for stuffing gift bags and cut it into napkin-sized squares. It makes a more rigid rose.

I perform this routine to a piece from an orchestral movie soundtrack. The piece begins quietly and gently as I start folding the rose. It reaches the top of a mighty crescendo when I finally say, "From the bottom of my heart... thank you." More on the music later.

"I used to live in Spokane, Washington. Ever heard of it? There wasn't much nightlife when I lived there, but Open Mic club nights were just getting started. My friends and I caught them on the weekends.

I went to one of these clubs on a memorable evening in early summer. There were singers, rock bands, slam poets, magicians... you name it! Each was better than the last and the audience was on fire.

At the end of the night, an elderly gentleman who had been watching from the bar took the stage. He moved the mic aside and the crowd fell silent. He reached into his pocket and took out a single red napkin. He didn't say a word or do a magic trick. He simply started twisting and folding.

The audience could see something beginning to form as he twisted the napkin. Can anyone see what it is? [It's a rose!] That's right. Anyone can *grow* a rose and anyone can *buy* a rose. But there are very few people in the world who can *make* one. This guy made something with his hands, with his imagination, from the bottom of his heart.

In the same way, ladies and gentlemen, you all came here tonight. You participated graciously. You each brought your imagination. And for that, I'd like to thank you.

[I finish the rose and hold it high.]

From the bottom of my heart. [Cue music] Ladies and gentlemen, thank you for bringing the magic tonight. Goodnight and aloha!"

γινώσκω: Sig

A few years ago, I had the opportunity to perform for Sig Anderman. He is a businessman and entrepreneur who built several million- and billion-dollar companies during his career. He's also one of the kindest men I know. His book, 'It Pays to Be Kind', is one of my favorites.

For his 80th birthday, Sig flew his family and forty close friends from all over the country to Maui for a week-long celebration. They hired a restaurant on the beach for dinner and a magic show.

I closed my show with 'Roses From Spokane'. When I got to the music at the end, something very unusual happened. The couple sitting in the front row reacted as if they had witnessed a miracle. I found this puzzling since, of course, there's no actual magic in this routine.

After my show, they immediately approached me with a rather excited look in their eyes. They asked me if I knew anything about them before this evening. I admitted that I did not. The man introduced himself to me: he was the composer of the piece I used for my rose routine! Then it was *my* turn to act as if I'd witnessed a miracle!

No, he didn't sue me for using his music. He was moved that we were able to share an artistic moment together in a tiny restaurant somewhere in the middle of the Pacific Ocean.

I've often struggled with 'why' questions. Why magic? Is this *really* what I should be doing? Then impossible moments like these happen and I'm forced to remember that just because I stand in the spotlight doesn't mean the work is about me. It's for them.

When I finally stop worrying, I can savor these strange moments and get a passing glimpse at a grand weaver leading me in the way everlasting. I catch my breath, and two words remain: 'Thank you.'

6: Armchair Philosophizing

*"Ain't got a soapbox I can stand upon.
But God gave me a stage, a guitar, and a song."*

— Ed Sheeran, 'What Do I Know?'

Painless Practice Through Flowstate

"You can't just do a trick one time and have it work out. You have to do it over and over again until it flows and has continuity. You have to do it thousands of times until you can do it without thinking."
— *Dai Vernon*

Have you ever sat down to practice a routine or work on a project only to find yourself distracted by other cares on concerns? We all want to keep growing as artists and we know that growth requires dedicated time and focused effort. But the stress of everyday life and the lure of our phone screens disrupt our focus within moments of starting our practice. The following concept has helped many of my students. I hope you'll try it.

Perhaps you're already familiar with the concept of 'flow' or 'flow-state'. In simple terms, flow-state is when time seems to fly by because you are fully absorbed in a task or experience. We can all remember a reading session, workout session, gaming session, or, hopefully, a magic practice session that felt that way. The work was neither too easy nor too hard, you made noticeable progress and you didn't want to stop. Sometimes, when I end one of my classes, my band students continue practicing through recess or after school. They completely ignore the bell because they're in deep flow-state.

Wouldn't it be great if we could turn on that flow-state whenever we wanted and with any task? Well, we can! It's not easy, but like building muscle, we can do things every day to help us enter a flow-state more consistently. Let me show you how to get started!

Day One

- Set an easy goal e.g. 'I will read and practice one card trick from ____ book'.

- Complete your goal and keep working until you stop 'flowing'. In other words, stop when you begin to lose focus or motivation. It sounds lazy, but remember, it's day one.

- You might feel you weren't very productive today. Don't get either discouraged or frustrated. Your practice time, although short, was productive and fun.

Day Two

- Set another simple goal or two (e.g. start to script a routine for your act; read a chapter from a book; practice sleights X and Y, or maybe review the card trick from yesterday).

- Complete your goals and keep working until you stop 'flowing'. Then push yourself to work a few minutes longer.

- Set your goals for the next day.

Each day, experiment with different *combinations* of goals to keep yourself motivated. Experiment with the *order* of your practice routine. Push yourself to increase your practice time *a little more* each day. Not pushing too far past your flow-state guarantees that your practice session will always be enjoyable. You'll find yourself looking forward to the next one.

A few years ago, I decided to focus on reading. On day one, I read for ten minutes and fell asleep. On day two, I pushed it to fifteen minutes. At the end of six months, I read nonstop from six in the morning until noon. This was during the COVID lockdown so I had time. I read much faster after those months, and, most importantly, I was having fun.

Many people discover a new passion and, keen to master the necessary skills, practice impatiently, driven by their initial rush of intense motivation. Ironically, this can lead to frustration and despair once they realize that the skills they want don't come immediately. It's why just about every home in Hawai'i has a ukulele collecting dust. It's also why treadmills become towel racks. I've had to calm down many young music students who declare, "I don't have what it takes!" after playing an instrument for just *one* day!

'Passion' comes from the Latin *passio*, which means 'to suffer and endure'. Yes, you need grit to achieve your goals, but I don't think your passion should rob you of your joy. On the contrary, the joy that you derive from your passion can empower you to endure each setback and failure. Your goals will only seem further and further away if you're angry and torturing yourself. Remember, experiencing the arts should be fun. Take each day in your stride and build up your flow-state one day at a time.

This applies to advanced artists, too. I've seen doctorate-level music students endure a joyless grind as they prepare some of the most sophisticated music ever created. It's common for music students to spend six to ten hours a day in a practice room as they work out every nuance of a piece for their final recital. When one doctoral student asked my father (also a music teacher) if he had any advice, my father asked, "Are you having fun?"

In what area are you trying to grow? Be patient. Focus on your drop in the bucket for today without comparing yourself to someone else's fuller pail. Keep it fun. Soon, you'll have all the chops and knowledge you want with hundreds of dedicated practice hours behind you.

Further Reading: 'Flow: The Psychology of Optimal Experience' by Mihaly Csikszentmihalyi (1990).

Names: The Real Magic Words

"Aladdin! Hello, Aladdin. Nice to have you on the show. Can we call you 'Al?' Or maybe just 'Din?' Or how about 'Laddie?'"

— The Genie, Aladdin (1992)

When I have the opportunity to do strolling magic before my stand-up show, I ask as many people as possible for their first names. I tell them that in fact I try to remember the name of everyone in the audience. This happens to be true, but in reality I usually only remember about five or six names. However, when I start my act, I call on those five or six people by name as soon as possible. "Welcome to the show, everyone. How was dinner, Ann?" "Brad, what is the first fruit that comes to mind?"

Because I include a few names like this, the people in the audience whom I met before the show start to imagine that I did, in fact, memorize *everyone's* name. It causes them to be more attentive, knowing I might call out their name at any moment. I've reached the point where memorizing names is as important as checking my mic, music and zipper before showtime.

If you practice memorizing names and faces, you will inevitably get better over time. I don't have a particularly great memory but my record so far is 42 names. For smaller stand-up shows, I actually *do* try to remember the name of everyone in the audience. Your memory is a muscle you can build slowly. The more names you can remember, the more connected they'll feel to you and the more engaged they'll be early in the show.

Here's a useful tip. While you're still doing strolling magic, keep circling back to tables and groups you've visited and review the names you've already tried to remember. Ask simple questions such as, "Where are you folks from, Noel?" and "What do you do for a living, Karen?"

When you encounter people with unusual names, ask them for a mnemonic instead of trying to think one up yourself. Most people, even those with common first names, already have a mnemonic because they've been asked before. "How am I going to remember 'Merick'?" "Well, it's like Eric with an 'M'." Bringing up fun, trivial details about members of your audience during your show turns it into a unique experience. "Let's all count together. I'd better hear you, Noel, since you're an accountant."

This pre-show discipline can also help you to overcome anxiety or nerves. Before the show, stand in the wings and review the names you've memorized. This will get your mind off thoughts that might cause you to doubt yourself or feel overly anxious. It reminds you to focus on the most important thing of all: serving your audience.

A Cure for the Common Cold Feet

> *"Courage is resistance to fear, mastery of fear — not absence of fear."*
>
> — *Mark Twain, Pudd'nhead Wilson*

The Disappearing Baton

A friend of mine once mounted the podium to conduct for the first time. He opened the conductor's score and, after a few nervous moments, dramatically lifted his baton. Suddenly, people in the audience started ducking and screaming. I didn't realize what had happened until someone walked up to the stage to hand my friend's baton back to him.

Students often ask me how to calm their nerves before a big performance. It's a great question. Fear is an inevitable part of life but there are some ways to deal with it. Let's take apart some clichés about overcoming fear and see if we can discover some practical strategies.

'Face Your Fears!'

Telling kids (or even adults) to 'face their fears' is sound advice but incomplete. There's no shortage of stressful situations in life: performing a show, going for an interview, breaking hard news, arguing with your partner... and so on. Facing these fears *recklessly*, meaning *without preparation*, can easily make things worse. How can you mentally prepare to face your fears with poise and boldness?

You need to have a calm and quiet mind before you interact with an audience. As with any conversation, an audience can tell if you're really present and listening or frantically thinking about other things. To begin, step outside and look for a nearby landmark, such as a stop sign. Walk towards it at a comfortable pace and, as you do, practice what I call 'brain venting'. In other words, allow yourself to daydream and entertain all the thoughts that are swimming around in your mind. Overthink everything that is giving you anxiety. Feel the emotions you're holding in. No thoughts or feelings are off limits or out of bounds. I like to pray.

Once you reach your destination, stop brain-venting and quieten your mind for as long as you can. You may not last very long at first, but even a few seconds are a good start. As thoughts and feelings invade your mind (and they will), acknowledge them and place them aside. I tell myself, "You had your chance to brain-vent. You'll have another chance later. Now be still." Over time, you'll be able to sustain that stillness longer. At my peak, I could last about fifteen minutes. With practice, you'll soon be able to top that.

What if you don't have time to go for a walk? Well, drive to your gig early, park, and brain-vent before you leave your car. As I mentioned, practicing this before a hard conversation or new experience is a great way to prepare yourself before you step out.

When I started performing, I didn't want to look nervous to my audience so I tried to force myself to calm down. I'd then burst on to the stage full of adrenaline and enthusiasm — often leading to my own version of 'The Disappearing Baton'. Learning to tune my feelings and thoughts helped me feel focused and excited before a show rather than nervous and sweaty.

Everyone knows this quotation about fear:

> *"The only thing we have to fear is fear itself — nameless, unreasoning, unjustified terror which paralyzes needed efforts to convert retreat into advance."*
> *— Franklin D. Roosevelt*

A *small amount* of nervousness before you enter the spotlight is a good sign. Provided you have rehearsed well, it shows you care about your audience and want to honor their time. Fear has sharp teeth and a mighty roar, but it's not your enemy. Stand firm in your intentions and use tools like brain-venting to 'convert retreat into advance'.

The Cave

You can face your fears by facing yourself. Just as healthy relationships require mutual honesty and humility, brainventing as a daily practice requires you to be prepared to face yourself honestly. Be warned: the vulnerability that comes from a quiet mind might cause you to revisit painful memories, insecurity or trauma. It may cause you to recognize your personal flaws and failings. The possibility of harsh feedback from others or, in this case, yourself, is the very reason most people flee from stages in the first place.

We all have a place in our minds where our past and personal demons lurk; a dark cave we'd rather ignore. It's not surprising that caves often appear throughout literature and film. In many stories and fables, the hero enters the darkest cave, struggles and sometimes fails to discover his fatal flaws. He must master himself before he can become a true hero.

Consider, for example, the works of Homer, Plato and even George Lucas. Odysseus escapes the Cyclops' cave with his sharp wits, but his reckless arrogance results in the death of his best men and a curse from the gods. Many people bask in their talents and victories, not thinking about how their unexamined character and vices might be destroying their relationships and setting the stage for future suffering.

In Plato's 'Allegory of the Cave', the prisoners embrace shadows on the wall as the truth. Even when given the chance to turn to see what causes the shadows, their eyes cannot bear the shadows' fiery source. They turn back to the shadows, unable to endure the pain of reality and truth.

From time to time, perhaps we all need people to grab us by the shoulders, drag us out of our 'caves' and thrust us into the sun where the light — the truth — is unavoidable.

Only by rising out of the cave and bathing in the sun's light can we adjust our vision, discover who we are and maybe even see the world around us with new eyes or new understanding. Socrates observed that few people do this, but he believed it was essential if a philosopher or king wanted to be truly wise. I think the same applies to a magician. Ask yourself in which areas of darkness and shadow are you seeking comfort or taking refuge?

In 'Star Wars', there is a scene where Luke Skywalker, The Rebellion's *hero*, arrives at the cave that has been allocated for his training. He asks Yoda, "What's in there?" Yoda replies, "Only what you take with you." The audience immediately wonders what Yoda means by this. Bravery? Strength? Courage?

Luke enters the cave and discovers the very epitome of evil waiting for him: Darth Vader. Luke strikes him down and the audience cheers. But when he approaches Vader's body, the illusion fades and Luke's own face appears within Vader's mask. We realize our hero is deeply flawed, filled with rage and bitterness — known as 'the dark side'.

The Psalmist, David, cries out to God to reveal the inner darkness that he knows could destroy him:

> *"Search me, O God, and know my heart!*
> *Try me and know my thoughts!*
> *And see if there be any grievous way in me,*
> *and lead me in the way everlasting!"*
> *— Psalm 139:23-24 (ESV)*

It's easy to convince yourself that you're 'fine' (and tell others the same). It's tempting to rationalize or ignore your flaws and trauma. But if you practice brain-venting and quieten your mind, you may encounter your own 'cave'. Your flaws and regrets can swallow you; or you can face the truth and emerge with clearer insight into yourself. Journal your mistakes and flaws. Acknowledge past hurts that you're still holding on to. Once you have done this, you'll notice that you can begin to heal, forgive and grow.

Everyone has their emotional 'baggage'. But you're an artist. An artist's work demands self-sacrifice, practice and devotion to your craft and to your audiences. You can count the cost and conquer each cave if you see it as your professional and artistic duty. This process hurts, but you can do it.

You might ask, "Haven't artists through the ages created beautiful work despite their personal demons?" Certainly. But many artists have suffered, burned every bridge and, in some cases, died in misery because they refused to face their trauma. Don't let your artistic gift cause you to forget that your character will always need forming.

Every person in your audience is struggling, too. Imagine the power of a show that lifts the audience's spirit through the genuine and contagious joy that flows from a person who's faced himself and won.

I've not fully won yet, but for my audience it's my artistic mission. I'll continue to fight for it with a resounding soli deo gloria.

Thanks for reading my brain-vent.

Intermission: Why Would Anyone?

> *"Beauty is a relic of Eden — a remnant of what is good. It comes from a deeper realm. It trickles into our lives as water from a crack in a dam, and what lies on the other side of that dam fills us with wonder and fear. Glory lies on the other side. And we were made for glory."*
> — *Russ Ramsey*

During grad school, I was the music director at a small church in a rainy town called Manoa. Every Wednesday, I tended to rest in the chapel before choir rehearsal. On one such occasion, I'd just taken out my cards to practice when one of the older choir members popped in for a casual chat. We talked for a while and I showed her a trick I'd been working on. Surprised, she laughed and said, "Wow, I just don't understand... why would anyone want to do that?!"

Why indeed...

A few years ago, I almost left magic. I asked myself, "Why would anyone ever want to do this?" No matter how much talent and performing experience you have, you'll mess up sometimes. You'll have bad crowds, stingy clients and noisy venues to deal with. And yet getting on stage, again and again, is the only way to grow. Why would anyone subject themselves to this?

Not long after, I returned to Spokane for an unusual gig. Each year, Whitworth University hosts an event during which newly accepted high school seniors can get to know the campus and, hopefully, choose Whitworth. My show was the final event of the weekend. The big prize was a full year of free room and board.

The lively crowd of 250 high school seniors and their parents was among the best audiences I'd had in years. At the end of the evening, a young woman won the free room and board that had been promised.

When I returned to my hotel, all I could think about was taking off my shoes. As I entered the lobby, a thin man with gray hair and jeans approached me, together with his wife and granddaughter.

"We were just at your show," the man told me. "Our granddaughter was recently accepted to Whitworth but we weren't sure whether we could afford it. We decided to 'lay out a fleece' this morning before the Lord. We prayed and asked him to show us whether our granddaughter should attend Whitworth. She won the room and board at your show tonight. She'll be at Whitworth next year!"

Now, I'm no advocate of a God-is-my-genie spiritual life. We can ask whatever we want and He can answer yes, no or otherwise. But in this case, my act ended up being how this family's prayer was answered with a resounding 'Yes!'. It changed the direction of their granddaughter's life and by some miracle I got to hear the story.

Why would anyone ever want to be a part of this? Well, look at it the other way round. Who *wouldn't!*

I realized that I had considered quitting magic because I had started to focus on how it made *me* feel. How is this serving *me*? How can *I* get more shows? How can *I* negotiate a higher rate? Of course, you have to think about these things (to a reasonable extent) to grow and make this profession sustainable. But I had gone too far. That young lady's family gave me a very welcome wake-up call. They reminded me that there was more to magic and performing than how it made *me* feel. I had been given a gift that could and should serve *others*.

As entertainers, we are often servants to people who are anxious, struggling and hurting. At some level, this includes everyone. We can't heal them all, but we can bring some light into their personal darkness. Please appreciate how important this is. *We* are there to serve *them*. We endure our struggles — tough crowds, long flights, underpaid gigs, bombing and so on — to grow to serve them better. In my experience, when we step out confidently with a servant's attitude amazing and unexpected things always happen.

There's a passage in the Scriptures where the Ark returns to God's people (remember that scene in 'Indiana Jones'?). King David is so overwhelmed by this wonderful news that, we are told, "he danced before the Lord with all his might." In an act of 'undignified' vulnerability, the king explodes joyfully before his God and kingdom.

Like David, some have witnessed the greatest light — a light that "shines in the darkness, and the darkness has not overcome it." (John 1)

If you have, then get up there, magician. Dance with all your might.

Let it shine.

The Ginóskó Philosophy

A former student recently called me to tell me she decided to study teaching in college. During our conversation, she asked about my teaching philosophy. As I thought about this, I realized that, over the years, my teaching and performing philosophies had unexpectedly aligned.

Philosophy 1: Love Through Preparation

After landing my first band teaching job, my father, Noel (a band director), observed one of my first classes on the podium. I energetically plowed through my lesson: I made the kids laugh, shared helpful tips, assessed their playing and even had them cleaned up before the bell. I rocked!

I visited my father that night, excited to hear what kinds of glowing compliments he might have for his son, who had chosen to follow in his footsteps. Instead, without looking up from the newspaper, he said, "You're wasting a lot of time up there." He saw right through me. I hadn't prepared a

The author and his father (left)

Noel Kuraya conducting an orchestra

lesson plan. I was 'winging it'. He could see how my high energy yet lazy 'teaching style' was a straight path to future problems and failure. As you can imagine, for me to hear all this was tough love, but it was exactly what I needed.

In a classroom, misbehavior is usually the result of a teacher who persistently neglects preparation. Students act out because they begin to notice that their daily lesson is always the same whether they're attentive or not. Before long, students conclude that if their teacher doesn't honor their time, they shouldn't have to honor his or her's either. It's hard to argue with this logic.

Like students, audiences can feel whether or not we've prepared thoroughly. When they sense that we haven't, we open ourselves up to heckling or (even worse) agitated silence. You might have a gift for improvising or working under pressure. Still, whenever you fumble with a prop, lose track of what you're supposed to do or mess up a routine, the audience starts to wish they were elsewhere. These days, they *do* go elsewhere — to their phones.

At the beginning of each school year, I promise each class that I won't waste a second of their time. I make this promise to show them that I care about their daily class experience and also to keep me accountable. Any student who enters my classroom has entrusted me with their time. If I don't come to class prepared for each minute, I'm wasting the lives of children. How dramatic! But consider the eternal words of the Scriptures. Life is too short to waste, whether you're referring to your own life or the lives you have the privilege to influence.

> *"You do not know what will happen tomorrow. For what is your life? It is even a vapor that appears for a little time and then vanishes away." — James 4:14 (ESV)*

My students and my magic show audiences are entitled to no less than my very best.

Magicians often mention the way Howard Thurston used to whisper, "I love you all!" to the audience moments before he stepped on stage. Many modern magicians have adopted his mantra. But, if we only think about the audience seconds before showtime, is it true to say we 'love' them?

I invite my students to consider the following example. Imagine that your date picks you up two hours late, clothes and hair unkempt and with an empty gas tank. How would an 'I love you' make you feel at that moment? The point is that if you *truly* love your audiences, this should affect not only your performances but also your rehearsal, scripting, the tweaks you make to your act and even your willingness to receive feedback.

Jim Steinmeyer's biography of Thurston shows that his love for his audience was more than just a pre-show mantra:

> *"In 1903 he still wasn't satisfied with the act and enhanced it with a number of cabinet illusions. Months on the road allowed Thurston to evaluate every trick carefully. What was the audience's reaction? How did each piece of apparatus hold up backstage? How long did it take to prepare in each city? Gradually, he was working out the most elaborate lighting and fountain effects, pruning the show down to the best tricks."*
> — *Jim Steinmeyer*
> *'The Last Greatest Magician in the World'*

Notice that *the audience's reaction* preceded every other decision Thurston made. He thought about them before the long list of logistics that went into his massive traveling show. He pared down his act until there was nothing left except the best he could offer.

The scale of my show is nothing like Thurston's so the questions I ask myself are different. But, as I sort out the details that go into my act, I'm guided by my favorite question...

Philosophy 2: 'What if?'

People sometimes ask why my band programs seem so 'different' or 'original'. Similarly, magicians ask each other, 'How did you find your unique character?' In every field, people want to become unique or at least 'different'.

My program strategy and teaching style are not the results of extra talent, charisma or intuition. They come down to a simple question: 'What if?'

Assistants Tessie and Drew

Some of my favorite teaching memories are of sitting with my assistants, Tessie and Drew, in the bandroom office late at night, pitching crazy 'what if' ideas. We'd mull over music selections, teaching strategies, funding, trips and every other aspect of running a band program for over 200 kids. What if we did a skit in the middle of the band concert? What if we flipped the classroom around for a week? What if we hired a comedy hypnotist as a surprise activity?

Over the years, we must have tested hundreds of random ideas. Many of them turned out to be mostly a waste of time. However, every once in a while we stumbled across an idea that really worked. In time, these ideas became traditions and our distinctive style took shape.

Maybe you're reading this because, at some point in your life, you asked yourself a crazy question: "What if I became an entertainer?" In the next section, I'll introduce you to a few of my 'What if?' friends.

'What If?' Applied to Magic

The five magicians at Warren and Annabelle's on Maui can each perform for up to two hours without an intermission and keep the audience captivated. They have the tightest magic acts I've ever seen. When I first hung out with them after the show, I expected a late-night jam session with card tricks or other props. I was never more wrong.

They met at Lahaina Coolers and started asking each other 'What if?' questions. What if I moved this trick to later? What if I told the joke differently? What if I revealed the card sooner? To them, the smallest 'What if?' detail was an opportunity to tighten the act based on what the audience apparently prefers. They're a prime example of ginóskó — using experience and relationships to keep learning and growing.

Curtis Kam is one of the top creative minds in magic today. It may not surprise you that he's also a 'What if?' guy. A couple of my recent favorites are, "What if the coins turn into molten silver?", and, "What if coins are the silver lining that emerges from rainclouds?"

After numerous phone calls with Curtis, my act went through countless tweaks as I drove home from my shows. As I struggled to figure out why certain parts of my act worked and others didn't, he'd provide feedback in the form of 'What ifs'. What if you made the trick a game instead of a story? What if you're coming out with too much energy...or not enough? What if that presentation doesn't fit you?

These questions saved me from blaming the audience for a lousy night and getting cocky on the good ones. The 'What ifs' from Curtis challenged me to keep working and focusing on my next steps. No whining. No gloating.

By the way, if you find yourself agonizing over 'What if?' questions like, 'What if I screw up my lines', or, 'What if I forget the steps to the trick?' before showtime, you may need to revisit the section on preparation. Not all 'What ifs' are created equal, but they can lead us to the next step in our magic and maybe even our life goals.

'What If?' Applied to Goals

One of my closest friends, Derick Sebastian, is a ukulele virtuoso. Some years ago, he asked himself, "What if I could play ukulele for a Lakers game?" No one had ever done this before and NBA executives never take calls or emails from random self-managed musicians.

Most would have abandoned the idea, saying, "I guess it's a closed door." But Derick continued to reach out to people, build relationships and work toward his dream. It certainly wasn't an overnight success story. Nonetheless, *six years later*, Derick was on the court at The Los Angeles Staples Center playing 'The Star-Spangled Banner' just a few feet away from LeBron James and Kobe Bryant. The ESPN broadcast of his performance went viral overnight.

In the late 1990s, Warren Gibson, a tourist from South Carolina, came to Maui for his honeymoon. After a blissful week in paradise with his bride, Lisa, a nagging question began to haunt him on his return flight: "What if I opened a magic theater in Maui?" He went home, started talking to investors and drew up a detailed business plan.

The author with ukulele virtuoso Derick Sebastian

Today, Warren and Annabelle's is one of the most successful shows in Hawai'i, celebrating its 20th anniversary in 2019. You'll only get a seat if you make reservations two or three weeks in advance. And keep in mind that this is with world-class luaus, whale watches and snorkel tours on offer around every corner.

Derick and Warren could have dismissed their 'What if?' questions as passing thoughts and then forgotten about them. Derick might have become the top ukulele player for local parties. Warren might have become the top local

With entrepreneur Warren Gibson

magician in the phone book somewhere. There's nothing wrong with these choices but there's nothing original about them either. Instead, they both decided to chase a crazy idea no one had ever considered. The result? An original concept came to life.

These men are what T. E. Lawrence might have called 'dreamers of the day' in his 'Seven Pillars of Wisdom':

> *"All men dream, but not equally. Those who dream by night in the dusty recesses of their minds wake in the day to find it vanity. But the dreamers of the day are dangerous men, for they may act on their dreams with open eyes to make it possible. This, I did."*

'What If?': A Warning

As we've seen, 'What if?' people can't sleep until they start acting on the question that has occurred to them. They conduct research and seek honest feedback. They're obsessed with exploring their idea even if it seems crazy, logistically messy or costly. They set course for their long-term goals and even inform their mundane, daily micro-decisions simply by asking, 'What if?'

But 'What if?' people have to be careful, especially when critics say, "What if your idea fails? What if it takes too much time, energy or money?" Sometimes, the critics are right. Acting on 'What ifs?' can involve risk, especially when your failures could affect others' lives. Isn't it ironic that we can still end up in a humiliating mess while trying to give people our best? My most embarrassing moments and crippling regrets were in classrooms and on stages — places where I certainly *hoped* and *intended* to be at my best.

There were days when I was too lenient and my classes spiraled into chaos. There were days when I was too harsh, leaving some students feeling let down and discouraged. In my early years as a teacher, managing my time, energy, lesson planning and life outside of work was an exhausting process. I know that it cost me relationships that I may never rebuild.

I've spouted cringe-worthy ad libs in my magic shows. I've screwed up routines and forgotten lines during paid gigs. I've accidentally broken props on stage and dressed unprofessionally. Experiential knowledge — ginóskó — and the 'What if?' road often guarantee growth in the sense that you're sure to experience failure at some point.

If you wish to become truly original, you'll have to accept the sting of defeat once in a while for the sake of the joy that comes from reflecting and learning. In 'Expert Card Technique', Hugard and Braue call this the "hard work and bitter experience" path to success. Seek forgiveness (when you can). Forgive yourself. Step onward.

'What If?': Final Thoughts

How can we become original and find our unique voice? Don't ignore the 'What if?' questions that occur to you, even if they seem absurd. Dare to explore them. Seek honest feedback. As you take risks and make mistakes, let no experience go by without reflecting, finding the lesson within that experience and making positive adjustments.

What ideas have you cast out because they seemed too crazy? Maybe you've said to yourself, "People don't do that!" Maybe you're right. You could be the first.

Philosophy 3: Do the Best You Can

Ben, my grandfather, was born on a plantation pond in Kauai to first-generation Japanese immigrants. He was the youngest of seven. As a child, he fell in love with music and biked several miles over unpaved roads and steep hills for trumpet lessons each week. The second world war broke out when Ben moved to California for college. He was taken to a Japanese concentration camp but exited shortly after since he was a student. He worked as a household servant to make ends meet, washing dishes.

After the war, he moved to Honolulu, married my grandma, Aya, and started a family. He became a school band director and tuned pianos on the weekends to put food on the table.

Grandfather Ben playing the trumpet in his youth

To his surprise, all three of his children followed in his footsteps. Noel, his eldest son, also became a band director. His middle son, Mark, played double bass in the Honolulu Symphony, and his daughter, Sue, played clarinet for the Royal Hawaiian Band.

In 1988, Ben's wife, Aya, died of aggressive esophageal cancer. A month before she passed away, she named her newborn grandson 'David'.

I visited Grandpa Ben in the summer of 2008. Alzheimer's had set in, so he no longer walked or ate independently. His speaking voice was a soft mumble. One afternoon, Aunty Sue told me grandpa wanted to talk to me. As I sat beside his bed, he gripped my hand firmly, and in a clear voice that I'd not heard in years, he repeated the words, "Do the best you can, do the best you can, do the best you can."

His words, though sincere, confused me. 'Do the best you can' reminded me of colorful posters with bubble letters in a child's playroom (my mother is a kindergarten teacher). But as I reflected on his life, I began to understand.

Ben and Aya on their wedding day

Ben, Aya and Noel Kuraya

Even though Grandpa Ben's family was poor, they did the best they could, saving enough to send him, their seventh son, to college. Despite racism and hardship during the war, he did the best he could and honored our country, even when our country didn't trust Japanese Americans.

As he raised a family of musicians, he did the best he could to support their goals and dreams. As he and his wife entered their golden years and she started fighting cancer, they did the best they could to fight it as a team and cherish their last days together. And even now, as his own body warred against him, he did the best he could. To Ben, 'Do the best you can' wasn't a vague suggestion. They were the words that had carried him through life. He never chose to play the victim, and by the grace of God, Ben Kuraya always did the best he could.

I tell this story to my students each year before their culminating performance. After a few moments, I ask them, "By the way, what is excellence?" Think about it for a moment. How would you answer that?

Cousin Bobby, Ben and David

For me, 'excellence' is when something is so amazing, so beautiful, so thrilling, so delicious and so extraordinary that when you remember that moment, you feel what you felt all over again.

Excellent food still makes your mouth water when you remember the first bite. A thrilling sporting event makes us want to stand and cheer all over again when we recall the excitement leading up to the final buzzer. Remembering our first kiss still makes our hearts race years later. Excellent experiences create powerful, lasting memories.

Magicians, I'll wrap up this section the same way I end class on concert day. Tonight, you could create something that will stay with your audience forever — something truly excellent. You've put in the hard work and preparation. You've learned everything you need. There's only one thing left if you wish to become excellent:

Do the best you can.

Do the best you can.

Do the best you can.

7: Friends & Mentors

"Perfume and incense bring joy to the heart, and the pleasantness of a friend springs from their heartfelt advice."

— *Proverbs 27:9*

Dr. Ron Pyle

During my senior year at Whitworth University, I took Dr. Ron Pyle's course on Interpersonal Communications. It equipped me with concepts that have helped me daily as a teacher and entertainer — some of which you'll read about in this section. Ron and I became friends and have stayed in touch ever since.

In addition to being an expert in the field of communication, Ron is also a speaker and preacher who has spoken across the country and overseas. Like many of our contributors, Ron has years of experiential knowledge in his field. He is also a stellar magician, regularly performing for students, friends and Whitworth faculty.

When he retired, Whitworth University said this of him: "His title was Professor of Communication Studies, but Ron Pyle is really Whitworth's relationship expert. Pyle has taught generations of students, faculty, and staff about relationships — both communication's role in fostering them and what the Christian faith teaches about them. Chosen 18 times by the senior class as 'Most Influential Professor', Pyle has made a remarkable impact on students."

I know he'll have a remarkable impact on you as well. Welcome to Magic Communication 101!

Ginóskó, David and Me

I'm honored to be invited to contribute to this book. My reflections will, of necessity, be very different from the insights provided in these pages by some of the most renowned performers in the world of magic. The reader might understandably wonder, "What is a retired Professor of Communication doing in a book about magic?'" It's a fair question.

The answer rests in the beautiful concept that is foundational to this book: ginóskó. Ginóskó is the progressive activity of knowing deeply. Ginóskó describes my relationship with David and provides the rationale for why I'm writing these words.

I first met David at Whitworth University, a small Christian liberal arts university in Spokane, Washington. In 2010, David was a senior. In previous years I had seen David presenting his magic act from time to time at talent shows on campus. I was well aware of his impressive skill as a magician and entertainer. However, at that point I didn't know him as a person. To put it another way, I didn't ginóskó David.

In the spring semester of his senior year, David took my course in Interpersonal Communication. I was very glad that he did. My objective in that class was to explore the nature of healthy human relationships and to provide some skills for living those relationships. I loved teaching that class for many reasons, one of them being that I had the privilege of getting to know some of my students in a ginóskó way. As a professor, I described my job like this:

> *"I teach important ideas to smart people who want to learn and want to open their lives to me."*

David is smart and from the very first day of my course he readily understood and embraced the importance of relationships. He also opened his life to me and as a result, we're fortunate to have a ginóskó quality of relationship that continues to develop to this day.

Ginóskó, Communication and Magic

My relationship with David, however rich to us, does not constitute a reason for contributing to this book. I know very little about the art and craft of magic. I do, however, know something about human communication. I hope to promote a ginóskó relationship between readers and magic from a communication perspective.

There are countless connections between communication and magic — enough to fill this entire book and many more. In these pages, I'll highlight just a few of these connections. I'm confident that communication can help readers ginóskó magic because communication is the vehicle by which meaning and knowledge develop.

In exploring the world of ideas, the 'what' must precede the 'how'. When you picked up this book and encountered the concept of ginóskó, your first question wasn't, "I wonder how to ginóskó?" Appropriately, our first question is always about the 'what' — what does it mean to ginóskó? The 'how' is important, but the 'how' is nonsensical until you understand the 'what'. In the following paragraphs, I will help us think a bit about the 'how' but first, we need to understand the 'what' of communication.

There are many definitions of communication. I'll use a definition advanced by John Stewart in his book, 'Bridges, Not Walls'. Stewart writes:

> *"Communication is the continuous, complex, collaborative process of verbal and nonverbal meaning making."*

Stewart's definition of communication begins with the descriptor, 'continuous'. Just as the ginóskó kind of knowing progressively unfolds, so communication continuously unfolds. Communication is continuous because we're constantly making meaning out of what's around us. Stimuli come our way and we select, organize, and interpret those stimuli so they're meaningful to us. Meaning making happens so quickly and so spontaneously that we're often unaware of the process. Before you take the stage, your audience is already making meaning of the physical setting, the emotional tone, the identities of the performers, whatever they can see and hear before the show starts and a dozen other variables.

Communication is complex. It is a miracle that humans communicate at all. Consider what occurs even in a most simplified description of the process of oral communication. Brain activity helps generate ideas, we push air through our diaphragm, our vocal cords are stimulated, we manipulate our tongue in our mouths, sound emerges, and as others receive sensation, their brains are active — and somehow meaning results.

Just to complicate matters further, our meaning making always involves our languages, identities, genders, cultures, histories, goals, expectations and a range of other factors. Appreciating the complexity of communication invites us to be humble about the process. It is wise of us to be careful about assuming that what we meant to communicate is the same as the meaning others receive.

Communication isn't something that one person does to another. Communication is collaborative, something that parties create together. No one bears sole responsibility for communication. When your show goes well, it isn't simply because you're skilled at magic (though I'm sure you are). The truth is that you can't have any kind of show without the collaboration of the audience. How can a magician invite the audience to collaborate? While there are multiple ways such collaboration can occur, one powerful way is through relating to your audience as human beings.

In his seminal book, 'I and Thou', Martin Buber distinguishes between an 'I — It' relationship and an 'I — Thou' relationship.

'I — It' relationships are created when I (a unique human being) treat another as an interchangeable object (an 'it').

Conversely, 'I — Thou' relationships are created when I (a unique human being) treat another as a 'Thou' (a unique human being).

The quality of the relationship you create with the audience is affected by the degree to which you treat that audience as humans. I'll describe only three ways that you can treat an audience as human.

One of the differences between objects and humans is that objects only react. When you drop a rock, the rock doesn't choose whether to fall or not. As an object, the rock simply reacts to the force of gravity.

Humans, however, have the capacity to respond. Unique humans can choose to respond in a variety of ways. The contrast between reacting and responding may seem so obvious as to make the distinction unnecessary. It might be, if not for the fact that you and I have both experienced being treated as an object, as a being incapable of responding. Not very enjoyable, is it? Building audience choices into your show can be one way of relating to the audience as humans and thereby inviting them to collaborate with you.

A second quality that distinguishes objects and humans is that objects are non-reflective while humans are reflective. Reflectivity involves awareness of what is happening around and in us. Decks of cards don't feel inferior when their designs are not as beautiful as those of other decks. That's because objects don't reflect.

Again this distinction seems obvious until you recall times that you were treated as non-reflective. For example, we experience this kind of objectification when conversations remain superficial and allow little room for reflection. You may be experiencing reflectivity right now if your awareness prompts you to consider how your communication invites others to reflect. A magic show is a perfect place to foster reflectivity as audiences experience a heightened awareness of what is happening immediately before them.

A third way to differentiate objects from persons is that objects are not addressable while humans are. Non-addressable means that you can 'talk at' objects. When I'm on a golf course, I frequently 'talk at' my golf ball: "No, not in the sand again!" While I talk at my golf ball, I never expect the ball to answer.

Humans, on the other hand, are addressable. You can 'talk with' another person. This distinction may seem like common sense until we remember times when we were objectified by being 'talked at' instead of being 'talked with'. In a magic show, addressability is largely achieved by tone of voice (see the discussion of nonverbal communication below). As you 'talk with' your audience, you express an appreciation for their humanity and thereby begin to create a collaborative 'I — Thou' relationship. Responsiveness, reflectivity, and addressability are just three ways that performers can collaborate with audiences.

One of the most important realities collaboratively constructed with audiences involves identities. Every time we communicate with another person, we're involved in collaborating with them about their identities. Every communicative act sends messages about your own identity and also sends messages about how you see the identity of the other person. When you meet with magician friends and they want to see a new trick you've developed, they're sending you an identity message that you're interesting and important. They are also sending identity messages about themselves — that they care about you.

Your identity, who you take yourself to be, is a function of the communication that surrounds you. This process of identity construction is collaborative. You can only have a certain identity if the people you're in communication with allow you to have it. You may have had the experience of meeting a family who just moved into your neighborhood. Wanting to project an identity of warmth and acceptance, you try to engage your new neighbor. No matter how hard you try, the new neighbor simply won't accept that definition of you. At least with that neighbor, you can't have the identity as friendly unless the other person allows it.

In the world of magic, one of the important decisions you will make relates to the identity through which you will do your show. The establishment of identity, however, isn't done in isolation. The audience must accept your identity. Your language, the way you dress, the tone of your voice, your body movements and other factors are all part of your offering an identity of yourself.

Successful communication can be either verbal or nonverbal. These terms are often misunderstood. Verbal means 'by word'. Nonverbal means 'not by word'. The confusion frequently comes when we add the categories 'oral' (by mouth) and 'nonoral' (not by mouth).

It may help to think of a two by two matrix in which we have the categories 'verbal', 'nonverbal', 'oral' and 'nonoral'.

The 'verbal/oral' category is evident when the words come out of the mouth (as they do with oral speech).

'Verbal/nonoral' occurs when words are used, but the words do not come by mouth (when the words are written for example).

'Nonverbal/oral' communication happens when meaning is made without words, but by mouth. For example, a scream or a sigh are not by word but are by mouth.

The 'nonverbal/nonoral' category relates to communication which isn't by word, and not by mouth. Touch, props, and clothing are all examples of nonverbal/nonoral.

Misunderstandings tend to happen when the verbal and the oral are conflated. For example, a boss may tell a new employee, "You will have a performance review in six months. We can do the review verbally or we can do it in writing." The boss has confused verbal and oral. Since 'verbal' means by word, the review done in writing is also verbal, assuming that the written review is done with words. The boss probably meant that the review could be done orally or in writing.

The importance of nonverbal communication for performers of magic is hard to overstate. While research studies produce a range of estimates, somewhere around 70% of the social meaning constructed in communication is nonverbal. Some kinds of nonverbal behaviors in the context of magic include voice (tone, quality, vocal stress on certain words, etc.), silence, movements and gestures, facial expression, eye contact and gaze, proximity (how physical space is used) and touch.

The functions of nonverbal behaviors are many. Here, we will discuss two of the most important functions of nonverbal communication.

First, nonverbal behaviors (especially use of voice) influence how words are interpreted. For example, the sentence, "That's not my red car" can have four different meanings depending on the stress put on particular words. "That's *not* my red car" provides emphatic denial. "That's not *my* red car" suggests that the red car belongs to someone else. "That's not my *red* car" conveys that the speaker has cars of colors other than red. "That's not my red *car*" suggests the speaker owns other red modes of transportation.

Another example of the intersection of nonverbal behaviors and meaning is seen in sarcasm. Tone of voice and facial expressions are how sarcasm is done. The words 'smooth move' have particular meaning depending upon how tone of voice and facial expressions relate to the action described.

Second, nonverbal behaviors are a primary way that you and your audience will negotiate your identity. Imagine, for

The author in conversation with Ron Pyle

example, that the identity you want to present to your audience is one of suave sophistication. Nonverbal factors such as how you dress, the tone of your voice, your posture, your facial expression, and your movements will all affect how your audience perceives you.

As you consider nonverbal dimensions of a magic show, consonance is vital. The way that you use nonverbal behaviors must be consonant (meaning aligned and consistent) with your communication goals. Again, if you want to be seen as sophisticated, but your enunciation is sloppy, your clothing is messy, and your posture is slouched, your nonverbal behaviors are not consonant with your intended message.

Communication scholarship has confirmed that, when the verbal and nonverbal elements contradict each other, people will tend to believe the nonverbal. If you tell an audience that you're excited to be with them but your face and voice are emotionless, they're likely to believe that you wish you were somewhere else.

When dealing with the nonverbal realm, it is wise for us to be aware that, in lived experience, the verbal and nonverbal are difficult to separate. In every instance of verbal/oral communication the verbal and the nonverbal occur simultaneously because of tone of voice. Also consider that the meaning of nonverbal behaviors is largely verbal. For example, facial expression is considered nonverbal (since it isn't by word) but the way we assign meaning to the facial expression is generally done verbally. We use words to understand the facial expression as 'sad' or 'angry'.

Remember, too, that culture is always a factor in communication. This is evident in the interpretation of facial expressions. While there are a certain number of universal facial expressions (have shared meaning across cultures) what isn't universal is cultural prescriptions about when and where and how to express nonverbally.

Since the nonverbal realm of communication is always present, performers of magic could easily lose awareness of how nonverbal factors impact the show. To promote awareness, consider seeking honest feedback from peers who will give special attention to your nonverbal behaviors and carefully review video recordings of your show.

For my entire adult life, I've been fascinated by the continuous, complex, collaborative process of verbal and nonverbal meaning making. It seems to me that communication and magic share many similarities. Both have the potential to fascinate those who study them. Both have such depth and nuance that they require a ginóskó kind of knowing. Both demand the best of our hearts and minds in the ginóskó of them. Both invite and even demand our creativity to advance our understanding and practice of them. Both produce authentic human connection when done well. Both evoke joy. My hope is that, by providing a communication perspective of magic, you will ginóskó magic with more insight, creativity, and joy.

— Ron Pyle, Ph.D.
Professor Emeritus of Communication Studies
Whitworth University

Dr. Kainoa Harbottle

Kainoa Harbottle is a world-class magician and a high school literature teacher. On one occasion when I was watching him teach, a student shouted out, "Why do we have to learn this?"

In a situation like this, most teachers would choose from a short list of responses: ignore, apologize, rationalize or scold. Not Kainoa. He fired back with an equally snarky quip to provoke a second attack. The second attack came. Others joined in.

This led to a strange battle of whiny questions, literary concepts, grammar corrections and teenage attitude. The bell rang and the students got up to leave. The same student shouted, "I bite my thumb at you, sir!" (Romeo and Juliet, Act 1, Scene 1). She then realized that she'd actually *learned* something. Actually, the class had covered the whole lesson.

That's Kainoa. He lures in his audience (or class) with his friendly demeanor and then crushes all expectations through a stellar lesson or devastating sleight of hand. You're about to experience this.

You probably came here expecting a treatise on coins. Not this time. Instead, you'll get a rare glimpse into the mind of one of magic's finest teachers and scholars.

Méntoras

"Tell all the truth but tell it slant —
Success in Circuit lies
Too bright for our infirm Delight
The Truth's superb surprise..."
— Emily Dickinson

When I originally read David's discussion of the word ginóskó — about the importance of mixing experience with relationships — I immediately thought of the word 'mentor'. This term actually comes to use from Homer's epic poem 'The Odyssey', in which (you may remember) Odysseus leaves his kingdom to help Brad Pitt in the war against Orlando Bloom at Troy. While he's away, Odysseus leaves his son Telemachus under the watchful care of his old friend, Mentor.

Unfortunately for Telemachus and his status as heir to the kingdom, Odysseus is away for far longer than anyone expected. This leads many to believe he has died either in war or in transit. As a result, things at home become quite chaotic, with multiple suitors now wooing Odysseus's wife, Penelope. Telemachus knows that if his mother were to marry one of these ardent suitors, he would lose his kingdom to some new stepdad.

Mentor helps the tentative Telemachus to help his already devious mother resist these various challengers long enough for Odysseus to return. This only involves waiting a mere twenty years. When Odysseus does finally return, Mentor supports him in what is clearly an unfair fight against the swarm of suitors and even assists in their brutal slaughter. Good times.

The interesting thing about the character of Mentor, however, is that he's not actually Mentor at all. In a dramatic plot twist, he turns out to be Athena, the goddess of wisdom. She has been in disguise all along to ensure that her favorite hero ends up with a happy, albeit undeniably bloody resolution.

There are a number of conclusions we can draw from this regarding the nature of learning as well as magic:

- Wisdom does not come to the characters (or us) directly but through deception.

- True mentorship might best be thought of as learning in a state of controlled duplicity.

- Or, as Emily Dickinson puts it in her beautifully cryptic and succinct way, the truth is best told 'slant', and a circuitous route rather than a direct path is ultimately more helpful for the learner.

These conclusions might seem counterintuitive or even paradoxical at first: we seldom think of wisdom being adjacent to, let alone embodied by, deception. Also, we tend to think of our mentors as well-meaning guides rather than evil geniuses exploiting our credulous simplicities. Even Dickinson isn't championing the adage 'the longest way round is the nearest way home', where sticking to rather than deviating from the frustratingly involved process is ultimately the most productive way of successfully completing whatever task is at hand.

However, the more you think about it, you more you will realize that deception is actually crucial to how we're effectively educated. What Dickinson is really suggesting is that learning is strengthened when the learner is guided to an incomplete pattern that they must then complete for themselves. For Dickinson, that elusive mystery 'truth' is best experienced as a 'superb surprise' rather than as an overwhelming mass of facts, implying that such a moment occurs with an 'aha' rather than a 'hmm'. The mysterious, Dickinson suggests, should be suddenly apprehended rather than analyzed into awareness.

Of course learning by revelation is nothing new to successful educators, business and/or cult leaders and even magicians. Managing a classroom often involves deploying techniques to which students remain oblivious but that help them to achieve their goals, especially if retention based on discovery remains valued over rote memorization.

Too little information means inquiring minds don't have enough to go on. Conversely, too much information taxes minds, leaving them unable to process let alone determine the essentials. Just the right amount of information leads to a moment of realization where the pieces of the puzzle click into place by the effort of the learner rather than the force of the teacher.

Likewise, the astonishment of a magic effect is heightened by directing the audience to the impossibly inevitable — the face down card that the audience suddenly knows but doesn't know is their selection even before it's turned over. This is typically the climactic moment when an incredulous spectator yells, "No!" For the spectators, this isn't a case of Schrodinger's Card but rather the emotion arising from the experience of inescapable astonishment. So every performer is also a type of mentor, but that's not the takeaway this book needs.

Kainoa teaching a magic class

For what David's focus on the influence of others made me realize about the case of Mentor and deception was a totally different take-home message. It's a message that magicians regularly try (even if sometimes unsuccessfully) to convince audiences of: that being open to learning from everyone around us is a wonderful thing.

What's most interesting to me in the story of Mentor is that the Greeks weren't looking for a showy celestial intervention with flashy lights and boiling rivers, exciting as that might have been. They were hoping to turn to the person next to them and receive inspiration to accomplish what they already knew needed to be done. Indeed, Dickinson's qualifying of our delight as 'infirm' suggests that what we really need is that helpful push to discover what we already, on some level, know.

The insights we can receive from those around us can be useful if we're receptive to them. Sure, there are a lot of dumb humans spinning falsehoods that arise from decrepit critical thinking skills, lack of information and poor genetic breeding — but this has always been the case. Just because you're going to meet dipsticks now and again doesn't mean you should ignore everyone, no matter how handy (or lonely) that strategy can be.

Think about it: table-hopping magicians are constantly relying on the kindness of strangers. Every time he saunters up to a table in the middle of one of Dad's stories, the magician has to convince a family he's never met before that this seemingly random interaction with someone will be a worthwhile experience. It's not an easy thing to do by any means and yet good close-up workers somehow achieve this several times in a single evening.

The most valuable lesson we can glean from all this is that our audiences are people too, and that we should be learning from them. This requires the gathering of extensive amounts of data as well as the ability to weigh others' ideas with interior assumptions. Yet learning to listen actively and appreciatively, rather than half-heartedly, should remind us that magic only occurs when an audience is present, which means their opinions really do matter.

When you're doing a trick by yourself in front of a mirror, that isn't magic – it's just practice. If you're experiencing the magic as you practice it, then you (or one of you) should probably see someone about that. Actively listening is a struggle, especially considering how easily the ego can get in the way. However, as you've probably already noticed, many of the essays in this book are about burying the ego in order to create and curate the best magic possible.

So I encourage you to keep your eyes open, looking to the people around you and even those in front of you — the ones silly enough to take a card, any card — as they might very well be the most important people we as performers should be learning from. Of course, I didn't come up with this all by myself; I was lucky enough to have a good mentor point me in the right direction.

— Dr. Kainoa Harbottle, PhD

'Telemachus And Mentor Discovered By Calypso' by Edward Scriven. (1810)

Tom Dobrowolski

Tom loves practical card tricks, encouraging others, and bacon. I know what you're thinking: the perfect man! But wait. There's more.

Tom is an experienced teacher of magic, with years of experience lecturing for magicians. He's also a fiercely loyal friend who never fails to provide encouragement and insightful feedback to serious magicians.

Each year, Tom and I perform together in the 'This is Magic' show on Maui. His unique blend of Midwest friendliness, joyful energy and quick wit makes him a crowd favorite.

When you watch Tom perform, you're actually witnessing the rich history of Chicago magic. Over the years, Tom befriended several Chicago magic legends who entrusted him with their strong routines and the classic 'Chicago Magic' performing style. They also imparted a few life lessons that continue to live through Tom today.

My favorite of those lessons is the subject of Tom's contribution, to which we now turn.

Pass it On

I became friends with Jim Ryan in the last ten years or so of his life. If you had the opportunity to know Jim, I'm sure you remember a big Irish guy who was larger than life. When we first met, he was in his 80s and still did magic incredibly well. I have many fond memories of spending time with his family and driving him to magic club meetings.

My favorite Jim Ryan story took place when I went to The Houdini Convention with him and his wife in my early twenties. I'd saved up just enough money for the convention and had about $150 left to spend when I got there.

We got to the hotel, checked in, and went to lunch to celebrate all three of our birthdays, which were around the same time. When it came time to pay, I reached into my pocket to cover my part of the tab and found it empty. I ran up to the hotel room to look through my things, only to realize my money was gone. I'd paid for my room and registration in advance, but, somehow, I'd lost every cent for magic and food for the next three days.

I went back down to the restaurant and explained the situation to Jim. I asked if he'd seen some cash lying around. He hadn't.

Later that evening, Tommy Edwards, another Chicago area magician, came up to me and invited me to get a Coke at the bar. When we sat down, he said, "Hey, I'm kind of hungry. Why don't you get a sandwich, too? I'll treat you."

I thought to myself, "Great! I can eat!"

The following day I ran into a guy in the lobby with his wife. He walked up to me and said, "We're going to breakfast. Why don't you join us? I heard it was your birthday!" This continued for the next two days. At every mealtime, someone would pop up and say, "Let me grab you a meal."

Cut to thirty years later at a dinner with Jay Marshall. After trading a few Jim Ryan stories, I recalled the strange events that happened at The Houdini Convention and the

*Tom Dobrowolski with Jim Ryan (top)
and Jay Marshall (bottom)*

generous magicians who seemed to appear out of nowhere to take care of me. Jay started to chuckle. He finally admitted that Jim had told him that I'd lost my money. Jay went around to everyone at the convention and said, "Let's all take care of Tom. Make sure he has a meal and something to drink." On top of that, he made sure no one said a word to me about my situation so I wouldn't feel embarrassed.

That was at least 35 years ago. A couple of friends and I have decided to do the same thing for devoted young magicians around us. It's our way of repaying the immense kindness we received from those great Chicago magicians. And, except for this story, we won't say a word about it.

There are a handful of guys we've done it for at this point. Some of them know and some don't. On one occasion, a young friend wanted to attend the Magifest convention in Columbus, Ohio. So what did we do? We brought him along! He stayed in the room for free. We made sure he was taken care of for the weekend. We passed it on.

This gesture has nothing to do with us getting credit for our charity. Rather, I like to think that it's Jim Ryan, Jay Marshall and the others channeling through us. They passed it to me. Now, I get to pass it to my young friend, and believe it or not, he's already passing it on to others.

So, in honor of Jay Marshall and Jim Ryan, I ask this of anyone reading these words who's in a position to lift up a young magician: *pass it on*. It can be a small thing, like a trick they can't afford. It could be a meal. It could be including them in a session you're having with somebody they wouldn't usually have the chance to meet. All you have to say is, "Why don't you come and sit down with us?" It'll mean the world to them. They'll remember it.

And maybe, someday, they'll pass it on, too.

— Tom Dobrowolski

Dr. Jason Fleming

I once suffered a back injury during a visit to Oahu. The pain started in my lower back and moved toward my chest. I drove myself to the ER, and moments later, I was on an exam table, staring at the ceiling. I was scared. I hadn't experienced those symptoms before. I wondered if I was going to receive horrible news and how I would react.

At the peak of my anxiety, a doctor came in to see me. His voice was comforting yet clear and strong. He was gentle yet confident; to the point yet good-humored. He even got a laugh out of me before he left to arrange my tests. My anxiety was gone and I knew I was in good hands.

This ER doctor clearly had years of experience in front of people. Was he a musician? A singer? Actor? Magician?

In fact he was, and is, all of these and more. It was Jason Fleming — a dear friend and magician whom I'd known for some years when I had this accident. In fact, he and I had performed and taught magic classes together.

Jason is our next contributor, and just as I was all those years ago, you're in good hands.

The Magician Will See You Now

In the emergency department where I work, there's a telephone just outside the door. People who come along to the ER seeking medical care pick up the phone and it rings at the desk inside. The Unit Secretary answers the phone and typically asks, "Good morning. Are you here to see the doctor?" This is how the process begins. The patient replies in the affirmative and their response triggers the entire cascade of actions that comprise the delivery of emergency care in America.

There's a point here that I think is of interest to us, as magicians. Notice that the question isn't, "Are you here for some medical care?", or, "Would you like to see some skills that our doctor has been practicing recently?" The patients are there to see the doctor and that's what they say. The doctor, in this way, *is* the show.

What can magicians take away from this scene? I believe it reveals something important about the minds of the people for whom we perform. Consider the audience that comes along to see your next show. They aren't there to see some tricks. They aren't there because your sleight of hand is pure gold or you have recently acquired a new prop that you'd like to try out. They're not there simply to be fooled (there are plenty of other folks trying to fool them these days). These things may be important. But the audience is, fundamentally, there to see *the magician*.

It's not only in the field of emergency medicine that you can see this phenomenon on display. Think back to the last time you went to a music concert. In my own case, it was to see Elton John. Was I there to hear 'Rocket Man'? Well, that was cool and certainly *part* of the reason. But I was really there to see Elton John.

As magicians develop from excited beginners to more mature and seasoned performers, they typically progress from practicing moves to learning tricks and then crafting an act. Because we focus on details, we sometimes can't see the forest for the trees. The audience is there to see *the magician*. We ought to satisfy this expectation.

The performer, in crafting the act, needs to give attention to their performing character. This is both 'you' and 'not you'. Your performing character is a person that you manifest from the very first moment you take the stage — whether that 'stage' is actually your living room or a proscenium or a moderately busy sidewalk. It's the image you want the audience to meet and interact with, and that you hope will delight them. You get to craft your character through the choices you make, cultivating it over time and with the benefit of that wonderful teacher we call experience.

But don't lose sight of the fact that your audience really wants to meet someone special: *you*. Your performing character needs to provide them with the enjoyable and rather privileged sensation of having met The Magician. If

Dr. Jason Fleming with the author

they go away at the end of the evening feeling like they did *not* met this interesting person, they'll be at least a little dissatisfied. And who can blame them? It's what they came along for.

Many of us first got into magic because we were shy. Or felt awkward. Or preferred the solitude of the practice mirror to the mirth of a group of friends having fun together. That's perfectly okay. Magic is a fantastic hobby and one that has helped countless folks to break out of their shells. But as magicians and performers, we're subject to the expectations of our audience, just as the physician is subject to the expectations of their patient.

Your audience wants to see *The Magician*.

— Dr. Jason Fleming, PhD

Magical friends: David Kuraya, George Wang, Jason Fleming, Kainoa Harbottle, Curtis Kam, Jade, Matthew Holtzman and Brad Kerwin

Nathan Coe Marsh

A new magic showroom opened on Maui in 2021, and like any magic nerd on a tiny island, I found myself in line on opening night. The magician chosen to launch and headline the new theater was Florida native Nathan Coe Marsh.

Nathan and I became fast friends during his residency in Maui. I suspect part of the reason is that we have been on similar journeys through the world of magic. Like Nathan, I remember the specific moment I became hooked on the art of sleight of hand and the performance of magic. We both pursued mentors throughout our careers. We both started performing in odd venues to gain experience.

I asked him about his personal strategy for creating an act that manages to consistently connect with audiences. Without hesitation, Nathan referred me to what he calls The Four Signposts. These four words are his starting blocks for each phase of structuring an act and scripting individual routines.

Four Signposts & Seven Tips

The Four Signposts

Here are Nathan's four signposts for structuring your act or scripting new material.

Focus. The show's beginning must ensure the audience looks up and listens. What am I saying or doing in the first few moments of the act and of each trick to ensure they are attentive to me? How am I using my body to engage them? What can I say or do to capture their interest?

Rapport. Once I have their attention, how can I create an environment where I'm connecting with the audience? How am I giving them my attention? How can I get this group of strangers to think and feel the same things simultaneously for the most impact later?

Climax. In the act and each routine, what is the amazing moment to which I'm moving? What does it look like? Sound like? Feel like? How are my body and voice telling them how they should feel?

Emotional Reaction. Find specific words for how you want the audience to feel at the end of each routine or after your show. Enlightened? Inspired? Connected? Hopeful?

The Four Signposts provide a framework for conducting the audience's emotions at each moment of your act. They help us be aware of the energy exchange between performer and audience, and, most importantly, they allow us to remember that we're there to serve them, not our egos.

When choosing routines, use these signposts to decide where they fit in your act. Can a routine build engagement and create focus? Or maybe it's the big climax? As you write your scripts, are you taking time to build rapport, or are you just having them pick a card and move on? Are you abruptly jumping to the next trick, or are you strategically drawing out the reaction and emotion your magic deserves?

Working It Out

Any pro reading this will know that completing a thoughtful script does not mean the act is finished. As Nathan often points out, writing is just the starting block. The race has not even started. The next step is working out the material in front of an audience. It's intimidating to test routines the first time. What if they don't get it? What if the jokes flop? What if I don't fool them? I asked Nathan about his thoughts on preparing to put new material and working it out in front of an audience.

Practice and Memorize

This may seem obvious, but it shouldn't be overlooked. Now that you've done the work of writing a script, memorize it. Knowing your script cold frees up your brain to remain present and listen to the audience throughout your act. You won't constantly think about what to say next and you can ad lib and play with the audience without losing your place.

As you practice your lines and routines, keep yourself accountable. Nathan records what he worked on after each rehearsal. It may be a whole run-through of the act. It might be a slow beat-by-beat breakdown of a trick. Either way, he schedules specific blocks of time for rehearsal. As he says, "If it gets scheduled, it gets done. Put it on paper."

This method may not sound exciting. Creative types and artists often resist this kind of consistent and disciplined workflow. But try it. Many of my creative friends agree that a regimented schedule protects us from our minds always moving from one creative thing to the next.

Go 'Off the Grid'

Most working professionals use every possible resource to promote themselves today. They maintain an active social media presence, run a slick website and constantly send emails and leave voicemails to turn leads into gigs. Nathan is no exception.

But when it's time to test new material, none of these business strategies come into play for him. Nathan works 'off the grid' at places where his followers won't know he's working. This allows him to build confidence and discover presentational gems he couldn't think of when scripting. And, frankly, it provides a low-stakes space for new material to fail. After all, we can invest thousands in marketing but the show's quality must come first.

You may wonder if it would be easier just to buy a few dealer items, complete with props and script? Sure, it's much easier. But these days TV shows, streaming services, YouTube, TikTok and other online platforms have made magic highly visible — which makes it a lot harder to get away with doing what everyone else is doing.

Persistence and Honesty

Don't be surprised if a trick doesn't sing the first time as you work out your material. It may take a few repetitions before you connect with it. The audience will feel when that happens.

On the other hand, be honest about what's working and what's not. Don't try to talk yourself into doing a joke or trick the same way if it's consistently flopping. Even if it's a bit you love, make changes or maybe even throw it out. There's no point in working on material if you're not going to reflect honestly and adjust.

(Continued >)

Seven Pro Tips

In one of our late-night sessions during his residency on Maui, I asked Nathan whether he had any reflections or lessons learned after ten weeks of shows on Maui and 700 shows at The Great Magic Hall in Florida.

None of Nathan's seven tips were the typical 'imagine them in their underwear' suggestions. I recommend that any working magician print these as a checklist to read before every show. I've included them here in his exact words.

(1) Set yourself specific performance-related challenges. For example, "Today, I'm going to focus only on speaking when I'm looking at another human" (not talking into a case while fetching a prop); or, "Today, my focus is on moving intentionally and staying rooted to a spot unless there is a reason to move." "Today, whenever I ask someone's name, I will consciously lock it into my memory." "Today, my conscious focus is on eliminating all tension from my body unless it is there for a dramatic purpose."

Yes, these should happen in every show, but they can't all be in conscious focus at once with everything else the brain processes during performance.

When you're in a situation where you know the space and material inside and out, consciously focusing on just one of these aspects of performance helps lock it in as an unconscious habit when you're in situations where you don't have that freedom. These are all skills that need to be worked on individually and consciously as skills. Knowing isn't the same as doing.

Speaking of conscious attention, the keys to not becoming a robot when doing a billion shows are **(2)** conscious focus on your breathing to pull you into the moment before entering, and **(3)** conscious focus on the specific individual humans in front of you at each moment.

Every person, at a given moment, has a natural rhythm and pace. A group of people becomes an audience when that pace synchronizes, and they respond to things as one unit with its own pace, rhythm and energy level. An excellent performance happens when the pace, rhythm and energy level of the audience converges with that of the performer. It's rather like surfing: the more time you spend on the water, the better you get at feeling the waves and being able to catch them.

(4) A solid callback to a specific thing that the audience knows *only* happened at *this* show will get the biggest of all laughs.

(5) An earnest attempt to correctly address someone in their own language will earn you genuine goodwill from them. Knowing a few key phrases in several languages with correct pronunciation goes a long way.

Finally, **(6)** get enough water and enough sleep and **(7)** most importantly, get comfortable shoes!

— Nathan Coe Marsh

Tony Cabral

In 2018, Curtis Kam and I traveled to Boston to see Tony Cabral perform behind the bar at the 'Legal Test Kitchen'. Watching Tony present devastating card magic for his guests was an education. As they enjoyed every routine, people laughed, gasped in astonishment and raised their glasses to toast this delightful magical entertainer. Tony created that 'everybody knows your name' feeling — not far, incidentally, from the actual bar featured in the opening credits of the 'Cheers' sitcom.

After the show, Tony invited us to stay at his home. The next day, we took a road trip to New York together with Tony's wife, Sheeri, and toddler, Ruben, to hang out with that city's finest magicians.

On that trip, I learned that the name Tony Cabral meant different things to different people. Some people thought of him principally as a card magician, writer or jazz pianist. Others referred to him as a portrait artist or simply 'the guy who does the best ever impressions of Zoidberg and Allen Okawa'.

All these various descriptions are accurate. How did Tony acquire so many skills and develop such broad expertise? Practice? Reading? A fateful deal with the devil himself? Let's find out!

Connections

Whenever I chit-chat with my audiences or any group of laymen (or as I call them, 'normal people'), invariably somebody asks, "How did you learn how to do this?"

I know a great many people with expertise in diverse fields: doctors, computer programmers, chefs, artists, scientists, musicians, plumbers and engineers... to name just a few. When they're good at their jobs, people assume they went to school to study that field, or possess a talent, or otherwise just spent more time doing that one particular thing than the average person.

When you perform a magic trick — especially a really good one — people don't just think about your level of expertise. They wonder how you learned about magic in the first place. The one thing 'normal people' know about our art is that 'magicians never reveal their secrets'. They quite rightly see conjuring as a field of arcane knowledge that neither they nor anyone else can penetrate.

This is the world we've created. Any of the specialist areas I mentioned above involves *knowledge* that the average person doesn't possess. But we magicians take things one step further: we have *secrets*. We do intriguing, astounding, unfathomable and impossible things right in front of people's eyes! We make them demand 'How?!' and then refuse to say.

It's a tease. If a guy comes to unclog your toilet or fix your fridge, you might ask him for some advice so you can attend to the next simple problem that crops up. But you don't pump the guy for fifteen years' worth of appliance repair expertise. First, it's rude. Second, it's impossibly ridiculous and vice versa. Third, we all know those guys charge by the hour and don't come cheap!

Meanwhile conjuring, in the raised-eyebrow words of the late Max Maven, "wears its secrecy on its sleeve". We push people far past their level of comfort and demonstrate things that confound their intelligence. The more intelligent the audience, the worse the discomfort. And that's the reaction we're going for. To divulge a sufficiently significant enough secret as to shatter the illusion is like creating a painting and then taking a knife to it. It's not just that 'a magician never reveals his secrets'. The truth is that a magician *can't* reveal his secrets.

Therein lies the rub. If magicians never reveal their secrets, how does anyone learn how to do these amazing things? Harry Potter gets to go to an accredited school to learn how to be a wizard. But the (hopefully) well-dressed, charming gentleman who makes sponge bunnies vanish, reappear, and multiply... what's *his* story?

The truth of the matter is that most of us, early on, develop in a vacuum. Oh, sure, we may see a magician perform at a party or on television, and that's the spark. But then we have to seek out those answers. We beg our parents for a magic kit. (Good luck to anyone whose favorite child discovers a magic shop anywhere nearby, as I did when I was just a wee sprout.)

Is that how I learned how to do what I do? Not quite.

If we didn't before, we learn to appreciate the library. That's how I absorbed the bulk of my foundational knowledge of card magic. As an undergrad at Brown University, I had the H. Adrian Smith Collection at my disposal. I used to dive into it like Scrooge McDuck in a vault full of gold coins. Armed with a little information, we practice. We sit at home in front of a mirror and we start learning these weird things. Eventually, we venture out in public and ask the all important question, "Hey, can I show you something?"

Is that how I learned how to do what I do? Not quite.

When I was learning how to be a magician, I didn't talk with anyone nearby about my goals and ideas. On the one hand, I developed my own tastes and opinions, balancing what I wanted to do with what people most strongly responded to. On the other hand, I was on my own and able to fail, succeed and draw my own conclusions. Basically, I was free for about ten years to suck really badly at whatever I tried to do and still, on occasion, succeed.

Is that how I learned how to do what I do? Not quite.

I came up through the magical ranks at a particular point in time. I'd read a bunch of books, learned a bunch of tricks and taken my lumps in bars or at parties. Then I joined a couple of internet forums that allowed me to connect with a group of folks who in earlier times I'd have never met or gotten anywhere near. In the days before the internet, I'd have had to resort to letter-writing or costly phone calls.

That's an element of my magical journey that I've always known was tremendously special, and that I remind myself not to take for granted. Through years of study, a few solid opportunities and mostly pure blind luck, I've had the good fortune to meet a number of people whose books are on my shelves. Of all the pursuits I've ever claimed to be good at, magic — specifically card magic — has allowed me to meet and connect with my models, mentors and heroes. Many of those people became my friends.

It's easy at this point to start name-dropping. "Dai Vernon passed out next to me at the bar at the Castle and all I got was this lousy T-shirt...". What's more important is the conversations I had with these folks, sharing ideas and getting inspired. I'm tremendously lucky to have had conversations with some of the best magicians in the world — some you may know and some you may not.

As of this writing, Darwin Ortiz passed away just a couple of months ago (Oct. 13th, 2023). Darwin was one of the first major influences on me through his books. When I discovered his work, he had two books of his own material out ('Darwin Ortiz At The Card Table' and 'Cardshark'), one book of theory ('Strong Magic') and his 'Annotated Erdnase', which I've always viewed as less of a commentary on the book and more of an overview of the history of card magic. That was a lot to cram into my skull, but I lived with that information for a long time.

Sometime in the early 2000's, via some decent internet forums, I connected with some of Darwin's friends and, in time, with the man himself. I started sending him emails. I'd send him routines I was working on at the time, and he was very kind and generous with his replies. I remember a conversation with our mutual friend Andrew Wimhurst when I first arranged to meet Darwin in person. I said, "Don't get me wrong, I'm beyond excited about this, but he strikes me as someone who doesn't suffer fools gladly." Andrew replied, "He doesn't, but he really likes *you!*" I thought, great, I get to be Darwin's token doofus.

That wasn't the case at all — well, maybe a little. Darwin and I became good friends who could talk about card magic or other things we both liked: comic books, horror movies, old-style comedy like the Marx Brothers and Ernie Kovacs, 'The Twilight Zone' and so on. He was always generous with his time and knowledge.

I used to collect ways to cut to the four aces like some people collect stamps. Darwin said to me, "You know, the strongest ace cutting routine I've ever done for lay audiences is Ed Marlo's 'Miracle Aces'." After he said this to me three times (which I've since dubbed 'The Beetlejuice Rule'), I thought, okay, time to figure out what he's on about. I thought I already knew the routine but I revisited it and came up with my own handling. I showed it to him and realized I'd done what he hoped I'd do: take the suggestion and turn it into something personal. He was very complimentary and I took it as a point of pride.

In 2012, I put out a DVD set for magicians. This wasn't actually my idea. A couple of friends decided they wanted to help me get my material out into the magic world. They asked Darwin if he'd be part of the project. Not only did he agree, he offered to be *in* the project. He sat with me as we taped the explanations, lending not only his guidance and expertise but also his presence and cachet. We sat, talked, joked and created a wonderful document of our friendship. As far as I know, I'm the only person he ever helped in this way and I'm forever grateful. (Then again, maybe I'm also the only one of 'his boys' who *needed* that much help.)

I have other stories about Darwin as well as other people whom were incredibly generous with their friendship and knowledge. Some are still with us, some are gone, and I miss them dearly.

At roughly the same time as my DVDs came out, a magician friend of mine moved to Boston for a while. We started up a regular Sunday dinner with a couple of young college kids interested in magic. After we'd been doing this for about a month I had a shocking realization. I'd always made a point of seeking out what I called the 'cool older dudes' — the ones who had been performing magic for as long as I'd been alive. The ones with connections to the past masters I'd never met. After all, that's how you learn.

What I realized after a month of these Sunday dinners was that, at this little table, I had *become* one of these 'cool older dudes'. I was the one with experience and connections to the old masters like Darwin and others who wrote the books on my shelves. I realized I had the opportunity to take the generosity that others had shown to me and pay it forward.

I hate the phrase 'the real work'. To me, there's no such thing. There's only 'the work'. I love seeing my friends do good work and I try my darnedest to return the favor. I aim to do what others did for me: I meet someone, we hit it off, I see what they're working on and I offer what I can.

Another of my mentors and dear friends is Lance Pierce — one of the greatest magicians you've never heard of. He told me a story about a young close-up magician who approached him at a magic club and asked for some lessons. In due course, Lance made the time to meet up with this keen young student and go through the finer points of some close-up routines. (If you're familiar with Lance's work, you know he understands that 'details make perfection'.)

After a handful of these sessions, the youngster offered to pay Lance for his time. Lance's response sticks with me and serves to remind me how lucky I've been on my magical journey. He said, "The real secrets of magic can't be bought or sold. They can only be shared."

— Tony Cabral

Lance Pierce

Many of my readers will own a wonderful magic book called 'In Concert' by Lance Pierce. In the introduction, Lance shares a memory: "When I attended my first magic convention, I must admit I felt somewhat overwhelmed and rather left out. Magicians can be a cliquish lot."

Lance goes on to mention that there were some legendary names at that convention, such as Dai Vernon and Charlie Miller. Of course, Lance was delighted to see these 'giants' of magic perform. However, as things turned out, they were not the highlight of the convention.

Lance resumes the story: "The one thing that stands out in my mind is that for the entire duration of the convention, only one person made the effort to introduce himself and talk to me about my magic. That was Roger Klause."

When I attended *my* first magic convention, in 2016, my experience was largely the same as Lance's. I felt rather nervous, lonely and surrounded by cliques — even though I was delighted to meet some people whose work I'd studied in print or on video. Only one magician, upon seeing my plight, said hi, introduced me to his friends and made me feel welcome. On this occasion it wasn't Roger Klause.

It was Lance Pierce.

Six Weeks

A long time ago, I walked up to my very first table in a fairly demanding environment. The room was packed, every seat filled. The ambiance was loud and boisterous. The sheer wall of energy in front of me was, to put it mildly, intimidating.

But I had what I felt was a solid pocketful of material, strong effects and routines. I had lines... lots of them. I definitely had a little skill — moves for days, as some of my friends might have put it. I had everything, or so I initially believed, to do the job.

None of this prepared me for how terrible I was. The guests were polite but their reactions were measured and reserved. Everybody was very friendly — encouraging, even — but I knew as I walked away from each group that I was far from where I needed to be. There was some applause, but for some reason it felt gratuitous.

This feeling of falling short despite supposedly having every advantage, every element in my favor, lasted from table to table. In fact, it persisted from one day to the next. The days turned into weeks that turned into months — and I still felt the same way. Oh, I made some progress, but I knew there was a great deal of ground I hadn't even mapped yet, let alone conquered.

If it weren't for the patient guidance of certain very close friends and mentors, I might have ended up believing that I would never improve. I might have carried on feeling that I'd gone as far as I could — with nothing more to offer than a pleasant but nondescript few moments of diversion, forgotten before the evening was done. At this point in my life, I was an excellent student and technical practitioner... but *only* that.

I might have been okay with that, to some degree, except that I'd made a major change in my life to be in that particular place doing magic for those particular people. In fact, I'd broken a cardinal rule in my life to do it: never do business with friends.

But there I was, trying to make it work to the best of my ability, in Boca Raton, Florida, working at Bill Malone's Magic Bar. I was immensely proud to be working for Bill. He had taken a chance on me and I didn't want to fail him or cause him to lose face because of me.

One day, Bill said to me, "I think you need to learn how to talk to people. You have everything else but you're just not connecting with people the way you want to. When people talk to you, you don't seem to respond to them because you're still stuck to your script. It's not working."

"Bill," I said, as reassuringly as possible, "I know what you mean. I'm actually working on this, trying to improve. Give me a little time, and I think you'll be able to see it."

"How much time?"

"Six weeks."

"Six weeks?!"

Bill seemed puzzled by my specificity and also rather exasperated. But he could tell I was serious. Shaking his head slightly, he simply said, "Okay". I'd asked him to take a leap of faith and he'd done so.

When Bill said I needed to learn how to talk to the guests, I took this to mean I needed to learn more about the art of conversation in a performing context. For me, it wasn't as simple as loosening up a script or responding to the guests more attentively, which I felt was what Bill basically wanted. It felt as if there was much more to it, and I was trying to break it all down in my head.

Up to that point, I had treated performing magic as a mostly intellectual exercise. Do *this* for *this* reason at *that* moment to get *these* results. It was all very analytical, like following a computer program full of 'If > then' statements. Nothing about it felt emotional and I wasn't following my heart. Intellectual analysis is useful but it *is* only the first step. At some point, you have to move from practice to praxis — in other words, to achieve ginóskó.

I knew what my goal was. I needed to be better at relating to audiences; to make my performances more conversational and less driven by a stiff, inflexible script. How could I learn to do this? I knew I could try to respond more naturally to things people in the audience said. I could try to adjust the timing and delivery of my lines so they felt more organic and less prepared, preserving 'the illusion of the first time' and all that. But I sensed there was a larger issue I needed to address.

After several days, I realized that while it's wonderful to perform magic, and we're in front of the audience to *be* magicians, it's not the *primary* thing we're there to do. I realized that my reason for standing in front of an audience was *not* to do magic. It was to converse with them, interact with them and relate to them as vital human beings. Magic was just a unique, awesome medium through which to do these things.

The people watching me at each table weren't *spectators.* They were *people.* They aren't just there so we can impress them with our superpowers. They are *with* us, experiencing magical events and sometimes asking what they mean. I realized that this was going to change everything.

I pondered this new direction and emphasis. If I'm going to make conversation the point, and use magic to make the conversation successful, what am I going to say? Most of us don't enter conversations of any kind without knowing what we intend to say or the overall message we're trying to deliver. Why do we share jokes with friends or mention recent events or share how we feel about what's going on in our lives? In general, we're going for a certain reaction, ("Harry did *what?!*"), or hope to get a laugh, or perhaps just want to build better relationships. Whenever we talk to someone, we nearly always know ahead of time what our intended goal is.

So why do so many magicians, when they're performing, just recite their scripted patter without considering their *message* — what they actually want to say with their words and actions and miracles? Why has this become fairly standard practice within the art of magic?

Bill Malone always promises his clients that he'll come to their event and lift the atmosphere in the room so everyone has a good time. He promises that he'll take their event 'to the next level'. That's his business message to his clients but, if you watch him perform, you'll realize it's also his message to his audiences: "We're going to have the most amazing time together — beyond what you'd ever imagine."

Nearly every successful magician has implicit messages in their work. They might be saying that nothing is as it seems, or that they want to share wonderful art, or that barriers are made to be broken. Each of us can choose a one-sentence statement that will be our message to our audiences and drive every artistic choice we make.

After some thought, I finally decided my message would be, "Magic is more than you were ever aware and when we leave tonight, you'll know that in your bones." It's clear enough and doesn't have any ambiguity. It's easy to remember and broad enough to accommodate almost any type of act.

Once we've decided what we want to say, how do we actually say it? For me, it meant re-evaluating every routine I performed. Which pieces carry my chosen message the best? When I looked at my repertoire list, almost immediately a few routines seemed inadequate. I didn't have a way to do them that said what I wanted to say. I took them out and replaced them with other routines that would allow me to reinforces my *message*.

After working on these new routines, reworking some old ones and writing new presentations, I started adding them to my performances. Throughout all this, I also focused on talking *with* people rather than just aiming my patter *at* them. Every comment from them deserved a response or at least recognition. Most of the funny lines were about *them* or things that were happening in *their* lives. I began teasing them mercilessly but also lovingly as though saying, "Hey, we're all in this together." I learned everybody's names and used them at every opportunity. Most importantly, the reactions were getting better and the laughs were genuine and appreciative.

I found myself developing a much better rhythm for the routines and for the room as a whole. The heightened reactions energized me and I felt I was making progress. I was moving beyond theory and into the realm of praxis.

One night Bill visited the bar after being out of town for some time. He sat quietly in a corner, as he often did, watching the business and making sure the crowd were happy. I moved to a table near him and sat down with a few guests, conversing with them and getting them involved. I only performed two coin tricks. When I was done, they erupted into spontaneous applause and cheered. I took a sincere bow, thanked them and walked towards my next table. This involved passing where Bill was sitting. I leaned in and said, "It's been six weeks." His smile was all the reward I needed that night.

Too often, we forget that there are human beings on the other side of that pack of playing cards. They have jobs and families and people they love (as well as a few people they don't like at all). They have problems and bills to pay and responsibilities. They have successes and failures and needs and wants just like we do. It's not only okay but actually *better* if we relate to them while implicitly acknowledging these things. We can't do that, however, purely from a script or out of logical analysis. We need both mind and heart in our magic. We need to have a more intimate and meaningful understanding of why we're there in the first place.

This in no way means that I was a consummate performer from that night on. Far from it. Becoming the best performer we can be is an ongoing process. Hence the praxis — the continual, never-ending exercising of theory into reality. What that night represented for me was the culmination of an effort just to get started on the road, to get out of my own way and start performing skillfully rather than just demonstrating my skill. Magic, like any other endeavor, is constant work.

Until the day he was no more, Roger Klause demonstrated this like no other. He had an absolute love for magic that few have equaled. Even on his worst days toward the end of his life, he still talked with other magicians, helping and guiding them, and never stopped trying to refine ideas on tricks and moves he'd long since mastered. Just by being who he was, he showed me that you may believe you have a trick perfected down to the last detail but the quest for improvement never ends. To put it another way, just because you think you're done with something doesn't mean it's done with you.

If you want to do magic, you have to ask yourself a few significant questions. Who are you? What's important to you and what are your values? What do you want to say to the people for whom you perform?

Once you know what you want to say, you'll have a much better idea of the material you should perform and how to perform it, because your choices will be driven by your intended message. Your intent will be the framework that guides the rest of your journey, and it will be an endeavor of both heart and mind, because 'scio qui sum' ('I know who I am') leads to praxis (exercising theory into reality). This is the path to ginóskó, the intimate understanding of what you do that can only be attained by doing it thoughtfully, artfully and intentionally.

About a year and a half after the events I've described, I was still trying to improve how I related to audiences. Things were going well and the reactions to my performances were getting better all the time. More importantly, I was getting different types of compliments than before. They used to say, "Wow, you're really good". Now thay said, "Wow, I've never really cared for magic before, but you've changed my mind." One of the more touching comments I received was, "You know, we've seen all the magicians in this place. When you're not here, it's just not the same."

All audiences will tell you you're good, but when they start telling you how *you* have impacted *them*, you're truly in new territory full of new possibilities.

One night, Bill came into the bar again and watched quietly from his corner seat. I was working behind the bar on the other side of the room and hadn't noticed him enter. After I finished, he called me over, paused, and said, "I saw you completely engage that group. You really commanded the room, and I've never been more proud of anyone. You're truly an entertainer." I hardly need to add how proud I felt to hear these words.

Such comments aren't a metric for success. They shouldn't be taken as validation of your being a hotshot performer. They're just signs of progress. They indicate that you're on your way and that the path you're on is the one you *should* be on. You're not done, you're doing.

So, with all this in mind, what questions will you ask yourself today and what messages will you take to your audiences? How will you say it?

And who comes first? Your magic? Or them?

— Lance Pierce

Jack Carpenter

Have you ever tried to create new effects or routines only to find yourself feeling frustrated and discouraged? You feel that you have some ideas with great potential in your notebook, but for some reason you can't figure out how to develop them into practical performance pieces. If so, our next contributor will help you.

All serious students of card magic know the name Jack Carpenter. Few others in the history of conjuring have created card effects with as much elegance and clarity as Jack. He's also one of the humblest guys you'll ever meet.

In 2017, I performed a few shows in the Seattle-Tacoma area. On my last night in Washington, Jack and his wife JoAnne graciously opened their home to me. As you might expect, dinner became a card session that lasted hours into the night.

One of the many subjects we discussed was Jack's unique approach to creating magic. I can honestly say I found the discussion truly fascinating and inspirational. With Jack's permission, I'm delighted to be able to share with you some of the lessons he taught me during that memorable night in Seattle.

The Pursuit of Elegance

Notes from Conversations with Jack Carpenter

Intention

Jack's published work has brought him numerous accolades from the global magic community, yet he believes inventing magic should never be for bragging rights. If you intend to create only for recognition (he says), you're more likely to rush and settle for something that's less than excellent. In other words, your intentions can either help or hinder your creativity. Put in the time and effort until you've found the most elegant solutions before attaching your name to a trick or project.

Jack's selfless attitude reminded me of Indiana University's trumpet guru, Bill Adam, whom I knew very well. He always used to tell his students that, "playing the trumpet is ten percent physical and ninety percent mental". Many young musicians tend to concern themselves with their gear, gaining the respect of other musicians or mastering pieces to they could use to show off. Their distracted mind leads to more frustration. Mental tension creates physical tension. Physical tension negatively affects the sound of any instrument.

According to Jack, the same can be said of creating magic. He says that, when he reflect on his creative output, his best work came out of his love for the art and not for attention or praise. What are your intentions? Why are you creating? Start there.

Resistance and Elegance

Any time we set our mind to doing anything creative, an anti-muse will inevitably attack. In 'The War of Art', Steven Pressfield calls this force 'Resistance'. Pressfield says, "It's a repelling force. It's negative. It aims to shove us away, distract us, prevent us from doing our work." When you attempt anything creative, expect Resistance.

To overcome Resistance, Jack says he must 'fight with the trick' to find the right solution. For some, this could mean sessioning with other magicians for ideas and feedback or putting down the props and disciplining yourself to study.

For Jack, 'fighting with the trick' means being willing to constantly experiment. He believes "we cannot visualize something that cannot be." With that attitude, he refuses to take no for an answer until the trick has achieved what he calls 'innate elegance'. In his book, 'The Expert Portfolio No. 1', Jack quotes this passage from 'Expert Card Technique' to summarize this process:

> "Where the expert shines is that he has gone through the hard work of thinking out the correct method; he has experimented by the hour in searching for the easiest and best technique. For him, it is a labor of love, rewarded by the inner glow that comes when he, at last, sees how to improve the sleight or when he devises a clean-cut method of attaining a result required in a given trick. It is this secret knowledge which makes him the craftsman he is…"

Searching for a 'clean cut' method doesn't necessarily mean semi-automatic or self-working. Jack's work ranges from self-working to 'knuckle-busting'. Wherever the trick falls on that spectrum, his goal is to find a handling that achieves simplicity and neatness and complements the routine's effect and essential premises. Only then will Jack allow himself to stop.

This attitude may be why many who have studied Jack's work often find it unnecessary to recommend or add anything. He has spent hours looking at the trick from as many angles as possible, considering every strategy.

Does Jack possess superhuman workflow or focus? Perhaps, but he is still human. He admits he finds it necessary to take an occasional break from cards. Does this mean that he surrenders to Resistance? Not at all. If you're torturing yourself trying to force creative work, stepping away might be the wisest step toward winning the fight. In the next section, we'll see what Jack has to say about this.

Stepping Away to Step Forward

(These are Jack's own words.) Some magicians feel guilty about exploring different things other than magic. They think they have to devote all of their attention to their one passion. But if you want to be creative, consider seeking inspiration from experiences besides magic. Have a family, go to work, take up botany, try knitting, get off your butt.

I regularly take breaks from magic throughout the year. I once took a whole year off. I can't help but be curious about other things. If there's a random interest you've always had, scratch that itch. Be curious. When I eventually return to magic, picking up the cards feels fresh and exciting again. I can revisit my notes and see things in a new light.

Too many magicians constantly look down at their hands as if the world doesn't exist. If you don't have a clear picture of the world around you, how can you create amazing and unreal things? I've seen guys who only live for magic and nothing else. They may have a lot of skill, but they struggle to relate to different kinds of people in performance.

The best remedy is participating in life. It's the most important thing a magician can do. Magic can be *part* of life but don't make it *all* of life. Simple things like spending time with your family and kids go a long way. You can watch how they tick. What makes them smile and laugh? What makes them cry? If you can relate to people, your magic will be enjoyable and not just a demonstration of skill.

Furthermore, having a family, career and other interests adds focus to the time you devote to your art. Some say, "I'd be much better if I didn't have to do all these other things", but the truth is usually the opposite. When you have unlimited time, there's no urgency to get something done. It's easier to put things off. On the other hand, if you have a variety of healthy things in your life, you can say, "Let's make it count!" when you finally have a few hours with the cards. You'll buckle down and focus.

There's richness in a diversified life. That richness can be felt in your magic. That richness can be given to magic.

Jack and Igor

The internet and technology make gathering and consuming information fast and effortless. As magicians, we love learning new tricks and ideas and feel tempted to bury ourselves under our books, videos and websites to fuel our magic.

It may surprise you that artists throughout the ages have found that creating without restrictions often leads to frustration instead of inspiration. In 'Poetics of Music', Igor Stravinsky reflected on his struggles as a composer:

> *"I experience a sort of terror when, at the moment of setting to work and finding myself before the infinitude of possibilities that present themselves, I have the feeling that everything is permissible to me. If everything is permissible to me, the best and the worst; if nothing offers me resistance, then any effort is inconceivable, and I cannot use anything as a basis, and consequently every undertaking becomes futile."*

Even in 1942, Stravinsky saw how having too many options brings creative paralysis. What was his solution?

> *"My freedom thus consists in my moving about within the narrow frame that I've assigned to myself for each one of my undertakings. I shall go even further: my freedom will be so much the greater and more meaningful the more narrowly I limit my field of action and the more I surround myself with obstacles. Whatever diminishes constraint diminishes strength. The more constraints one imposes, the more one frees oneself of the claims that shackle the spirit."*

We don't know what went through Stravinsky's brilliant mind as he wrote each note of his music, but by giving himself restrictions he could break some of Resistance's chains. Here's a practical example for true music buffs:

> *"Let us take the best example: the fugue, a pure form in which the music means nothing outside of itself. Doesn't the fugue imply the composer's submission to the rules?*

> *And is it not within those structures that he finds the full flowering of his freedom as a creator? Strength, says Leonardo da Vinci, is born of constraint and dies in freedom."*

Jack certainly embraces the notion of constraints as an *aid* or *spur* to creativity. He refuses to use gimmicked cards. He strives to make all his card work angle-proof. And, as we've seen, he divides his time between magic and other interests and relationships. Following his example, you may like to ask yourself what kinds of limits and constraints you can place on *your* creative projects?

At the time of writing, Jack has taken up the piano and has also started flying lessons (yes, in real planes). At the end of the call, he said, "I won't take the cards out until the sun comes out in Seattle."

16/16 Vision

> *"How much better to get wisdom than gold, to get insight rather than silver!"*
> — *Proverbs 16:16*

Jack is a devout man of faith. In one of our phone calls, we discussed how the most remarkable artists throughout history harnessed their vast knowledge and converted it into beauty and elegance. For Christians like Jack, the ultimate example of this is also the source and giver of all good things: the creator, God.

As we saw earlier, Jack's search for innate elegance in his magic involves constant study and experimentation. His mind focuses on strategies, techniques and solving problems while his heart gazes heavenward. When I asked Jack how he applies his faith to inventing card tricks, he quoted Hebrews 4:16:

> *"Let us then approach God's throne of grace with confidence, so that we may receive mercy and find grace to help us in our time of need."*

Doesn't this suggest that approaching God should be reserved for life's biggest issues — rather than questions about card tricks? Jack argues quite the opposite. Although the God of the Christian faith is the omniscient, eternal creator, He yearns to be called 'father' by his people and to know (ginóskó) humanity instead of lord over them from a distance. Jack, therefore, involves God in every area of his life, including the invention of card tricks.

Jack's spiritual discipline isn't to be confused with treating God like a personal genie. Jack doesn't ask God for wealth, glory or Lamborghinis. The purpose of the asking isn't to demand things but instead to foster a relationship with his heavenly Father. Jack says, "When we 'approach the throne of grace,' we ask for a peek into His vast wisdom. It might be asking for wisdom for big life decisions or figuring out how to eliminate an extra card. As long as we are willing to accept God's response, we can ask."

That said, Jack feels he has experienced God through the elegant ideas given to him throughout his career. "All good things come from God," says Jack. "That extends to card tricks... maybe even coin tricks."

A Familiar Story

English Literature scholar Tom Shippey once quoted C.S. Lewis' description of an excellent literary myth this way:

"A story that everyone knows about even though they couldn't remember reading or hearing any version of it."

The story is new and yet somehow familiar. I find that I experience this sensation most often with regard to music. Whenever people ask me about my favorite pieces of music, I always think of ones that seemed to have a timeless, universal and familiar quality the first time I heard them. Bedřich Smetana's 'The Moldau' is an excellent example. The first time I heard it in Music Theory class, I had the strange feeling that I already knew it and had been listening to it for years. I returned to my dorm and listened to it on repeat five more times.

I often hear magicians react similarly to Jack Carpenter's card creations, thinking, "Why haven't we always done it this way?" It's as though his solution to a card problem or sleight was always in front of us, waiting to be picked up.

In every generation, exceptional people like Carpenter, Lewis and Smetana appear and give us new pieces of lasting artwork. To the frustrated magic creator reading this, I believe the next important creation could come from you. Don't quit. The idea you were searching for could be as close as one more minute of perseverance. Maybe even a prayer.

(A note on the quotation. C.S. Lewis is one of the most quoted and misquoted authors. In my research, I couldn't find the word-for-word source for this quote. However, it perfectly summarizes his observations on stories and myths, a subject he wrote about often.)

Jack and his wife JoAnne with the author

Jade

My wife, Aileen, and I know many couples in the magic world. But none feel more like family than Jade and her husband Matthew.

Jade and I have performed, lectured and traveled together many times over the years. Whenever Aileen and I visit San Francisco, Jade always has hot noodle soup and a room for us. We go out for dim sum and Jade, her mother and Aileen (also Chinese) chat in Cantonese while Matthew and I discuss card tricks. When Jade and I talk stage magic, Matthew and Aileen talk Teslas (Aileen is a Tesla technician and Matthew drives a Model 3).

In Hawai'i, any older loved one is referred to as an 'aunty' or 'uncle'. This can sometimes be a little confusing when parents have to explain to their children who their *actual* aunties and uncles are! But the notion that many people in our lives can be just as close as 'ohana' (family) is one of my favorite aspects of Hawaiian culture.

Jade and Matthew are my magic aunty and uncle. I hope that, as you read this section, you'll feel like part of the family too!

Roses in the Garden

An Interview with Jade.

Making Magic Beautiful

DK. Your magic is often described as 'beautiful and elegant'. How can magicians make their magic more 'beautiful'?

Jade: I like magic that's visual, so I always think about the images I'm creating on stage. Rather than thinking of the specific movements, I think of the moments or pictures I want to reach in a routine.

Like freeze frames?

Yes. I have my husband, Matthew, take photos of me to help me find those freeze frames. Then I can execute them when I'm performing.

That's a great idea. I have zero dance or movement training, so the idea of learning how to move gracefully is intimidating. Aiming toward a freeze-frame is less daunting. How did you arrive at that strategy?

I love dance and the visual arts. I studied dancers for my concept of elegance and gracefulness and paid extra attention to the body lines they create. You can learn the same thing from painted portraits. Expert painters create engaging light, shadows and body position with their brush. In a sense, I'm trying to do something similar. For me, it's all about creating pictures and lines.

Does learning dance help your magic?

I'm not a trained dancer but I do study Qigong. It's a Chinese system of movement, meditation and posture training. When I started practicing it every day, I felt much stronger and more grounded. I can stand taller and stretch my arms out further — which is helpful when you're only 5 feet 4 inches. Using these skills helps me to appear rooted and strong when I'm performing.

Physical Fitness

As a general rule, do you think magicians should be physically fit?

Yes! Many of us think that performing magic or putting on a show is only about the tricks, but your body is part of the entire picture you're creating. There's no way around it. And besides, if you take care of your body, you'll be in better health! So why not?

I recently heard a presenter at a magic convention say that magicians should invest in an exercise machine instead of investing in the newest tricks! I think there could be some truth to in that!

Brutal!

Very brutal!

What are some other things that magicians can do to get healthier?

Cut out fried food!

I think I'm going to struggle with that! I have to say I love French fries.

I'm not saying fried food doesn't taste great. Many people think it does… and that's the problem. It's really not good for you and your *body* doesn't like it. All those things cause inflammation. I think it's a good idea to practice moderation in everything. Not so long ago our family started eating more Mediterranean food and I feel great! It's very healthy. Consume less butter and carbs. Cut out pre-made, highly processed foods.

Healthy diet. Exercise. What else?

Get as much rest as you need. Learn to be kind to yourself. This one's easy to forget. Magicians can be very hard on themselves. Remember that everybody needs acceptance and love — even yourself!

Tasteful Costuming

Related to creating pictures on stage, you have the coolest costumes. What are your thoughts on how magicians should choose their clothes?

First of all, I envy the guys and their pockets. Second, look sharp! Don't squeeze yourself into something too small or too big and wear things that suit your character. I've seen guys dress like Lance Burton who behave like a country bumpkin. There's nothing wrong with that kind of character but they normally don't wear frilly shirts and tails.

Dressing a certain way doesn't guarantee you create the desired impression. You may have a cool outfit but if the way you move and talk doesn't match your look, you'll always be trying to be something you're not. The audience can feel that disconnect.

Ladies, choose your costumes with integrity. Too much 'T and A' cheapens your performance and detracts from your skill and talent. I'm not saying you always need to be fully covered but you can be sensual and feminine without being sexual or trashy. Think what you're trying to sell.

Becoming Multifaceted

Your act has elements from your silent Chinese act, routines where you joke with the audience and a part where you play your own mother! How did you put this all together?

The person on stage is the same person off stage. People are multifaceted — like a diamond. It's how we shine. I wanted to show the audience that I was interesting, so I knew that they'd have to see more than just one part of me.

When I first started, I was very shy. The silent act came out of who I was then, so that's all I was known for. As I matured and gained confidence, I added talking pieces. It was difficult at first, but it was one of my best decisions. They saw my real personality come through when I started speaking. Each element in my act represents a different part of my personal journey. During my run at Liberty Magic in Pittsburgh, people often left the show, asking the staff, "Wow! Is she really like this? Is this the real Jade?" They'd respond, "Yes! That's all Jade." And it is.

Other than reflecting on their personal journey, how else can magicians find interesting 'facets' from their lives to share?

Interesting people are interested in the world around them. People who are curious and who enjoy exploring different ways of thinking, looking, seeing and being are naturally interesting to audiences.

Some magicians aren't interested in the world around them.

And some magicians aren't naturally interesting to the audience so I wouldn't tell them to 'be yourself'. But that doesn't mean they're bad people or can't become successful performers. Those magicians should find a character they'd like to portray. They can ask who they'd like to be if they had a choice and then try it out. They can build the diamond from scratch.

The author, his wife Aileen, Jade's mother, Jade, Ethan Holtzman, Matthew Holtzman

Choosing Tricks & Self-Awareness

Once you've found your character, how do you choose tricks?

I think it's less about the trick and more about what you can make of it. Take the Rice Bowls for example. You can make it like a dance like I do or it can be a procedural talking piece. Both ways can work for different people. I enjoy comedy but I know I couldn't do a purely comedic act. But if the piece is like a dance, I can do it. Again, you have to know who you are and what sort of character you want to convey when you perform on stage. This usually comes with age and experience.

Once you know yourself, you can discern what you can and can't pull off. You can also start to identify areas where you may not be a 'natural' but you could nonetheless develop some skill and ability by putting in the work. This can be difficult because sometimes not even your closest friends or mentors — though they may be full of good intentions — can help you make those choices. You have to know yourself.

My decision to start talking to the audience is a good example. Some of my friends were encouraging but others didn't believe I could do it and, to be fair, I wasn't great at first. Some friends even tried to write lines and scripts for me to use in my act, but they all sounded more like them than me.

But I listened to everyone's advice and then chose the ideas that I felt were best for me. In the beginning, it's tempting to simply imitate good performers, especially if they let you! But in the end, you need to think about how you can bring the best out of yourself on stage. It's more satisfying to create your own character instead of just trying to copy someone else — which probably won't work anyway.

I decided to stick with it and the more I worked at speaking during my performance, the more comfortable it felt and the better I got at every part of it — the writing, rewriting and performing.

Young Magicians, Anxiety And Practice

How should younger magicians choose material, then? They might not have the life experience or self-awareness to know what would work best for them. Like choosing a costume, what if they choose routines that don't 'fit' them?

Of course it can be hard in the beginning. I've never minded learning by trying and making mistakes — it's really the only way to find what works for you. Try a lot of tricks. Some won't work and that's okay. Ask yourself who am I? Who do I want to be on stage? What do I want the audience to see and experience? Ask yourself as many questions as possible and then try to choose wisely. And remember to be patient because this process can take a long time.

I didn't want to be pigeon-holed into just one style so I keep my act very varied. At one point I might be very elegant and graceful but then in the next part I'm stooped over, playing my sassy, elderly mother! But believe me, my act didn't just form overnight. I had to experiment for a long time. Your art is never finished. Your act is never done.

Do you still get nervous before shows?

Yes but I thrive on it. Always prepare your mind and body. Breathe deeply. Your body wants to stop breathing if you get nervous. Next, I have a quiet moment to myself. I say to myself, "I love being here and what I do. I love the audience and I'm glad they're here. Go!"

Choosing the material takes time. Working it out takes time. Any thoughts on practice and rehearsal?

Practice more than you think you need to. When I was younger, I underestimated how long it takes to master something. Now, I give everything extra time. This is what I always tell my kids: expect it to take longer than you think. Visualize what everything should look like. Know your script. All of it is important. It's theater.

Pet Peeves About Performing

The first time you saw me perform, your advice about stage presence and posture made a huge difference. Can you share some tips and pet peeves?

Here we go... *plant your feet*! Don't shuffle your feet and shift your weight back and forth. Stay grounded. Connect with the audience by looking at them. Look up at the balcony and even the dark spaces in the crowd where you know people are sitting.

Don't look at the props that you need to pick up. Know where everything is and where it goes when you're done with it. Keeping your eyes on the audience keeps you connected with them and shows that you're confident and professional. It says, 'Of course, I know where everything is. I've done this a million times' (even if you haven't).

Use the full stage. Don't waste it but don't wander aimlessly around it. You don't always have to be center stage, but have a purpose for moving left and right. Are you connecting with different parts of the audience? Are you showing them something? Are you making a point? Try to stay downstage as much as possible.

We all know that no matter how much we rehearse, everyone needs flight time. Can you share any thoughts on how to polish the show?

Do it multiple times. It'll happen automatically if you're aware of the little things that happen during your show. Suppose I'm performing one night and I ad lib a funny line that happens to get a big laugh. I'll do it again the second night to see what happens. If it consistently gets a strong reaction, it stays in the show. You'll find gems in accidental things as you perform.

Try different things. A small pause can be powerful. Sometimes, eliminating words and simply pointing will bring out the strongest reaction. The pause might give them the space to say, "No way...".

Negotiation

Corporate groups always ask for rates instead of sharing their operating budget. What are some of your tricks for negotiating rates and pay?

It comes down to three things: food, how many people, and location. If they have a buffet, it's a low-budget event. If it's at a high-end location, they have a lot of money. If they have several hundred people, they probably have a large budget. Once in a while, the event will be for a small group of high-roller VIPs, but that's rare. Try to get as many details as possible before giving them your numbers.

Once I have all the information I need, I give them three price ranges and try to get them to choose the middle one. The most expensive option costs way more, but it will usually require me to get lights, assistants and a U-Haul. In the end, when you work it all out, I make about the same as the middle tier.

I also like to offer the client the option of 'giveaways'. These are customized magic favors to give out to the guests, like a packet trick with the company branding. You can sell these to them to score a profit.

Favorite Story: The Roses in The Garden

Some years ago, I had the chance to perform for Prince Albert of Monaco. I sat next to him at dinner.

When I came home to San Francisco, I couldn't wait to tell my parents about it: "Mom! Dad! I sat next to royalty! The signed bill vanished! It appeared inside my pantyhose! They freaked out! I almost got to ride on his yacht!"

They smiled and listened. And when I was done sharing my story, they nodded and said, "That's good. The roses in the gardens are growing beautifully."

What!? What does that even mean? Don't they care about my adventure?

As I thought about it, I realized that everything I'd shared was foreign to them. Instead of trying to understand, they decided to share a reminder with me in their own way: traveling and meeting interesting people is exciting, but they're fleeting moments. None of those things have deep roots, like the relationships that truly matter. Roses have roots. Family has roots.

This has become my fundamental and absolute truth: when people meet me in my travels, I never think or act like I'm anything more than your next-door neighbor. Because what's important? Fancy people and places? Fame and glory? Those things are short-lived. Stay rooted. Let people in your life who truly love and support you keep you grounded. Nurture those relationships. Keep the roses growing beautifully in the garden.

Jade with her mother in the garden

Ian Rowland

I spent many years writing this book, doing the interviews and gathering contributions from various friends. At that point, I got stuck. How to turn all these words, photos and illustrations into a finished book? I had no idea.

I asked around, watched tutorials and tried various bits of software. I'm embarrassed to admit I ultimately gave up. Ginóskó sat idle for a year. Then one evening I saw a post on Ian Rowland's Facebook page: "I'll help you finish your book!" After a quick Zoom call, it was clear I'd found the expert help I needed.

Ian is a professional writer-for-hire and ghostwriter with over thirty years experience. He specializes in helping people to self-publish their work. He's also a magician, mentalist and self-proclaimed 'bad guitarist'. If you google him, you'll see his expertise goes *much* further.

As Ian and I worked on this book, we became firm friends. He's 7,200 miles from Maui, in 'sunny' England, but our ongoing communication made him seem more like a neighbor. Sadly, with all the tea he consumed while editing and laying out every line of this book, Ian turned into a *Camellia Sinensis* bush*. Before the incident, and at my invitation, he contributed this essay.

*It should wear off soon.

Magic Is Hard

Magic is *hard*.

It's seriously, *searingly* hard to do. Magicians don't talk about this enough, which I think is a shame because it *really* matters — and I'll explain why in a moment.

Performing magic is hard because it calls for a five-track mind. Let me break it down for you.

1. First of all, you have to take care of the *effect* — the story you tell the audience that leads to an impossible yet impudently real conclusion. Every trick is a sly symphony of cognitive vandalism that feeds the logic of cause and effect through a shredder of incantations, like this:

Step 1. I can follow this and understand it.
Step 2. I can follow this and understand it.
Step 3. That's impossible! No way! How?!

When you perform magic, you have to tell this story clearly and efficiently.

2. While you're doing that, you also have to take care of the *method*. I'm referring to all the secret stuff you're doing that the audience must remain unaware of.

3. At the same time, unless you're a 'silent' act, you have to deliver your *words* or 'patter', usually a mix of script and improvisation. This means you have to be clear, eloquent and listenable, with vocal projection, appropriate pacing and a range of light and shade in your voice. Depending on the type of act you do, you may also be trying to deliver gags and get laughs.

4. On top of all that, you have to handle physical *props*. As we know, some tricks involve incredibly deft sleights that can take a lifetime to master. But handling any props at all calls for skill and care. Even if you just need to hold up a mystery envelope, you have to display it clearly, be aware of your sightlines and angles and make sure everyone can see what they need to see.

5. Finally, you have to interact with *spectators*, which involves taking your carefully rehearsed performance and shaking the spice of unpredictability all over it. You might get a polite, attentive spectator who follows instructions perfectly. You might get an ape who thinks it's hilarious to disrupt your act and 'make the tricks go wrong'. Whoever you get, and whatever happens, you have be able to deal with it.

There are your five tracks: *effect, method, words, props, spectators*. Your mind has to be able to run all five tracks at the same time, minute by minute, second by second. Unlike actors shooting a movie, you don't get retakes or second chances. You have to get everything right in one take, the first take and the only take.

Needless to say, not everyone has the necessary aptitude for this. Different minds excel at different things, such as driving a bus, laying bricks or negotiating a nuclear arms treaty. The question is, what percentage of our species has the five-track mind required to perform magic well and make it look easy? My guess is that's it's a vanishingly small percentage. It's just not something most minds can do.

Most magicians, most of the time, don't think about this. They rarely if ever take a moment to reflect on just how grimly, fiendishly hard it is to perform even a simple card trick well. This is a shame because it's truly, desperately important — for at least *two* reasons.

Here's my first reason. If we remember that magic is hard, we might also remember to feel immensely proud of one another. It doesn't matter whether you're amateur or pro, famous or just the best magician in your kitchen. Everyone in this community has spent years learning to make something formidably difficult look easy. We should look at one another with respect, admiration and love.

Being able to perform magic for people is, ironically, almost a genuine magical power. Think of the things you can do. Fill a cabaret club with laughter, wonder and delighted amazement. Turn a drab party into a great one. Make a child's eyes light up with giggling joy — even if she's in a hospital bed at the time. That's a pretty good set of superpowers. Superman can fly but he has the slight benefit of being fictional. We're stuck in the realm of the real, yet still the magic happens.

By the way, I don't think there's anything wrong if we turn into one big 'mutual admiration society'. No one else knows enough about what we do to fully appreciate it. Outsiders don't know a Dye Tube from a Lateral Tenkai. We have to admire one another because nobody else can do it for us. Only we can see the invisible skills we have.

Here's the second reason to remember that magic is hard: it might remind us to look after one another. You see that expert close-up worker with three weekly residencies? Perhaps you think he's so busy and successful he must be happy. Maybe he is. Then again, maybe he's still hurting inside from his ghastly divorce two years ago and doesn't feel he can say anything because 'big boys don't cry'.

See that brilliant cabaret magician over there who gets all the classy cruise gigs? Maybe she's worried sick about her teenage daughter hanging out with a 'bad' crowd and she thinks drugs are involved. See that big headline star with his own illusionist show? Maybe his timing was a bit off this evening because Mom's in hospital and the medics say she only has a few weeks left.

Magic is hard and life can be harder. All the more reason to be there for one another; to reach out and say, "Hey, I gather things are a bit rough right now. Can I help? I'm here if you want to talk (and not just about magic for a change)".

I think we can all learn to do this. We can remember that magic is hard, and therefore show one another the respect, admiration and love we deserve. And also remember to look after one another. We can and we should, because that's when the real magic starts.

Magic is hard. Share the pride, help with the ride.

— Ian Rowland

The sign outside the main entrance

8: Warren & Annabelle's

"Each evening, from December to December
Before you drift to sleep upon your cot
Think back on all the tales that you remember
Of Camelot.

Ask every person if he's heard the story
And tell it strong and clear if he has not
That once there was a fleeting wisp of glory
Called Camelot."

— *Alan Jay Lerner*

Camelot

It's not always the case that life gives us smiles or tears. Sometimes, they come along at the same time, the sweet with the bitter, the light mixed with a darkness never wanted or invited.

I've heard wise men talk about paradise and sometimes, rather clumsily, try to describe it. Well, I can describe it — or at least a part of it. I can even tell you how it got started. In 1995, a Los Angeles magician called Warren Gibson and his wife, Lisa, visited Maui on their honeymoon. After strolling Front Street night after night, Warren had an idea so crazy you could use it to uncork wine bottles: to build his own bar and restaurant with a theater devoted entirely to magic shows!

This was clearly a non-starter of a notion. Maui already had about 400 places chasing every tourist dollar. What's more, people came to the island for many reasons but 'to see card tricks' was not, in general, very high on the agenda.

But Warren worked some miracles, raised the money and built his dream. Warren & Annabelle's opened for business in 1999. Since you ask, Annabelle was the ghost, always heard but never seen, who played piano in the cocktail bar each evening.

Tides turned, seasons passed and fortune smiled. After a shaky start, Warren & Annabelle's became a success story. Word got round, smiles and laughs got shared and the 'sold out' nights on their booking webpage became the rule rather than the exception. And that's when the story of Warren & Annabelle's became part of my story.

The venue presented two magic shows, six nights a week (dark on Sundays). Initially, Warren himself performed every show. Later, he recruited a small team of truly *great* magicians to help out: Dana Daniels, John Shryock, Chris Blackmore and John George. All seasoned professionals with years or even *decades* of performing experience.

I was drawn to this venue like a Sphinx moth to jasmine by moonlight. To begin with, I just went along to watch the shows. Then I hung around after the shows and, rather awkwardly, tried to meet 'the guys' — the magicians Warren had recruited — and get to know them. Fortunately for me, they turned out to be friendly and welcoming. They could see I was a serious student and keen to learn but they tempered their encouragement with realism.

"Look, David, if you want to get good at this, it's going to involve a *lot* of practice."

I replied with my best 'give me a break' face. "Hey, I'm a *musician*. You want to talk to me about *practice?*"

But they were right. I had a deck of cards, good questions and some chops, but I was not yet an entertainer. Warren & Annabelle's became both my second home and my first magic school.

John Shryock, John George, Warren Gibson, Chris Blackmore and Dana Daniels

Why did I love the place so much? Well, let me take you there now and you can see for yourself.

You and your party are given a warm welcome at Reception. With a little coaxing, you find the secret keyhole in Annabelle's Chamber and... hey presto! A brick wall slides back, revealing a luxurious parlor buzzing with excitement. Tom Thomas greets you with a hearty "Aloha!" and escorts you and your friends to a comfy sofa near the piano.

The smell of coconut-battered shrimp, crème brûlée and fresh coffee fills the air. Adrian is at the bar ready to make you a signature cocktail, such as 'Warren's Wit and Wisdom' (vodka, Southern Comfort, amaretto, grenadine, pineapple juice and sweet'n'sour mix). Once you're seated with glass in hand, one of the servers might jump on the mic and treat you to a jazz standard such as, 'I've Got You Under My Skin', accompanied of course by the tireless Annabelle.

> *"I've got you, under my skin /*
> *I've got you, deep in the heart of me."*

"Do we have any honeymooners in the house?" asks the singer. Of course we do. It's Maui. "How about anyone celebrating their anniversary? Fifty years?! Amazing! This next song's for you, honey bunny!"

Your evening at Warren & Annabelle's is just getting started. Eventually, Tom stands next to the piano and announces, "It's showtime!". You make your way into the beautiful, 88-seat theater of magical wonders.

Backstage, the magicians are getting ready. They take a moment to watch the Lahaina sunset from Warren's second-floor office. Down below, couples saunter along Front Street arm in arm, heart to heart, in love with love itself. Two minutes before showtime, Tom peeks into the office, gives his 20-second read of the audience and double-checks that the performers are ready. Mic on. Tie straight. Zipper up.

As the magicians stand behind the curtain, they remember Warren's briefing. "Make these people into missionaries. Make them want to tell their friends to come. Everyone working here has invested their lives into this business. And what gets butts in seats? The show. I don't care if they're a dead audience — don't quit!"

The next two hours are a whirlwind of non-stop magic, fun and laughter. At the end of the night, the magicians personally bid farewell to every guest as they leave the club. It's clear that everyone has had a *wonderful* time. The guests' faces are practically glowing, their eyes bright with evidence of tears from laughing so hard. Their gait is light and eager, the handshakes firm and sincere. They've been part of something truly special. Magic on Maui, with drinks, laughs and a ghost.

"Aloha! Come again!" "We will!"
"Tell your friends." "Oh, for sure!"

That's what it was like. Night after glorious night, joy after radiant joy. I harbored an ambition and didn't care who knew it: I wanted to perform on that stage; to be one of the privileged few, alongside the others. This was the dream I couldn't un-dream, so I continued working awful gigs outside of the club to get more flight time (practice). There was no kid's birthday party, dance floor or rowdy bar I wouldn't face if it meant inching closer to my stage debut at Warren & Annabelle's.

'The guys' became my friends, my family, my strict-but-fair guides through magic's maze of mysteries. They were endlessly helpful, impressively generous, relentlessly kind. When I rehearsed, which I did often and at great length, they gave me wise and constructive feedback. They allowed me to open for them whenever I could make it over after a full day teaching middle school band. They even encouraged me to use some of their routines and music in my act. They did all this knowing that if I got hired, they would lose some paid stage time.

Eventually, it happened. I became the sixth magician at Warren & Annabelle's. The first time I saw my name on the poster, I teared up a little. And if you think I'm even remotely embarrassed to tell you that, well, you just don't know me at all.

Warren & Annabelle's went from strength to strength. I enjoyed more evenings there than I can count, sometimes performing and sometimes just spending time with my friends in the happiest, greatest, most magical venue of them all. It should have lasted forever.

It was not to be. On August 8th, 2023, a fierce wildfire reduced much of Lahaina Town to ashes. Warren & Annabelle's perished in the fire. Warren's dream, the show, our fleeting wisp of glory, our Camelot, was gone forever.

Sometimes, in the place in our hearts where there are no words, we can tell how special something was by the chill, the involuntary shiver of knowing it can never come back.

Thankfully, there are still memories. How did that song go?

> *"So deep in my heart /*
> *That you're really a part of me."*

— David Kuraya

- - -

For this book, I interviewed Warren Gibson and all four of 'the guys' who regularly performed at Warren & Annabelle's. As will be obvious, these interviews took place before the tragic events of August 2023. As you read these interviews, you'll get to know the extraordinary performers who mentored me and, together, built one of the finest entertainment venues ever known.

John Shryock

Curing Stress With Preparation

DK: The other Warren & Annabelle's magicians say you never get stressed out or frazzled. Do you ever get anxious?

JS: Yeah! Stressful situations come up all the time in magic just as they do in life. I try to think, "What do we do to fix it?" Stressing out doesn't help or solve anything. That's not to say I never stress over things. But I try to ensure that when I approach a situation, I'm prepared for it, not just 'winging it'.

I did a show last night here in Arizona. When I got to the theater, I had a simple cue sheet for the sound guy, the light guy and the guy pulling curtains. Imagine what a mess I would have been in if I showed up frantically trying to tell each of those guys what to do. Good preparation is a great way to keep stress levels down.

We all need R&R: repetition and rehearsal. When I started in magic, video cameras were harder to get than they are now, but my buddy Allan Rasco ran the camera for the evening news. When the news was over, we had the TV studio to ourselves, so we could rehearse all we wanted. We'd stay there all night and practice our acts and get video and personal feedback from each other.

We made a rule that you couldn't add something to your show until you executed it perfectly ten times in a row. Whether it was a sleight or producing a dove, whatever. It was a grind, but we stuck to that 'ten reps' rule.

I still follow this rule today. The Torn and Restored Newspaper is a pain to set up. There's no difficult sleight of hand, but I put in a ton of reps at home before I added it to my show. The first time I performed it, I had already rehearsed it dozens of times, so I didn't feel nervous.

Ultimately, I didn't want to embarrass myself on stage because I didn't rehearse enough. People with a passion for something — be it music, writing or art — don't find it a chore to practice. They *want* to practice because it's fun (and even better if you have friends to jam with).

This not only applies to practicing sleight of hand and reading books but, for the performer, you also have to be willing to organize the logistics of your show. I got home from Maui on Saturday night. I spent Sunday going through the props and stage illusions, ensuring everything was prepared to bring into the theater. It was hard work after a day of flying, but it was fun.

Videotaping

Videotaping your rehearsal and performances is a recurring suggestion in this book. You started in a TV studio. Now we have smartphones.

It's the best thing anyone can do to clean up their act. If you can take the ego out of it and watch yourself with an eye of trying to learn, you'll quickly improve.

I distinctly remember videotaping a rehearsal session where I did card manipulation and tried to be cool, like Lance Burton. I just looked like an idiot. I could never pull off being the dramatic 'stare at the audience' guy. What worked for me was smiling and having a good time. By taping myself, I soon learned who I was and, more importantly, who I was not.

If you record a live show, look at how you're standing and what your eyes and face are doing. Which of your actions or lines earned a positive reaction? Enhance those. Did anything come across as off-putting? Reduce those things. For most people, their stage persona is an exaggeration of who they are. Only a few of us are good enough actors that we can just take on a whole new character. Find your best attributes as a regular person and enhance them.

Was there anything else that helped you tighten your act and persona on stage?

I learned a lot from my wife, Mari. She's a dancer, so of course she's excellent at moving on stage. When we first started performing together, I remember watching videos where she kicked my butt! She was so much stronger as a performer that she inspired me to up my game. Over the years, she's also chosen a lot of our music. And as a dancer, she is great at choreography. We're partners.

John performing a Tabary rope routine

Music

You choose and edit the music for your routines. Any tips for magicians thinking about including music in their act?

I believe that music is necessary to build drama into a magic show. I start by asking, "What *feeling* do I want this routine to have?" I'm always collecting tracks I might want to use. The newest piece Mari and I put together is a Compressed illusion. I didn't want it to be scary or too dramatic, or else it might suggest, "I'm squeezing my wife!" I wanted it to be fun. We found a song called 'Booty Swing' by Parov Stelar that we both thought captured the right mood.

You want the climaxes in the song to line up with the climaxes in the magic. I use a Yello song in my Torn and Restored Newspaper routine. I edited it so that one hit happens when the newspaper opens, fully restored. Then I thought it would be cool to reprise the music when I show the inside of the newspaper. If you get the music just right, you can achieve some powerful moments in your show.

So you rearrange the music to fit the magic?

Not always. Sometimes I do the opposite. When I started at Warren & Annabelle's, I did a rope routine to an Enya song. There was a slow part in the music where I imagined the knot sliding down the rope but it didn't fit the timing of my routine. Instead of editing the song, I rearranged the rope moves to line up with that moment in the music.

I see. Sometimes you edit the music to fit the magic, and other times, you edit the magic to fit the music.

Right, and I never use a song just for background music. I've seen magicians, during tech rehearsal, say, "Play this song and when I get to this point, fade the song out." They're not performing to the music, they just have it as background. That's all right but I prefer always to choreograph the magic with the music. Of course this involves more work but I think it's worth it. You get a stronger emotional response from the audience when the music and everything you do and say are in harmony.

Telling Jokes as a Non-Comedian

Warren chose Dana and Chris because of their comedy. You and John George aren't 'comedians' as such but you still get several laughs a minute in your shows. How did you learn to include comedy without being a 'comedian' as such?

Since I'm not a natural comic, I had to learn through repetition. I sometimes watch old videos of myself telling the same jokes that I still do now and they're not as funny. The jokes themselves are funny, but my timing wasn't as good back then as it is today. Repetition and performing honed my timing and my ability to deliver jokes and lines well. You can learn how to do it, but obviously it takes time and a lot of practice.

Whatever skills I have as a performer come from the number of shows I've done. After fifteen years at Warren & Annabelle's, routines that ran three minutes are now eight minutes long because of all the lines with built-in laugh breaks and applause breaks. I know some people say you have to be born funny or likable but I believe you can learn to be likable and tell jokes well. Those instincts will grow in you over time.

Chris and Dana are great at improvising with the audience, so they have different approaches. In my case, most of my ad lib skills come from being in particular situations often enough that I know how the audience is going to react. I have lines ready for those moments but to the audience they appear off the cuff.

If you watch Warren's show, many of his funniest lines look improvised, but he's delivered them thousands of times. Warren creates situations throughout his act just to get to the 'ad libbed' punchline.

In my show, I do the standard slow-motion gag with music from 'Chariots of Fire' as part of a coin trick. Sometimes, someone in the crowd will say, "Do it again slower!" When the music starts, it's twice as funny because it looks spur of the moment. Over the years, I've found ways to cue them to say, "Do it slower!" to get that fun moment every time.

Entertaining 'Bad' Crowds

You've performed all over the world and in all kinds of situations. How do you handle a bad audience?

I keep in mind that the audience isn't there to entertain me. I'm there to entertain them. Even if the crowd isn't as responsive as I'd like, it's still my job as the person they paid to entertain them to give them 100 percent.

I don't think it's fair to call any crowd a 'bad' crowd. It's not as if they all came in thinking, "We're gonna be a jerk to this guy!" They're just who they are. Your job as a performer is to do everything you can to get as much energy out of them as possible.

Sometimes I'll go out and the crowd starts out slow. I just keep on trucking and very often, after keeping my energy going... bam! Suddenly they come alive! It happens a lot. However, some crowds are quiet no matter how hard we try to get them going. It's still our job to entertain them.

I have a few strategies to get them with me, though. My first few routines are designed to get the crowd behind me and to teach them how to applaud and react. I want them to actively participate instead of acting as if they're watching TV. I want them to feel like they're a part of it.

Creativity Through Problem-Solving

One of the things you're best at is problem-solving and working out ways to make a trick practical.

Yeah, some people are good at inventing new tricks. My buddy, Eric Buss, just dreams up the fun and crazy stuff and then finds ways to build it.

I was never great at creating new stuff. I take on a problem and then try to solve it. For example, I wanted to do an Ambitious Card, Triumph and a Color-Changing Deck back-to-back in my show. I asked myself how could I do all that with one deck?

How can I do Gary Kurtz's 'Trio in Three' with a Copper/Silver/Brass set instead of Two Copper/One Silver? I'm better at solving problems than devising new wild ideas.

Another good example is your take on Alan Wakeling's billiard ball routine.

Yes, I wanted to do the Wakeling routine, but I didn't want to have extra balls on my person. My solution was to build a special box for the balls to appear in. In the routine, each time a ball vanishes, it visually reappears in the box instead of in one of my pockets.

I don't think it necessarily improves Wakeling's routine, but it fits my performing style better. I find it plays bigger that way, too. I did it on cruise ships for years.

It's helpful to know that being 'original' doesn't necessarily mean that you have to create tricks that no one's ever seen before. It takes creativity to solve problems and develop your unique way of presenting magic.

Balancing Family & Magic

I admire how the magicians on the Warren & Annabelle's team can spend months on the road and yet remain happily married. How do you balance being a traveling entertainer and a family man?

Yeah, it's pretty tough. When we started a family, I decided I wouldn't be on the road more than I am at home. That was the rule I chose for myself. This was a tough rule in financial terms because I make most of my living on the road. But for those six months when I'm home, I spend practically all my time with my kids. I don't go to work early in the morning and come home at six or seven. I'm picking them up from school, dropping them off at events or taking them to sports practice and so on and generally being as involved with them as much as possible. When you average it over a year, I probably end up spending as much time with my kids as a father who works a 40-hour week because I can give them all of my time.

In keeping with that rule, have you turned down big opportunities?

I'm fortunate to have a long relationship with most places I work. I try to work with them to schedule bookings as far in advance as possible. I'll look at when the kids are out of school and see if we can make travel and family work together. I might try to book a week at The Castle in the summer so that as a family we can go to Disneyland the week before.

At the end of the day, I've often said, "No, I can't take that job." I know it's tempting for magicians to want to say yes to everything. I believe that family always comes first. Give yourself rules and stick to them.

The X-Factor: Sincerity

You're one of the very few sleight-of-hand magicians who also performs stage illusions. You've worked at The Magic Castle, Caesar's Empire, The Magic Island in Houston and Wizards in California. You've performed on cruise ships and at Warren and Annabelle's. You've certainly seen a lot of magic acts. What would you say is the main difference between merely good and really great performers?

I think it comes down to sincerity. People say that guy has 'it' or she has the 'it' factor. Well, what is 'it?' I don't know whether it's defined, and I'm not saying I have the definition, but I do believe sincerity is a huge part of whatever 'it' is.

Take Doug Henning as an example. He had unbelievable sincerity when he performed. You couldn't watch him without noticing that he believed in what he did. He sincerely wanted to share the experience of magic with the crowd. He was there for the crowd.

Sammy Davis, Jr. is another example of someone whose 'it' factor was through the roof. Charisma oozed through him, and when you watched him, you felt that he was truly present, sincere and with you.

Great performers never just go through the motions — even though there are times we might want to. If the audience thinks you don't give a crap about them and what you're doing, there's no way they'll get behind you and feel the emotions you want them to feel.

That reminds me of the line in your show where you look at the audience and say, "I know it <u>looks</u> like I'm having a great time up here... I <u>am</u> having a great time!"

I am! Maybe there's some cheesiness to that line, but I really do love what I get to do. I appreciate the audience being there and I'm sincere when I say it. They're getting my very best, and I want everybody in the crowd to have as much fun as possible.

My goal is that everybody will leave saying, "Man, that was a great time. We need to come back here. We need to tell our friends to come." That's how Warren built his business. He always says that our job is to make missionaries for the show through our performance.

Be sincere. Your demeanor should say, "I'm here for you. I appreciate you. This show matters."

Supporting Other Magicians

You and I share a love for the magic fraternity. There are many genuinely kind people in magic. On the other hand magic can be competitive and toxic.

In my experience, there's a lot more good than bad. I've said this before and I still believe it: you could drop me in the middle of any decent-sized city without anything and I could go on my phone, look up a magician and probably make a friend. The magic fraternity is great because, by and large, we're very supportive of one another. We help each other out and want to be friends.

Yes, magic can get competitive. Don't let somebody knock you and don't get into some ego war. Saying or even thinking, "I'm better than you", or, "I got this gig, and you didn't" doesn't help anyone. Constantly putting down others is a sign of insecurity. I find it's more fun to be friends and partners. Congratulate people and be proud of them. Learn from what they did.

You helped many magicians become more successful in their careers. Is there anything you want to add to that?

A lot of guys give lessons that they charge for, which is fine. I'm not dissing this in any way. They're providing a service. But if some guy in the magic club offers me money to help with their act, my response is usually, "No! We're in the same magic club. I want to help you. Let's jam!" That's how it was when I joined the magic club. No one charged me for lessons. We were just a bunch of guys who loved magic. It's fun to be creative and help each other out.

So again, no harm in charging for lessons. Some people do it very well. But for me, it never feels right in the magic club. We're a community, so we help each other out.

Any more advice?

Don't give unsolicited advice.

Hah!

Well, sometimes, magicians ask, "How'd you like my show?" I usually don't get into critiquing their show unless I feel like they really are curious about how they can make it better. I'm not gonna be the guy who says, "Hey, I saw your act; you should do this." I'd rather have them want my opinion or at least respect it. I'll give the most honest and sincere advice I can, but I won't do it uninvited, you know?

I found that hard work and kindness led to being in the right places and right times many times throughout my life. Those qualities also led to many long-term relationships in magic. I've worked for Warren for 15 years. I worked on the same cruise ship for nine years. I was at The Magic Island until they closed. I've had great relationships. When one door closed, another opened. Keep working hard. Keep being a nice person to work with.

You have a story about a few shows you did in the early 90s. It's one of the most inspiring magic stories I've heard. Please share that with us.

At Midnight, It Ain't Sunday

In 1989, I was in my early twenties. My buddy Dal Sanders sold a show called 'The Magical Mysterious Suitcase Science Show' to a company called the Bureau of Lecturers. They were an agency that sold school assembly programs to schools throughout the Midwest.

My job was to perform in different small towns — three schools a day, five days a week. I was given a small salary but had to cover my own gas, food and lodging. I built a bed in the back of my van to sleep, stocked it with bread and peanut butter and found a cheap motel to get a proper shower every other day.

I'd drive into the school's parking lot each morning at around eight o'clock. I'd find a fountain to brush my teeth and wash my face. I'd load in, do the show and drive to the next town. The second show was at noon so I'd eat lunch in the school cafeteria. Then I'd hit the road to make the last show at three. I did that for three months in hundreds of little towns.

Early on in the tour, my van broke down in a small town near Jacksonville, Tennessee. I pulled into a shop to get it fixed and the owner looked at it and said it was pretty bad. He couldn't get the parts for a week. I told him about the shows I had coming up, and he said, "Borrow my truck. Drive it to your shows."

For a week, I took the garage owner's truck to different towns and schools in the area. In the evenings, I went into Jacksonville to find table-hopping work to pay for the repair. I'd walk in, find the manager, and say, "I'm a magician. I'm on the road. My van broke down. I'm trying to get it fixed. Can I entertain your guests and work for tips?" It worked. One restaurant belonged to a hotel, so they gave me a room for a night.

The parts arrived at the end of the week, but it was Sunday and I had to be on the road on Monday. The next run of shows was too far from the town and the van still wasn't working. The garage owner told me, "John, when I bought this gas station, I promised my wife I'd never work on a Sunday." I said, "Man, you've already been so incredibly kind. I totally understand. Don't worry about anything." Then he said, "No, no, John. At midnight, it ain't Sunday no more." He returned to his shop at midnight and worked until morning so that I could make it to my next show.

I don't know what I would have done if it weren't for the people who showed me kindness that week. I do know this: there's still some good in the world.

John George

International Champion Of Magic

As an International Champion of Magic, how do you feel about magic competitions today?

They're not for everyone but I've done them and enjoyed them. Whenever I wanted to develop a new skill, a competition helped me have a structure. I was a successful student in college because I knew the steps to achieve my goals. I noticed I could create a similar structure if I took part in magic competitions. I could treat the preparation — research, study, practice, seeking teachers — like a college class and the performance like a final exam.

But you can't 'win' an exam. Was your goal to win?

The main purpose was to become a better magician, but yes, I also wanted to win. I knew that I'd be in front of other magicians, so I refused to make a fool out of myself.

You did win.

In the end, I won First Place at the IBM's Golden Cups Competition, First Place at SAM's Gold Medal Competition, the People's Choice Award at SAM, and the Silver Medal of Merit, which only a few magicians have received.

How did you get ready for these competitions?

Doug Brewer and I periodically had my parents invite ten friends to their home. We'd set out cheese and wine and perform two eight-minute magic shows. Then we handed out a questionnaire, saying, "Just be honest. It's nice to know what you liked but we'd rather know what you *didn't* like or found confusing. Don't just say nice things because that won't help us." The comments we got helped us to make improvements. We did those shows for over a year.

You made flight time and practice happen in your own home!

Sure. If you only think, "Man, I just wish I was a better magician," it won't happen. If you only work on sleights in front of a mirror, you won't become a better entertainer. We knew we needed to put our magic in front of people, so we made them come to us.

It seems like collaboration was a huge part of your career.

It still is. If you're wise, you know no one is good at everything. It's great to collaborate with others because you can share your expertise with each other and grow together. I wouldn't be the magician I am today without Doug Brewer, the director Glenn Kelman, Johnny Ace Palmer, Chipper Lowell and all the guys at Warren & Annabelle's. I even learn from my magic students. I'm always open to them bringing in something new or clever I hadn't thought of.

Networking

DK: The Warren & Annabelle's magicians say you're the master of networking.

JG: I don't think of it as networking. But it's true that I like to find something fascinating about the people I meet. It's a habit I inherited from my father. When I meet someone new, I'm always searching for things about them that fascinate me. Everyone has something. That's what I want to talk about. It sounds selfish, but that fact is people like to talk about themselves.

How do you dig for that fascinating thing?

Well, you can start with the regular questions. "What do you do? Where are you from? Do you have a girlfriend?" But you can move on from there. Something always turns up. Don't have motives or a secret agenda. Just talk to people and listen. The agenda is just to make a real connection, no more and no less. Taking an interest in people leads to all sorts of opportunities that you can't foresee. One time at Warren & Annabelle's, a gentleman named Sunil came over to me after the show. He was very friendly and complimentary and we chatted for a while.

Two days later, my wife, Devon, and I took a submarine tour, and Sunil was there carrying a drone. Devon had just bought me one, so we had a chat about drones. I asked him, "When are you going to fly it?" He said, "As soon as we get off the submarine." We stuck around to watched him fly it and afterwards made plans to fly our drones together.

Sunil works in Northern California as a venture capitalist raising money various startups. We stayed in touch over drones and magic and when COVID hit in 2020, I told him I was doing virtual shows. He said, "That sounds interesting." Those three words aren't to be taken lightly when they come from a venture capitalist and they turned out to be life-changing. I got tons of work from Sunil's business connections when I launched those shows.

I couldn't have known that would happen when I first met him. We found our common interests, talked about them and became friends.

You weren't trying to exploit him to take advantage of his connections. You just enjoyed hanging out with each other.

Right. I was never thinking about getting gigs or money from him. That's just the way things happened to work out. I genuinely like the guy and enjoy being around him. Our friendship just turned in that direction years later. That said, I believe gigs are bound to happen if you're putting yourself out there and making new friends with the people you meet. Don't force it.

Many magicians only hang out with other magicians and are only interested in magic. You have tons of random interests: drones, table tennis, swing dancing and playing the drums are a few that come to mind. And you're always open to discovering new ones.

I think I'm naturally inquisitive and curious. That's something that children have that most adults lose. Kids see something new and immediately want to know more. What is this? How does it work? Can I try it? They seem like silly questions but those questions have always opened doors for me, not just in magic but in life.

Restaurant Magic: Paid to Advertise?

Not all of your work comes from serendipitous relationships like Sunil, right? How do you intentionally secure gigs?

That's true. Magic is work. My best advice for a close-up magician is to be open to working restaurants. Think of it this way: each table is a mini audition. When I table-hopped at restaurants, I set my mind on a few personal goals. One: even though I didn't know who the customers were, what they did, or how much money they had, I was determined to find a way to insert myself into their lives tastefully. Two: even though I was paid to be there, I would use that time to actively seek more work.

That doesn't mean I was a sleazy used car salesman about it. When you show people that you are interested in them and that you find them fascinating, it's hard not to find a way to connect with them on a personal level. You're right that some magicians criticize restaurant work. Sure, it's not as rewarding as performing in a theater, let's say. But think about it this way: you're getting paid to advertise.

At one time, I did six restaurants a week, making enough money to pay my bills. That doesn't include tips. I no longer have to do restaurants, but I have table-hopping to thank for launching my career. I've never needed an agent, and I bought a house in southern California thanks to doing close-up magic in restaurants.

That said, even though you're using the restaurant gig as a vehicle to find more work, the first priority is still the establishment. The restaurant has to be happy with you. Not just the magic, you.

When working at a restaurant, I think of myself as a brand ambassador, head of hospitality or even an extra manager on the floor. If I walk up to a table and they're unhappy about something — maybe a spill or something undercooked — I don't make them sit through my card routines. I go to the manager or a waiter and let them know, try to fix the problem somehow.

People will be likelier to share things about their experience with you than with the restaurant staff. They may tell you the fish is spicy or the A/C is cold in a particular spot. That kind of information is valuable to the restaurant.

Focus on being good for the restaurant. There will always be time to do more card tricks. How are you helping the culture of the establishment? If you want to be successful, then the restaurant has to be successful.

Working With a Director

When you were putting your act together, you hired a director. Why?

Many magicians get most of their advice and feedback from other magicians. I think that's a mistake. Sure, listen to your magician friends but also get advice from experts who aren't magicians. A director is one good choice. He might get you thinking about aspects of your show most magicians wouldn't consider. For example, how are the beginning, middle and end of your show distinct from each other? What is the purpose of each part of your act? What's the overall message you're trying to convey?

A director's job is to know how to tell a story and to answer some of those questions. Often, magicians just do trick after trick. A director might help you combine all the tricks and create a complete story so you've got a show!

What were some specific ways that your act improved with his guidance?

He knew me pretty well so he could challenge me in a very personal way, which made for a very productive relationship. There was a moment in my show where we both agreed that an olive should reappear. However, I couldn't figure out a method during our meeting. I said, "I can probably figure it out, but I might not have the answer today." He responded, "Well, why don't we just call your mentor Johnny Ace Palmer? He would know."

I went home and thought, "Why did he say that? I can't believe he said that. Maybe Johnny would know, but I can do this, too!" I came back the next day with a solution. He said, "You did it! I knew you could do it."

Another time, Disneyland asked me to do mentalism for a Christmas show for kids. I told my director friend, "This doesn't make any sense. Mentalism isn't going to work for a group of kids! I should sell them on sleight of hand and magic tricks instead."

He said, "Well, Santa Claus knows if kids are naughty or nice, right? So if Santa knows, why couldn't you?" It was so smart! My director could see different angles and solutions because his job is to envision creative ideas to put on a great show. The more I worked with him, the more I realized I was only thinking like a magician. I started trying to think his way, too.

That understanding was useful when I had to perform in a Disney show set in the Victorian era. The cast had to dress a certain way and we could only use props that were appropriate to that era.

My director friend happened to be overseeing the show and he asked me about the effects I was going to perform. I told him that I wanted to make a bowling ball appear. He said, "John, we talked about this. You can't have a bright orange bowling ball appear in a show set in the Victorian era! It doesn't make sense!" I said, "Wait a minute. The kids in the park aren't from the Victorian era, are they? I'm asking the kids to think of things *they* can imagine appearing in the bag. The bowling ball didn't come from *my* era. It came from *theirs*." I used his thinking against him. And he said, "That works! I like it!"

During the show, when the bowling ball appeared, I'd ask the kids, "Who was thinking about this thing?" At every show, one or two kids would obligingly raise their hands, thereby 'proving' that the idea didn't come from me. In fact, I'd act like I didn't even recognize what it was. This notion went over so well that I used the routine in Disneyland for a whole season.

Becoming Funny

Another time I sought help for my show was when Warren told me my act wasn't funny enough. Now, I don't think that all shows need to be funny to be great, but in Warren's showroom, he wants applause, astonishment, and laughter.

I went to my comedian friend, Chipper Lowell, and I asked him if I could hire him to write a few jokes for my act. His response surprised me. He said, "I won't write any jokes for you. I'll teach you how to become funny."

Is that possible?

I think it is for some people. In my case, I had to adjust my thinking. He taught me to trust my instincts before I started writing jokes. He said, "If you think of something you think could be funny, just say it. See what happens. The audience will tell you immediately if the line or joke is funny."

That's scary. And it's hard to believe that such a small change in your thinking made you funnier.

It didn't happen overnight. By no means am I suggesting I'm as funny as Dana Daniels or Chris Blackmore, but I will say that our reviews used to say something like, "That one magician did great magic, and the other was super funny." Now many of our reviews say, "Both magicians were hilarious!"

It worked!

But I had to work on it actively. Sometimes, the audience won't agree with what you think is funny. It takes time and even some crickets before you have an act with many laughs per minute. Using Chipper's method, I could organically develop funny lines or situations that are unique to me. If I had just tried to create jokes out of thin air, I might have imitated other people I found funny.

Most magicians start as kids, reading a magic book or watching a video to impress their friends. The problem is many of us carry on thinking that's the only way to keep growing. We don't consider other skills that can elevate our magic. Learning about woodworking, dance and acting has made a huge difference in my magic shows. We should be learning from the world, from everything. Comedy was one area that I had to back up and learn.

Many magicians want to figure out who they're supposed to be on stage. I figured it out by asking myself, "Where am I at my best?" and "Where am I the funniest?" After some thinking, I remembered being a kid at home at the big

John performing at The Magic Castle

round dining room table. I owned that table. My family tried to say grace, and I'd make my brothers or sisters laugh. I'd crack jokes and poke fun at people. My mom tried to get me to calm down, but she'd be laughing, too.

That was my answer. When I'm on stage, you're at my dining room table. And I'm that kid having fun. Everyone's path is different, but remembering times in my life outside of magic where I was funny and felt comfortable helped me.

Details and Preparation

Chris Blackmore likes to go with the flow on stage, whereas you pay attention to every minute detail. Is one way better than the other?

That's a hard question because a lot of that is built into me. I'm detail-oriented. When Johnny Ace Palmer mentored me, he taught me to organize my props. He'd say, "When you reach into your case, you should be able to find everything with your eyes closed." That's how I work to this day.

Does that work ethic only apply to props?

No. I've made sure that every sleight is practiced and ready. My angles are good. The music cues are programmed correctly. My script is tight. Then I can focus all of my attention on the audience at showtime. They always have to be our highest priority. All these details are for their benefit.

The first time the Magic Castle booked me, I did a lot of lapping in my act. The height, size and angles around the table were all important, so at home I built a table identical to the one in the Close-Up Gallery. That way, when I showed up at The Castle to perform, I was ready.

Wow, that's very detailed!

For a long time, I believed that tiny details had to be perfect in a magic show. Over the years, I've loosened up a little. I realized that there there are some things that you can't plan for. Once, I attended an event where I was supposed to perform on a four-foot stage. When I arrived, the band had already set up on it. They said, "This is our stage, and we're not moving. You'll have to perform on the ground." I talked to the client and they weren't much help.

I knew I had to immediately get the audience's attention *without* the stage or I'd lose them. I grabbed a chair, stood on it and did my first trick that way. It's important to prepare and work out the details but you must be ready to adapt and improvise if necessary.

John George vs. Warren!

The way you got into Warren & Annabelle's was different from the other guys. Please share the story.

Warren is a very blunt and honest man, and I wasn't used to that. On my first night there, I thought I did my magic fairly well but I wasn't as good an entertainer yet. If you asked me what I was, I'd say, "A magician." If you ask me what I am today, I'd say "An entertainer." I've since learned to share solid magic while at the same time making people laugh and telling jokes and stories. I wasn't doing that on the first night.

After the show — which I thought had gone pretty well — Warren came up to me and asked, "How do you think you did? Do you think you could put butts on seats night after night with that show?" I said yes, I thought I could. Warren said, "No, you couldn't."

We got into a huge argument over it because I felt that I needed to defend myself. After all, I'd worked all over the world and had won quite a few awards by that stage. Who was Warren to tell me I wasn't funny enough, entertaining enough, or, in general, good enough to be working at Warren and Annabelle's?

I thought I'd never be asked to work there again. I returned to my hotel room and thought, "Am I even going back tomorrow night?" We had had a pretty heated argument. I went back and did my shows the next day, and when I saw

Warren everything seemed friendly. At the end of the week, having finished performing all my shows, I talked to Warren and asked, "Should I plan on coming back?" He said, "Of course!"

I went home and my friends asked me why I would ever *want* to go back. They were quite loyal to me and didn't like the fact that Warren had said I wasn't good enough. But then I thought... he's inviting me back. He's telling me I'm not good enough but he's also inviting me back. So what does that mean?

Other magicians had tried out at Warren & Annabelle's and, in most cases, Warren hadn't made the time to give them any feedback. He just said, "Thank you." But Warren *had* given me some feedback and had also invited me back. Regardless of his intentions, I began to suspect that he saw more in me than I even saw in myself at the time. Maybe he wanted to see me grow.

And by the way, I'd seen Warren work in his showroom. No question about it, he was leaps and bounds better than I was as an entertainer. I remember thinking that I'd never get up to his level. When my friends were saying, "Don't listen to him!", I started thinking, "He wouldn't have invited me back if he didn't truly believe I had some potential and could improve."

It was an excellent learning experience for me. Looking back, I'm glad that Warren and I had that argument and that I wasn't stupid enough to listen to my friends and run away because of my ego. Warren made me work harder at a time when I thought I'd already reached the top. Because of what happened, I've become a much stronger and more capable magician and entertainer.

Not every magician may have a chance to work at Warren & Annabelle's, so what do you think magicians can learn from that story?

Don't ever think you're done learning. Be a student for life. After all these years, I think I have a solid act, but I can still improve. Always strive to be better.

The Head & Heart of Magic

You've said that being an artist is an exercise of mind and heart. What does that mean?

To answer that, we have to talk about swing dancing. Before I met my wife, I had a girlfriend who made fun of my lack of musical talent. I was always on the wrong foot when we danced and I couldn't even clap to songs on the right beat. Despite this, I decided to learn swing dancing because it looked fun in the GAP commercial. But again, it was hard for me to hear the music so I hired someone to help me listen! Eventually, I learned to swing dance on the beat and that's how I met my wife.

My swing dance instructor always said, "The most important thing is to dance on the beat and have fun." But I was very mechanical and rigid. I 'danced in my head'.

Dancing in your head?

I learn in a very logical way. Step one: swing your body this way. Step two: move your foot that way. It's who I am. I'm very particular about getting each detail perfect. It's a strength and also a weakness. I was too studious and precise about something that had to be more from the heart. I was thinking too hard so I couldn't have fun.

How did you overcome that?

I decided to practice the moves until they became second nature. Then, I could focus on having fun. Once I did that, I danced more from my heart, and it became much more fun for me and my partner.

It took me a while to realize that I performed magic in my head, too. I had to memorize every detail of my act so thoroughly — script, moves, angles — that during my show I barely had to think about any of those things. I could focus on creating a conversation with my audience. These days, I even try to get the *audience* to make *me* laugh! I can perform magic from my heart and focus on being fun and amazing because the technical aspects are already mastered.

Make-A-Wish

One of the highlights of your career was creating an experience for a Make-A-Wish recipient. It's a story that I believe every magician needs to hear.

For a long time, if people asked me about my all-time favorite gig, I said performing for Paul McCartney. That changed a few years ago.

One night, the owner of the hotel where I was the house magician for twenty years called me. He said, "I'm on the board of the Make-A-Wish Foundation and I was wondering if you'd be interested in doing magic for their annual gala." I immediately agreed. My sister's son, Daniel, was a Make-A-Wish recipient.

When I went to the planning meeting for the event, I assumed they wanted something like an hour of strolling magic. I was surprised when they said, "We want you on stage in front of a thousand people." I said, "That would be great! No problem!" They continued, "...and we'd like you to make someone's wish come true."

This may sound silly because I don't have a bucket list. But in hindsight, if I did have one, I think this would be on it. I think making a child's grand wish come true is the coolest thing in the world.

They said the event was in six months. At that time, they had to choose a recipient and figure out how to fulfill the child's wish using my magic show. We talked about the different types of wishes. For example, if the child wanted to meet someone, we'd use a stage illusion to make that person appear. If they wanted to be a magician for a day, we'd make that happen.

Weeks went by and they finally called me with some answers. They said, "We've found this perfect little girl. She's five years old. Her name is Tori. And she wants to fly on a magic carpet with Princess Jasmine."

I said, "No problem, we can make it happen!"

Now, in the magic world, I'm known for my close-up magic. I do stage performances in the corporate world, but this was out of my comfort zone. I said, "No problem" but in my head, I thought, "That's nothing like we talked about! I don't have a flying carpet in the garage!"

But I was committed and didn't want to disappoint anyone, especially Tori. So I called all my magic buddies and started asking for advice. I also went to a magic get-together called the Board of Directors, a group of magicians including Dana Daniels, Chris Blackmore, the Passing Zone and others. They get together and workshop magic. When they got to me, I said, "I don't have anything to workshop, but I've got this problem." After explaining everything. someone there said, "Why don't you talk to Mike Michaels in Vegas?"

I immediately called John Shryock, who then connected me with Mike (they're old friends). When I spoke with Mike, he was excited to help. He has a big heart and was eager to be a part of it. There were many hurdles along the way but after a few trips to Vegas and countless phone calls, Mike ultimately designed and built an outstanding illusion I could perform.

John Shryock happened to have a friend who looked just like Princess Jasmine. Her brother was actually the actor who played Aladdin around the park in Disneyland. All the pieces were coming together.

Fast forward to the day of the event. The illusion and all the pieces were ready to go. I was taken to meet Tori in her hotel room just before the show but, being very shy, she didn't want to talk to or look at me. So I said, "Where's her brother and sister?" I was told they were on a different floor." I said, "Please call them up here right now."

I sat them all down and started doing magic for them. Tori looked out of the corner of her eye and saw her brother and sister laughing and having fun. All of a sudden, Tori saw me as safe. She began to join in. When we were done, I asked her brother and sister if they wanted to be on stage. They said, "Yes!", so I told them they could come on stage if they could convince Tori to come on stage, too.

I did my show at the gala that night and at the end of my set, I said, "We have a special surprise tonight. We're going to make someone's wish come true on this stage!"

I looked over and saw Tori with her family in the wings. I could tell that everything would be okay. Tori smiled right back at me with a twinkle in her eye. The music started and Aladdin came out. I wanted the audience to think that Tori's wish was to meet Aladdin. He took out a magic lamp and smoke puffed out. A curtain opened, and a bigger lamp appeared, producing Princess Jasmine from an even bigger puff of smoke. Maybe the wish was to meet Princess Jasmine? I went up to Tori and said, "Tori, this was fun… but we haven't granted your wish yet. What was it?"

Tori said, "To fly on a magic carpet with Princess Jasmine."

We had given everyone in the audience a light-up magic wand. I put Tori on the magic carpet and told the audience, "Wishes don't come true by one person alone. It takes a community like everyone here tonight. Pick up those magic wands, turn them on and wave them!" Suddenly, a sea of wands lit up the darkened banquet hall.

At that moment, the music started and the carpet flew up ten feet and then twenty feet across the stage. When Tori came down from the carpet, I gave her the magic lamp and said, "I want you to remember this night forever."

That was, hands down, the best experience I've ever had doing magic. Part of it was the collaboration and working with other magicians. It couldn't have happened without John Shryock. He made sure everything ran smoothly.

I don't like when people say fake it 'til you make it. There are a lot of magicians out there who are faking it and it doesn't give us a good name. You really do have to practice. I've worked hard at everything that I've done. I never just go halfway. I always give 100%. In this case, I took a chance at something that I had never done before. It ended up changing my life and, hopefully, other people's lives too.

If there's something that you're passionate about and you're willing to give 100%, then take risks. But at the same time, don't think you have to do it all alone. Don't be afraid to collaborate and call upon your friends for help and advice. It was a great night and a huge success but it was our combined effort that made it happen.

Today, Tori is in recovery, leading a happy and healthy life!

On a flying carpet with Princess Jasmine!

Chris Blackmore

Finding Who You Are on Stage

DK: How did you discover your potential as a comedic performer?

CB: Looking back to my school days, I was always the class clown, you know? The goofy and funny guy. I enjoyed making the others laugh. That may seem like a good quality for a performer, but I had to learn not to take it too far. Only being a goofball didn't pay. I had to find how to gather respect while also being a joker. You have to appear genuine and honest on stage. People will sense when you're not authentic and when you're not comfortable. One of the nicest compliments I get is when people tell me I look comfortable on stage.

Warren and Lisa always say that about you.

I guess I somehow figured out how to make being a wild monkey pay. One thing I do know is that the best way to find out who you are on stage — in fact, the only way — is to perform as much as possible. Take every gig and perform at every opportunity. Then videotape your performances. Have others review the videotape and ask them for their feedback. Make it clear you want their *honest* views, without sparing your feelings.

It's hard to be aware of your physicality and personality while performing. When you see yourself on video, you can tell if you were thinking to yourself the whole time or relaxed and comfortable. And do you command your stage or are you a little tired and distant? Remember, you're the ringleader. Even if you do a silent act, lead the audience with your eyes, body language, and attention. The audience needs to focus on you.

Growing up, I was influenced more by comedians than magicians. I started to imitate people like Steve Martin or George Carlin. Over time, I learned to keep a few traits of the people who influenced me. In the beginning, you might feel the need to imitate others to build confidence. Eventually, you need to sort things out and innovate.

How long did it take you to find your stage character?

It's a gradual process. You're always yourself. You're physically up there and can't much change who you are (unless you're playing a character). I was wild and chaotic at first and it was more about me than the audience. When I realized the show is *about* and *for* the audience, I found my stage personality. It's not about you one bit.

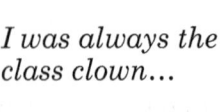

I was always the class clown...

Flexibility

If a magician wants to make a living doing magic, should they focus on one style of magic or try different kinds?

If you want to be a professional magician and you want to stay employed, it helps to be well rounded. At one time, you could tour the world with a twelve-minute silent act. There were revue shows everywhere. But the shows changed and didn't really employ as many short silent acts. If you weren't well rounded, you lost a large portion of income.

I have experience doing close-up, stage, illusions, backyard barbecues, parlor, trade shows, cruise ships and corporate shows. I've made a decent living by being willing to do many things. So if I had to go restaurant table-hopping for a while to feed my family, I would.

Being flexible also made me a better performer. What do you do when the ballrooms aren't set up right to do a big show? How do you entertain guests during dinner without being annoying? These are all learned skills that can apply to your whole life. If you want to stick with a specific niche, that's okay, but if you want to make magic a career, aim to be able to entertain anybody, anywhere.

Clean or Dirty?

What do you think about dirty jokes?

In today's society, it's more marketable to work clean. No foul language, no suggestive material. It's part of my DNA at this point, though. I worked at Disney World in Florida for five years and another eight years in Anaheim. There's zero tolerance for ethnic jokes, cursing, swearing or any suggestive material. And it was excellent training because these days corporates do the same thing.

I once did a show for Federated Department Stores, which owns Macy's and Bloomingdale's. I arrived while they set up the banquet room and introduced myself as the magician to the organizers. A woman came up to me in tears and said,

"Do you make any blow*** jokes?" At first, I wanted to be flippant and almost immediately said, "That's what I close with!" But I saw that she was under stress. She said, "We had an entertainer last year who made inappropriate jokes with the matriarchs of our company. He thought it was amusing. You'll be fired if there's anything inappropriate tonight." There was a heavy burden on this person to ensure that the entertainment was clean and appropriate for her clients. She felt she had been let down very badly by that other entertainer.

What's the point? Too many entertainers have an attitude like, "I'll clean up my show for those types of things." Are you sure? At Disney, we did seven shows a day. We had kids who peed, bit, kicked, clawed, scratched and pulled down their pants so... it was a challenge. Suppose you're not in the habit of keeping it clean and professional. Do you really think you can control your tongue in those frustrating, awkward and exhausting situations? Don't chance it. Unless you only work in comedy clubs, there's no need for dirty jokes or cussing in a magic show. Keep it clean.

Children and Families

Tell me more about working with kids. I know you take it very seriously.

I take great offense whenever an adult belittles a child on stage. Too many magicians treat children more like a prop than a participant. If you bring a child on stage, everything must revolve around the child. Are they comfortable? Do they feel safe? Are they enjoying themselves and having fun up there?

I've brought up over 6,000 children on stage at Disneyland. This is a once-in-a-lifetime experience for each child and bringing them on stage is a special moment for them and their families. I never wanted them to feel uncomfortable. Many people, adults included, find being on a stage extremely intimidating. Do everything you can to make them feel comfortable. Treat everyone you bring on stage with dignity.

Years ago, I took my family to The World Series and Jim Hill, a local CBS sportscaster in LA, was there. He was in between things, so I went up and introduced myself to tell him that I had always liked him as a sportscaster. We chatted for a minute and at the end of it, he said, "You have an absolutely lovely family." And I could tell that he meant it sincerely. Even now, twenty years later, I still remember that conversation.

What can entertainers — or indeed people in general — learn from this? When you compliment a family or, in particular, the children, you win them all over. Always take photos with the kids. Be funny and silly with them. Most importantly, never hesitate to tell parents what a lovely family they have. They *do* have a lovely family. Tell them sincerely, and they'll never forget that gesture.

The Real Work on Corporate Events

Many magicians want to perform at corporate events but aren't sure how to go about it. Can you share some advice about working with corporate groups?

The first rule is: arrive *very* early. You should never be in a position where you feel rushed or panicked. You have to anticipate potential traffic and parking problems. Expect to have to tow your luggage to a ballroom on the other side of the hotel. Expect to realize that you left your socks in the car! There might be a sound or lighting problem that you have to resolve. All these various types of stress are eliminated if you just arrive at the venue in plenty of time. I'll find a place in the corner and read my phone for two hours if it means not showing up in a panic and stressing out my client.

Dress appropriately when you arrive at the gig. You should be carrying your show jacket in, not wearing it. You do not want to get sweaty and wrinkled while setting up. On the other hand, you should not be in a T-shirt and flip-flops either. You need to look presentable when you meet the client. Think about how hotel workers dress — comfortable yet professional.

Second, find the restroom when you arrive and ensure you look presentable. Take a good look in the mirror and smarten yourself up. You should look clean and relaxed when you meet your client.

Third, find the ballroom or venue, roll your luggage in, and put everything in the corner out of the way. Do not have things in your hand when you meet the person in charge.

Fourth, when you find the people in charge, look them in the eye, shake their hand and thank them for inviting you. Ask to see where the stage is and confirm when you're scheduled to perform. It's not unusual for things to be running behind. Once you've confirmed the timeline, say, "It was a pleasure meeting you. I want to ensure I'm set up and ready to go. Do you mind if I do that now?" They will usually say, "Go ahead." They've got a zillion other things to see to.

Fifth, immediately go to the sound and lighting booth. Introduce yourself to the tech crew and get your sound set up immediately. That's the thing that can give you the most problems. You don't have a show if they can't see or hear you. Give them a simple lighting cue sheet. And I mean *simple*. They have a lot to see to — seven mics, lights and PowerPoint slides. Make life easy for them. Test your mic, look at your side angles, get the lights filtered and then quietly set your stuff off to the stage's side. Stay out of everybody's way.

When you're done, return to the client and say, "I'm all set up. Is there anything I can do to help?" Ninety-nine percent of the time, it's a no, but it's a good gesture to show that you're there for that client. The bottom line is this: don't create problems. They've got tons of problems.

You're thinking about the client's needs hours before you even meet them.

That's right. I worked with the Disney Approach to Quality Service program in Florida. They're so guest-centric that it changes your philosophy. The focus is on ensuring the guest is having a good time. As long as they have a good time, your job is secure.

As soon as you make it about you ("What about me? My lighting's not right! I need this or that...") you're in trouble. Do what you can in a gracious way to get things fixed, and realize you can't always get your way.

The people organizing corporate events have worked months and months to get these things right. How do you think they feel when the entertainer who pops in, does an hour and pops out, starts complaining to everyone when everything isn't just the way they want it? You won't get repeat business. On the other hand, if you come in thinking, "No gig is perfect, but let's work together to make everything as good as possible to make the client look good and feel good," you'll get called back.

Collaboration

You've done many shows with a cast. At Warren and Annabelle's, we work in teams. You spend years on the road performing with your wife and doing variety shows. Do you have any tips on collaboration?

Suppose you're going to work in variety shows. In that case, you'll work with stagehands, sound and lighting crew, assistants and performing partners. You have to learn how to collaborate with all these people. They'll all come to you with questions and deserve answers because you're the entertainer. You'll work with all kinds of personalities — especially in high-stress situations. Strive to be patient, organized and gracious with everyone.

We're blessed at Warren & Annabelle's because all six performers get along great. We don't have egos. We're all very complementary to each other yet we critique each other in a helpful and friendly way. We support each other.

That kind of collaboration reminds me of Steve Martin, who famously said, "Be so good they can't ignore you." If your act is really good, you'll get noticed. Eventually, you might get really noticed. But being 'good' goes for how you interact with people off stage, too. Be kind. Be organized. Be professional before and after showtime.

I worked with my wife, Dolly, for 25 years, traveling the world doing illusions and comedy. We certainly had situations where we were at odds with each other. She'd get frustrated with me because sometimes I'm too laid back. I'm comfortable winging it, but she wants to know her cues and when to come out on stage. After all, she's the one who has to change costumes and get into uncomfortable props. I told her, "You'll know! I'll wave you on! You'll know!"

But as you know, I can be kind of unpredictable. It was frustrating to work with me sometimes. I had to learn to be more aware of the other entertainers' needs, whether a whole cast or my wife. They must be able to shine, too.

Breaking in Routines

Some magicians plan every detail before putting new material on stage. You once told me to focus on "getting the highlights." What do you mean by that?

As I think about the routine's beginning, middle and end, I make sure that I know what I want to achieve and what I must do at critical moments — the highlights. I make sure that I know what I will say at those moments. From there, I let it flow.

Other magicians might recommend scripting every second. The danger is looking like you're more focused on reciting a script. I like how you have some script for the highlights while leaving room to explore and remain present.

I know others prefer to be very scripted, which works for them. There's nothing wrong with finding the way that works best for you. I'm more comfortable letting it flow as much as possible. Once I figure out the working script, I can work on the details.

The details?

Yes. Some rock bands test songs with crowds before putting them on their album. Each piece has the words, melody, bass line, chords and so on before they perform it on stage.

But with each show, they make adjustments and figure out where to punch it and where to pull back. Those are the details. That's the best way for me, too. Most of the 'song' stays the same as I tweak small details with each show.

Staying with the music analogy, how can you tell if a 'song' is good or you just got a kind audience? And if you get a flat response, how do you know if it's the routine or the crowd?

Don't add more than one or two new effects in a single night. In your professional-grade show, hopefully, you already have reliable tricks, lines and moments that you know work with most audiences. Even if the new trick is a little rough, you can trust the show will go well because you've done most of the show hundreds if not thousands of times. That way, you can determine whether it's the audience or not.

Generally speaking, there are fewer bad than good audiences, or we probably wouldn't do this business. Even then, don't underestimate the power of a good performance. An excellent performance can turn around a lousy audience.

Are we having fun?

Tough Crowds & Tips for Beginners

Is it more fun to have a great crowd or win over a hard one?

Almost by definition, everyone likes a lively, responsive crowd. They allow me to improvise even more than usual because they'll accept my wild ideas. On the other hand, there's professional satisfaction in taking a crowd that lacks energy, or doesn't get you at first, and then managing to turn them around so that they have a great time.

That's something I've learned from Warren. You don't stop fighting to win that audience over. This is my act and I can't change who I am but I'm not going to give up. I'm not going to rush it or finish early. I will fight to win them to my side. It's exhausting sometimes. But if I didn't do it, I'd feel like I gave up. I can't do that.

Any pro tips for winning over tough audiences?

I once learned a great lesson from Dana Daniels. We did a show together at Huntington Beach in a huge ballroom. Lots of distractions. There were probably 300 tables, and he had a small area with a stage and some chairs. When he was due to start, there were still guys on stilts, face painting and all sorts of stuff plus loud background music. No one paid attention when he came out and started his show.

He just kept a steady, calm pace, and within ten minutes, people started noticing. I remember hearing people say, "Hey, this is fun!" Within 15 minutes, he had the majority of the people focused on him. The audience eventually realized that his act was great and became interested right after that. It was a great lesson. Trust your act. Don't panic.

What do you say to a beginner who may not have a trustworthy or polished act yet?

Work, work, work. I don't care where. Work anywhere where someone will hire you to do magic. Work free shows if you have to. Building any skill requires repetition. Working is where you get the repetition to get better at performing. And rehearse your butt off before you work.

The Gift of Funny

At Warren & Annabelle's, we say goodbye to every crowd as they exit. I've heard many people tell you you're the quickest wit they've ever seen. Where did that come from?

I genuinely believe that it's just God's gift of quick wit. That's how it feels to me. I know that I've always been extremely fast with a response. In fact, thinking back over the years, I can still remember the first time it happened. At the time I was just a third-grader in Mrs. Montgomery's class. Someone said something, I made the whole class laugh and I never looked back.

I think we were all given gifts by God and it's up to us to figure out what they are and how we're supposed to use them. I had the gift of being funny but I could also be snarky and even a little mean. So even though I was quick, I had to learn how to use this ability in a fun and loving way.

It's a challenge. I'm human and I still think of funny things that aren't appropriate. I have to be careful because Warren & Annabelle's is a clean club. But even if I have to bite my tongue occasionally, I believe it was a gift given to me. I must be careful with it but I must use it.

I've probably watched your act a hundred times, but it never gets old. Your interaction with the audience makes each show unique.

Thanks. The guy who inspired my stage name, Richie Blackmore, was the lead guitarist of Deep Purple. He's a controversial figure in music. He didn't like to play the same song the same way twice. He said he'd play in an orchestra if he wanted to do that. He famously said, "When you hear us play as a band, we're all improvising. Every night, it's different even though it's the same song; there are subtleties, there's cadence and flow that's different to fit the crowd and the mood of the musicians."

As a fan, I enjoy that! I also don't want to hear the song done the same way over and over and over. Otherwise, I'd just buy the album.

I encourage everyone to listen to live recordings. Not doctored. Live. Then you can hear the band 'warts and all'. Mistakes and all. But you will also listen to them stretch. They try to do some things that aren't in their wheelhouse one day, but the next thing you know they're doing something new that adds to the song.

In the same way, magicians will have nights with misses and mistakes, too. You have to be willing to take that. You have to have tough skin in this business.

How else has your faith impacted your life and career?

I say a prayer right before I go on stage. Then I say 'love' because that's what I want to convey.

Christianity has tempered me. I think many entertainers live for those high highs and suffer from those really low lows. We want to be great every time, and it can be depressing when you don't get that love back from the audience. My faith has helped me stay balanced. I was rough and a little ruder before. It calmed me down from who I was, allowing me to have more fun on stage. It's helped me find a way to be compassionate while still being everyone's favorite class clown.

Giving Back

What else helps you stay humble and tempered?

Charity work. I highly encourage any entertainer to share their gifts with children. There's a place in Kissimmee, Florida, called 'Give The Kids The World Village'. It was founded by a gentleman named Henri Landwirth — a Holocaust survivor.

It's a space for children with terminal diseases who want to experience something like Disneyland. They built a cafeteria, pools, waterslides, train rides and fun activities for the children. It's basically a small village that families can visit. The children who visit need around-the-clock care, so the villas have medical equipment in the walls, behind paintings and stuff. It looks like a fun family home but at the same time emergency medical equipment is always available. They also have a theater for live shows. For me, working for these children who happen to be sick really helped me to put what I do into perspective.

You quickly realize how insignificant our show business worries are compared to what many others are going through. On the other hand, you also get to see the importance of what we do. We're in the business of wowing and entertaining people. We get to help people forget their troubles and enjoy a laugh for a moment. Over the years, people have come to me after shows, telling me some hardship they or their family were going through. Then they say my show was their first laugh in a long time. For these kids, their troubles and pain were first and foremost for most of their lives. If you give them a few brief moments where they forget and just laugh, you're doing them a wonderful service.

We're lucky to be able to do what we do. Use the act you've worked hard to build up over the years and give back.

Dana Daniels

Origin Story: 'It's a Bird!'

DK: Every working magician has to decide what style of magic they want to do at some point. How did you choose?

DD: When I started magic at the age of eleven, I did close-up magic. Later on, I did a dove act, a manipulation act and even illusions, trying to discover who I was on stage. I realized that the one common thread was always comedy. I loved jokes.

How did you end up choosing stand-up and using the bird?

I did my first audition at The Magic Castle in front of an audience — which is what you had to do back then. My show went really well and the audience loved me. Peter Pitt came up to me after and said, "I can't book you." I was stunned! Hadn't he seen the audience's reaction? I killed! He said, "You have good timing and a good sense of humor. You have a great personality on stage. But I have ten other magicians doing the same act. They're doing the same tricks and the same jokes."

I couldn't come back with an argument. I had to face it — he was right. He said, "Come back with something original." That's easier said than done.

How did you do it?

I had a parrot. I thought I'd produce it in my dove act, but parrots aren't like doves. They're difficult to contain and produce. So I was left with a pet who couldn't do magic. For fun, I created a bit I performed for friends when they came over. The parrot liked chewing things, so I came up with a routine that involved the parrot chewing on a playing card. Someone picks a card and shows it to the parrot. Then I read the parrot's mind to figure out the selection. While I showed the card to the parrot, he'd chew on the corner 'unbeknownst' to me.

I'd put the card back in the deck and then try to read the mind of the parrot. I'd then run through the cards until I came to the quite obviously chewed-up card. At that moment, I'd have an amazing 'psychic revelation', allowing me to find the selection. People who saw me do it at home cracked up.

At that time, I belonged to a club called The Long Beach Mystics. We had monthly meetings at a school auditorium to work out new routines. One time, I was assigned to host the show. I remember feeling anxious, thinking, "They've seen everything I do!" My mother said, "Do that thing with the parrot. It's hilarious."

Dana and parrot, 1983

I shrugged her off. I knew the routine was funny in my living room but I didn't think it would be as funny on stage. It wouldn't translate. But as the show got closer, I became more desperate, so I took her advice.

That night, I brought the parrot out between acts and did the bit. It killed. Even though it wasn't a magic trick, it went over better than anything I had ever done for them. Afterward, the senior members came to me and said, "More bird." That's when I decided to develop an act around the parrot. It was the spark I needed for an original act.

It's amazing how the answer was in your house the whole time. A little pressure and helpful friends and family launched you in the right direction.

Right, that's what it took for me to see it. Once I saw the potential, I grabbed onto it and went forward. Once I had my hook, I could ask, "What tricks can I do with a psychic parrot? What tricks have I never done that could work with this psychic parrot act?"

The next step was writing down tricks and then figuring out how to present them using the parrot. How am I going to play it? I was creating an original act. It was exciting.

Finding the Funny

When you create routines, I know your goal is to 'find the funny'. How do you do that?

Right. I brainstorm by creating lists to look for jokes. When I developed my routine using a phone, I wrote everything I could think of that had to do with a phone. It didn't have to be funny. It was just something to look at while writing my script: phone line, phone jack, phone book. Push two to hear it in Spanish. I wrote lines from commercials: "Can you hear me now?" That helped me write lines like, "Is it funny now? Is it funny now? Let me know when it comes in funny." I tried to think of situations with a phone. What do people say when they're talking on the phone? What do people do with their phones?

I get my best ideas when I'm in my hot tub. That's where I came up with many ideas for my characters, jokes and even the names of shows, like the 'No Show'. There's something to say about a quiet and relaxing place where you can think.

Find friends who can help you brainstorm and find ideas. I even went on Facebook for ideas a few times. When looking for funny names for a character in the 'No Show', I posted, "I need a funny name for an escape artist." And man, they just poured in! People had tons of funny names. I see comedians do that, too. A comedian friend of mine sometimes posts different versions of a punchline and say, "Okay, comics, which is funnier: A, B, or C?" If it helps you out, why not? But the ultimate test is still the audience.

What do you say to those who prefer to ad lib on stage?

I highly recommend ad libbing on stage but you should also discipline yourself to write out the script for the trick. They go hand in hand. Everyone should take an improv class, whether you're an entertainer or not. It helps you think faster, relax on stage and get comfortable with yourself. A script can start as simple as, "Hello, ladies and gentlemen. I'm Dana Daniels. And now, here is a piece of rope." It might not even be funny... unless you're holding a deck of cards.

Have the list next to you that has everything associated with your routine. Sometimes you get lucky with the ideas, and they quickly gel together. Sometimes it takes longer.

When to Stop Writing and Start Performing?

Put together what you can and get the routine on stage. Go somewhere (not a high-stakes show) and do it. Sandwich the new material between routines that are already polished. I used to try things out at showcases or comedy clubs. You don't make much money, but you're in front of an audience.

For my phone routine, for example, I booked a week in the parlor at the Castle and aimed to make it a solid bulletproof routine by the end of the week. After you script and plan, work it out in front of a real audience and set goals.

Most importantly, listen to your audience. That's all of Comedy 101. I've always included comedy but that doesn't mean every joke I write works the first time. Sometimes a joke gets a huge laugh after the first try and sometimes a joke you thought would kill falls flat. That's okay. If I ever feel like a joke should work but doesn't, I give it three tries on stage. If it still doesn't work, I throw it out even if I think it's funny. Only things that consistently get laughs stay in the act. The goal is three or more laughs per minute. You'll only know if you're listening to the audience.

When I was breaking in the phone routine, I remember one time when I said to the guy on the phone, "I'm on stage with a psychic parrot." The guy on the phone misheard me and replied, "Ferret?"

I repeated it to the audience: "Ferret?! No, not a *ferret*! A parrot!" It got a big laugh, so I thought, "Well, that's in the show now. I'll say that in every show, even though they don't actually say that. I'll pretend they misunderstood me and say ferret."

After the show, I went backstage and wrote it down. Then I thought of a line to tag the bit: "A psychic ferret would be ridiculous." So I got two laughs out of a moment that happened by accident. Those things happen when you perform a lot and listen.

Sometimes it just comes to you. Years ago, I worked out a Confabulation routine. When I first did it, the final revelation was a shopping list from my wife. It wasn't the funniest routine, but the trick went over great. I was still trying to figure out how to make the bird part of it.

After doing the trick that way for a while, I filled in for Mac King in Vegas. I was backstage five minutes before showtime and thinking about that trick. Suddenly, it clicked: what if the letter was a desperate cry for help from the bird? What if he says he's being forced to do this against his will? I started cracking up. I quickly grabbed a piece of paper and I changed the whole trick just before showtime. The revelations read, "He only feeds me [___], and only pays me [___], and makes me live in [___]." It killed.

Learning Funny

Can anyone learn to write jokes or become funny?

That's a good question. You can learn to write comedy with practice. At the same time, you do have to have a certain sense of humor about yourself. It's a matter of trusting that sense of humor. For a long time, I didn't trust it. There would be something in my head that was funny to me, but I didn't think it would be funny to an audience — like the parrot at first. You have to step out and try it.

Delivering Funny

It's one thing to write jokes and another to deliver them. Any tips for telling jokes?

How you deliver jokes and lines can change your character to the audience. I'm always experimenting with my delivery. Speaking at different pitches is one way. Am I bringing my voice up higher or lowering it? Tempo is another way. Is it funnier if I talk faster or slower? I'm always discovering new things about my stage personality.

As I get older, I can't keep acting, speaking, and moving like the same young guy who worked at Disneyland in his twenties. Someone my age talks about things differently on stage. I have different experiences to share.

Calling Back to Funny

Related to jokes are running gags and callbacks. I have several in my show.

They can be all kinds of things. For example, I have a silly dance that comes back a few times in my act. Then there's a simple line: "It's a bird!" It can also be a person you keep coming back to. I have an ongoing souvenir gag with one member of the audience.

I recently put something new at Warren & Annabelle's that ties a nice little bow to the end of my show. I tell a true story about a magician I saw as a kid. Part of his act was an

Appearing Cane, but I don't actually produce the cane until the very end. After my final bow, the cane appears. I twirl it, have the bird jump onto it and walk off stage. It's one last little callback at the very end.

Clean and Funny

I know you prefer to work clean. There's no profanity or blue humor in your act.

You have to know your audiences and what is appropriate for them. The kinds of audiences I work for usually prefer me not to use bad language or blue humor.

Using bad language can also hold you back professionally and artistically. Sometimes you have to work clean. It's easy to start relying on profanity to get that shock factor. For example, I've seen George Carlin live and I always thought he was brilliant and hilarious. But I always thought he was funnier on television because he had to work clean. TV forced him to be just as funny and effective without the profanity. I'm sure many would say he was funnier with the profanity, but I think he was funnier without it.

"Is it funny now?"

Nothing is Beneath You

I know you take all kinds of work, no matter the payout. Not many gigging magicians these days share that attitude.

I love doing my act. If I have downtime, I'm happy to find ways to keep performing. Sometimes, it's just for working out material, staying in shape or connecting with people. It's fun to meet other entertainers. I was lucky enough to hang out in the green room with people like Garry Shandling, Ray Romano, Arsenio Hall and Robin Williams. When it's people like that, you're just observing and learning.

If you're going to be in this business, you must love performing. Low-paying gigs can lead to bigger ones. Keep showing up. Nothing is beneath you.

It's also exciting to follow people's careers. I've met people who were 'unknowns' in these clubs who are now big stars! One of them has a movie coming out in a couple of weeks. It doesn't seem so long since he started as an emcee!

The lesson is to be kind to everybody. You never know — the guy pulling the curtain could be the same guy who gives you a job someday. What if he becomes a CEO who could hire you for an event? Maybe he'll open his own club. There are tons of stories like that. Treat everybody with respect.

Tenacity

Any tips on finding gigs for someone just starting out?

Tenacity. Work to create opportunities. I'll give you an example. There was a show called 'Sugar Babies' that used to be on Broadway. Later it toured around the country. It was a burlesque show with variety acts like singers and dancers. But it also had comics. I remember thinking, "I want to be in this show. This is right up my alley."

One day, I saw the first dinner theater production of 'Sugar Babies' coming to Anaheim at The Grand Dinner Theater. I lived in Anaheim, and the theater was across from

Disneyland, where I worked. Even though it was a dinner theater show and not the big Broadway version, it still looked like a fun show to be part of. I decided to audition for it. But when I looked at the drama log, it said: 'Actors audition Tuesday. Dancers audition Wednesday. Variety acts submit a videotape.'

Live auditions are always better. Even back then, I knew that if I could do a live audition I would increase my chances of getting the job. I told my mother that they just wanted me to send in a tape. She said, "Why don't you go to the dancer's audition and do your act?"

I told her, "That's crazy." She said, "Exactly!"

So that's what I did. The next Wednesday, I went along to the dancer's audition. I took along my bag, a tuxedo and of course the parrot. And I just sat in the hallway surrounded by all these dancers in leotards, practicing and doing all their warm-ups and stretches.

They all sort of stared at me but I didn't say anything. The director came out from time to time to call in the next act, glanced over at me for a moment and then brought in the next dancer.

Eventually, he came over to me and said, "Can I help you, Sir?" And I said, "Yeah, I'm here to audition to be your variety act." And he says, "Well, this is for dancers only." I said, "Wow, good news! No competition!" He laughed and said, "I'll tell you what. When we're done auditioning dancers, you can audition if we have any time left over." I said, "Fair enough."

At the end of the day, I auditioned for him and subsequently got the job. I found out later that Johnny Thompson had submitted a tape. I told the director, "You could have Tomsoni? You're insane!"

That was one way I got a job and it was just by tenacity. Go after it, make calls and suggest yourself. It doesn't always work but it's worked more times for me than not. After all, if you don't try, you know for *sure* you won't get the job.

Beyond Tricks: Friends

What were some of the things that helped fuel your passion for performing over the years?

First and foremost, my friends. I wouldn't be where I am if it weren't for the magic club I belonged to, The Long Beach Mystics. As a teenager, it created a community for me. I felt accepted even though we all critiqued and razzed each other all the time. Some guys didn't last long with that. Sometimes, you'd make a mistake on stage and, boy, the guys wouldn't let you forget it. But I stuck it out because I loved it so much.

The Long Beach Mystics fed my passion for magic by having that meeting to look forward to every month. To this day, they're all people I admire as entertainers and are very dear friends. We share ideas and trust each other. Without that club, I could have easily gone into something else — like photography. They kept me going and motivated me to the point where magic became a living.

Beyond Tricks: Balance

Balance is another thing. Always balance your life with your career. Many entertainers seem unhappy because they only focus on one area. If you're married, you must maintain your marriage and manage your life outside of performing. I'm at Warren & Annabelle's half the year. I don't want to be married part-time, so Jayne often comes out here.

When we were younger and the kids were growing up, I wanted to be home more, so I stopped working cruise ships. At that time, I approached Disneyland and told them I was interested in being a consultant. That consulting opportunity turned that into a job performing there. Even though it was only two days a week, it kept me in town. I just did other gigs.

I could be home for family events and birthday parties. I turned down many terrific opportunities — tours and various shows. But even if they had benefited my career, they wouldn't have been helpful for my family.

Any regrets?

No, none at all. I always told myself that other opportunities would come along once the kids were older. And sure enough, that's how things worked out. For example, I got the opportunity to tour the world and perform on Broadway with 'The Illusionists — Turn of the Century'.

Beyond Tricks: Vices

I also never took drugs and I don't drink much. When I worked at comedy clubs, that stuff was always around. Sometimes, other performers would shun you if you didn't party with them. I had that happen to me a few times. What can I say? It's not the way I party. I'd rather see a movie or go out for a meal.

If you're in that environment a lot, it's natural to want to fit in. But that's not a good excuse. At corporate events, they might want you to have drinks with them and I did on a few occasions here and there. But I never drank to get drunk. Thankfully, nowadays, it's no longer such a big deal if you say you don't drink or smoke.

Steve Martin

You've performed for and with dozens of celebrities over the years. Madonna, Morgan Freeman and Ryan Gosling are just a few. Do you get starstruck?

The most nervous I ever got meeting a celebrity was Steve Martin. I was a teenager when I first saw him. He was on the Mike Douglas show and I remember thinking, "Wow, you can be funny doing magic?" He did a comedy 'magic' act but he didn't do any actual magic. He had lots of funny lines and gags. Seeing his act opened my eyes to a different way of performing.

His career exploded shortly after that. He was on Saturday Night Live and started making hit movies. I saw him at the Universal Amphitheater during my senior year in high school. That was when they recorded his live show.

How did you finally meet him?

I've met Steve several times, but the highlight was when he saw my show in Santa Barbara. We got to chat after the show. He gave me a great line that I still use in my show. Who do you want to meet?

I want to meet Steve, too. His book 'Born Standing Up', was an essential read for me.

He's different from his on-stage persona in real life. He's very quiet. In another one of his books, Steve talks about how people are often shocked because he isn't the 'wild and crazy guy' they expect.

I totally relate to that. Offstage, I'm reserved and quiet, too. When people see that you're like that, they sometimes feel disappointed because you didn't meet their expectations. I have to consciously remind myself to be more engaging and animated when I meet people after my shows, or they might assume I'm cold or rude.

So you don't have to be the most extroverted or exciting person all the time to be a good entertainer.

Right. When people ask Steve Martin for an autograph, he hands them a business card that says, 'This certifies that you have had a personal encounter with me and that you found me warm, polite, intelligent and funny.' He hands these out instead of signing autographs because it's funny but also so he doesn't have to put on a show for people.

Sensational!

Here's one of the best things I learned while working at the Golden Horseshoe. I was only 22 when I started there — the youngest guy in the show. There was a hilarious singer and comedian named Fulton Burley who was a treasure to work with and I wanted to learn everything I could from him. I'd pick his brains after every show.

I noticed that whenever someone asked him, "How ya doing, Fulton?", he always responded with, "Seeensational!" And it always got a smile. It's such a different response from what you typically get. So one day, I asked him if I could start saying it too. He goes, "Yeah, I *want* you to do it!" So I did, and later added, "But I'll get better!" It's a funny tagline.

That's wonderful. Do you do it only when you're performing?

Anywhere. I do it in grocery stores. When the cashier asks, "How are you, Sir?" I say, "Sensational!" And it always gets them. They always say, "Oh! That's great!" Then I say, "But I'll get better!" And that gets a laugh. People always ask me, "Hey, do you mind if I use that?"

I was just about to ask you that.

Go ahead. Spread it around. Everybody should do it.

Warren Gibson

How It All Began

DK: How does a police officer become a magician?

WG: Long story. You want the whole story?

Yes.

I started as a police officer and ended up working for South Carolina National Bank as a criminal investigator. My specialist area was investigating credit card fraud. They also sometimes asked me to present talks and seminars for chambers of commerce and merchant's associations to educate them about how to prevent credit card fraud in the retail sector.

One time, I was teaching with a Secret Service agent who was there to talk about counterfeit money. He opened his talk with a magic trick to get people's attention. I thought this was a pretty good idea. Afterwards, I asked him if he'd teach me that trick, which he did.

It was the Torn & Restored Newspaper. He'd say, "Imagine a criminal comes into your store and uses counterfeit money or a stolen credit card. They can tear your business and others to pieces. The investigator's job is to take the pieces of the crime, put them back together and determine who committed the fraud." Suddenly, the paper was restored. It was a visual way to describe a criminal investigation.

With his permission, I started using it in my seminars. About three months later, I started wishing I had a couple more magic tricks — maybe one in the middle and another at the end to round things off. Unfortunately, the guy who taught me said he didn't know any more tricks. I asked him where he learned the newspaper trick and he referred me to a magic shop in Charlotte.

I went to the magic shop that weekend and bought about $200 worth of magic tricks. When I got home, I started working on them but quickly realized that most were small close-up tricks. They wouldn't work in front of audiences of 50 to 200 people. The magic shop's demonstrator got me excited because he fooled me left and right. All I could say was, "Yeah, I'll buy that. I'll buy that one, too!"

I drove back there a weekend later and bought a few magic books. I don't remember which ones now but I began practicing sleight of hand as a hobby. While working on cases, there was a lot of dead time. Very often, between interviewing witnesses or waiting to interview a suspect, I'd practice. I'd typically carry eight or nine tricks in my pockets. I constantly practiced.

When did your hobby become a career?

Maybe six months after I started practicing, I was in a hotel's restaurant bar with a group of friends. We were in a booth around the edge of a dance floor and I started doing tricks for them. A crowd began forming around us. The hotel manager was dining in the restaurant and saw the group.

He sent the bar manager over to me, who said, "The hotel manager would like to speak to you." When I walked over to him, he said, "I want you to work for me." I said, "Excuse me? Doing what?" He said, "You're a magician, aren't you?" I said, "Well, not really. I know a handful of magic tricks." He said, "It doesn't matter. I saw what you did with that crowd, and I want you to work for me."

I said, "I really can't. I have a full-time job. I travel a lot, too." He said, "Don't worry about it. Any night that you're in town, just come in. Go from table to table like you were doing at your table over there. I'll pay you by the night."

But I knew nothing about table-hopping or performing magic. I was 26 years old, and it wasn't even a year since I had seen my first magic trick. Guys who grow up in big cities have exposure to magic clubs and shows but I grew up on a farm with cows and hay. My childhood was farming in our gardens, castrating calves and butchering our own beef. I didn't know what I was doing but I started working two or three nights a week at this hotel. I ended up doing that for four and a half years.

That's how I taught myself sleight of hand and how to perform. I learned a lot of things wrong since I only had books. I made it work for me.

Do you ever wish you had had a mentor or a community of magicians around you?

When I first started performing in South Carolina, I did go to see Tom Mullica three times at The Tomfoolery in Atlanta. That planted the seed in the back of my head that, someday, I wanted to have my own close-up show. But in retrospect, it was a blessing in disguise that I learned from books instead of from other magicians or from going to a local magic club. I had to develop my own style. I never copied anyone because I didn't have anyone to copy.

I find it almost a disadvantage for younger magicians to be around performers they want to emulate. Instead of developing their own personality and style, they tend to copy who they're impressed by. That's why many performers never reach their fullest potential.

They may develop a large vocabulary of sleight-of-hand techniques, but that doesn't benefit them as performers. And the bottom line for me is this: a person's performing ability is without doubt far more important than their technical ability or knowledge about magic. There shouldn't be any argument about that.

I've heard it many times at magic conventions. "Magic tricks don't entertain people. The *performer* does!" But very often, the guys I hear saying that are the ones who are the most guilty of expecting a trick to entertain people on its own merits. Many of them aren't very good performers, which is why they're teaching magicians or doing lectures versus performing for the lay public. People may not like that opinion but that's how I see it.

Neil Foster and Los Angeles

Magic eventually took you away from your home in South Carolina. How did that happen?

After four and a half years of table-hopping, I decided to pursue magic as a career. I'd heard about the Chavez Course, so I contacted Neil Foster and told him I wanted to be his student. He accepted me and I moved to Michigan.

Neil Foster said something to you when you graduated.

I'm reluctant to talk about it because it'll sound a little self-serving, even though it's true. But in a nutshell, I wasn't a good student. The other students developed much better routines and were much better with their sleight of hand and technical skills.

When we graduated, Neil gave each student their diploma and ushered them out the door. When everyone else had left, he sat me down and said, "Look, you have a gift. And that gift is with people. Take that gift. Go out and perform. I don't tell many students to pursue magic as a career because they don't have what it takes. You do. Go do it and make me proud."

So he was a prophet! Is it true at one point you developed a a silent act?

I never really polished a silent act for stage. Even though Neil encouraged me to perform (and he probably meant a manipulation act) I'd already been table hopping for years. That's what I was good at.

In fact, during my first week at the Chavez Course, I picked up a table-hopping gig at a restaurant outside of Kalamazoo called 'Sharon's on the Lake'. After graduating with Neil, I stayed there for ten months. During this time, I realized that if I did have a gift with people, I couldn't use it doing a manipulation act on a big stage. I decided my career path was to figure out how to do close-up magic in an environment other than table-hopping.

Is that when you decided to build Warren & Annabelle's?

No. I moved to Los Angeles. On my second night there, I found a job as the house magician at 'Bobby McGee's' in Burbank. That was the beginning of my full-time magic career. I started doing private parties and corporate work and for the last five years in LA worked at 'Wizards'.

So it was all going well. Why did you leave all that?

My wife Lisa and I went to Maui for our honeymoon in 1993. By the fourth night, we realized there was nothing for adult couples to do at night except go to a luau. So I said to her, "This might be a great place to open my own magic theater." We had no real desire to move to Hawai'i. That wasn't a motivating factor for us. I just saw it an opportunity. After our honeymoon, back in LA, I spent the next two years writing a comprehensive business plan.

The Business Plan

Two years! That's a lot of planning.

I've seen many young magicians attempt to open their own venue over the years. Many do not invest the time and research necessary to create a business plan that spells out every detail about their theater or show.

When I began planning Warren & Annabelle's, there was little information on the internet compared to today. Furthermore, Maui County's visitor and travel statistics needed to catch up by at least four or five years. I had sparse and old data. That was a challenge right away.

I hired an experienced attorney to write a private placement memorandum (PPM) for me. It's like an IPO on a much smaller scale but it still costs $25-30k to have done. It's lays out for investors all the risks associated with a project and their realistic expectations. It also sets out the legal rights and protections of all parties.

My PPM painted a rather dismal picture of the prospects for my venture. Think about it — a magic show in Maui? People don't go to Maui, or Hawai'i in general, for a magic show. Regardless, I took my business plan and PPM and began knocking on the doors of former clients. I asked if they would give me 15 minutes of their time to hear about my new project. Surprisingly, the vast majority said yes.

It took me a year to raise the money ($1.1 million) to build Warren and Annabelle's. Unfortunately, once Lisa and I moved to Maui, complications set in. Finding a location, getting architectural plans prepared for the theater and then actually constructing it was a monumental task — a hundred times harder and more challenging than I expected. All of the pre-opening hurdles were hard enough. But the years after opening were the two most difficult years of my life.

How so?

Three Days From Closing

I'd planned on having about $200,000 in working capital when we opened. However, we opened with very little due to construction delays and costs. A few months after opening, I was three days away from closing. I told Lisa that we'd close on Friday because payroll wasn't going to cash.

One Wednesday night, my walk-on music started and, behind the curtain, I lifted my head, turned my palms to the ceiling and said, "Lord, all I ever asked you for was my shot, my opportunity, and you gave it to me. I have no regrets. Thank you." I stepped through the curtain and it felt like a huge weight had been lifted off my shoulders. Even though I expected to close on Friday. I felt a huge sense of relief.

After the show, one of my employees came up to me and said, "Oh my gosh, you were goofy tonight!" Until then, I had never considered comedy when I performed. But in that particular show, I guess I was suddenly humorous and funny. Frankly, all I could do was laugh because of the dire financial situation.

Luckily, we got *just* enough people in between Wednesday and Friday for us to make payroll. The next three or four payrolls were touch and go and I still thought we might have to close. I returned to my investors who, luckily, had enough faith in me to invest more money. Even then, we lost a lot of money that first year. The second year we made very little. Around year two and a half, we began selling out. Only one marketing strategy was working: word of mouth.

The rest is history. It was difficult and painful in the beginning. In those first few years, during all the business challenges, I took very little time off from performing. But Warren & Annabelle's was extremely successful. And that's how a police officer became a professional magician.

Marketing Secret: Create Missionaries!

Today, there are hundreds of online marketing services available. Digital media can get ads out in seconds. How can you be sure that word of mouth is still the best way to market your business?

Consider The Magic Castle. It's a nonprofit with a strong reputation in the middle of a metropolitan area. My business is the exact opposite. Warren & Annabelle's is a small for-profit business in an isolated community. As you can imagine, those factors (and others) make it very difficult to become successful.

I was competing with 400 other tourist activities when we opened. Virtually all those were outdoor activities like snorkel trips, riding bicycles down the volcano or hiking in the national park. People come to Maui to do outdoor activities surrounded by all the beauty Maui has to offer. You can't blame them.

But I naively thought, 'If I build it, they will come'. I figured if we advertised online, made brochures and filmed a TV commercial, everyone would realize they needed to see the magic show on their vacation. This just didn't happen. Magic shows are an odd duck in Hawai'i, and yet I never imagined it would be so difficult to convince visitors — set on Hawaiian activities — that they needed to see my show.

No form of advertising we've tried over 23 years has ever made a dent in our profits. Not a single ad ever paid for itself — and we track our marketing very closely. The only thing that consistently puts butts on seats and keeps my doors open is word of mouth.

I have a saying that the performers and every staff member hears me preaching ad nauseam. We all have one job — to create missionaries. By that, I mean it's not enough for guests to leave Warren & Annabelle's saying, "That was a good show." We want them saying, "Oh my gosh! I can't wait to come back here!", or, "I can't wait to tell my family and friends that when they come to Maui, they have to come to Warren & Annabelle's!" If they aren't doing that, we haven't created missionaries. The market is incredibly competitive on Maui, especially for an odd duck like a magic show. Without those missionaries, we wouldn't have survived.

The Guys

Over the years, dozens of magicians have approached you, wanting to work for you. How did you build your team?

For the last 15 years, I've had the same team of guys working with me: Dana Daniels, John Shryock, Chris Blackmore, John George, and most recently, David Kuraya. Who I did and didn't hire had everything to do with my philosophy of creating missionaries. I asked myself who would consistently put butts on seats over and over again?

I knew Dana from Wizards. Several things led me to call on him. First, Dana is funny and an outstanding performer. I also knew that he was reliable in character. By that, I mean he didn't have drinking problems, drug problems or women problems. That's true of all of the guys. I also knew he was a faithful Christian which is important to me. Dana began to fill in for me when I started taking some time off every once in a while.

John Shryock and his wife, Mari, came into Warren & Annabelle's when John was still working on Hawai'i cruise ships. The first night he and Mari visited, we stayed up talking until two or three in the morning. We became fast friends. Soon after, I booked him for a week for what he didn't know was an audition. Right from the start, John impressed me as a charming performer who paid great attention to detail. Furthermore, his magic was outstanding. He was always reliable to work with and a true professional.

I knew Chris Blackmore from LA. He called me when he was traveling to Hawai'i. He asked if he could perform one night to show me what he could do. I gave him a slot and he did a phenomenal show. Lisa often says that no one seems as comfortable on stage as Chris. He has years of experience

John Shryock, John George, David Kuraya
Chris Blackmore and Dana Daniels

working for top corporate clients and cruise ships. His knowledge of customer service and professionalism is vast. Chris is a comedy magician, so his strength isn't technical magic (that's not news to him). Nonetheless he's a phenomenal performer with a lightning wit — nobody ad libs like Chris Blackmore.

I knew John George from Wizards. He used to hang around there when he started magic. His mentor was Johnny Ace Palmer, who needs no introduction to anyone in magic. He contacted me ten years ago and asked if I'd try him out at Warren & Annabelle's. I said, "Let's book you for a week, and I'll see how it goes."

After the week, I told him I thought he needed a show more attuned to a lay audience. He was already technically solid but needed to grow as a performer. John went back to LA and worked meticulously on his act. Three or four years went by and then he called me out of the blue and said he'd like to perform for me again. He had become a much better performer. John George has created missionaries at Warren & Annabelle's ever since.

John George says one thing he and I have in common is that you could have given us the boot when we first started there and with good reason. We both had a lot of growing to do. You didn't give up on us. Why not?

Well, I like both of you personally and didn't want to see you fail. Both of you would have continued to be successful in your own right. But when I say 'fail', I'm talking about finding a place on stage at Warren & Annabelle's.

I wanted to give both of you enough opportunity to prove yourselves. Early on, I criticized you rather harshly because I knew you could become better performers (the magic was never in doubt). Over time, both of you rose to the occasion and became excellent magicians and performers. You're also men I respect. That's important to me.

As you said, I've had numerous other magicians from around the world contact me, wanting to work at Warren & Annabelle's. But many don't understand that Warren &

Annabelle's is a business intended to make money. It's not a place to showcase a variety of acts or for magicians to test new material. I have 25 employees who rely on me to ensure the doors stay open. I must ensure the acts on stage are true missionary-makers for the sake of my staff.

People sometimes think that businessmen only care about hoarding money for themselves. You're saying that Warren & Annabelle's success isn't just for you and your family but for your employees, too. That's easy to overlook.

That's right. My business is built on loyalty and my employees are extremely loyal to me. Our performers have all been close friends for years. Our kitchen manager has been with us for eighteen years. Our director of operations, seventeen years. Our office manager, fifteen years. My bar manager has been going on for twelve years. All our core staff have helped to create missionaries over the years, too.

But it's still the show that keeps the front doors open. We have a beautiful piano bar called Annabelle's Parlor, a magic entryway with a secret passage, and a delicious gourmet menu. All of those things are wonderful, but if the show isn't standing on its own and creating missionaries, our front doors will close forever. They almost did.

Ten Thousand Shows

You've done tens of thousands of shows on your stage. It's two hours with no intermission. How do you keep it fresh?

I've been asked that many times. My pet peeve is watching a performer on autopilot or 'phoning it in'. I think audiences deserve better. There are a few motivating factors for me to keep it fresh.

First, as I've said, I have to keep my business open. It would shock people to know what it costs per month to run Warren & Annabelle's, so I can't be less than 110% when I step through that curtain. Hopefully, I'm honest with myself when I say that in over 10,000 shows, I've never 'phoned in' a performance.

Granted, we all have those fleeting moments as performers when we realize that we just delivered a line from rote memorization. I've performed for three days in a row with a 103.2 fever and after minor surgeries. But I have never allowed myself more than that split second of lapsing into 'autopilot' mode. I tell myself off. "You just threw away that line. You didn't *mean* it. Snap out of it! Let's go!"

Every person in front of me paid hard-earned money to see me at my best. They don't care how good I was last night. They only want to see me at my best *tonight*. Anyone on my stage must perform on that level to create missionaries.

Secondly, I believe that God gives us all gifts. It's up to us to develop those gifts. One of the gifts He gave me is the ability to connect with audiences. God built me that way. Therefore, no matter how I feel and how many business or personal issues are weighing on me, I need to step through the curtain and focus on my audience to exercise that gift.

Third, I'm highly competitive. I've always looked at each show as a competition. Can I win this audience over or not? Even with tough audiences, I never quit. My show is two hours long. And even if they are a slow audience, I keep saying to myself, "I'm still going to win over this audience." Granted, I may not always succeed. Sometimes they're just a tough crowd. But right up to the last minute, I am never willing to give in to an audience. I give them all of my enthusiasm and energy in the hope that the show will end up being the highlight of their vacation.

Playing 'Warren'

You're quite a different person when you're onstage. Would you say that you play a character when you're performing?

My wife always laughs when people say, "It must be a riot living with him!" They think my personality on stage is the same as it is at home. Similarly, I once received an email from a lady who said, "When we saw your show, we thought at first that you were drunk. You were zany! By the end of your performance, I realized you were an absolute genius because it was all by design. I don't think I've ever enjoyed a show more." Yes, I'm playing a character who's a bit of a Southern country bumpkin. At the same time, he's someone who takes you by surprise.

Why have you chosen to play a character?

To be honest, half of my audience wouldn't like the Warren I am at home. I'm usually a very serious person. I'm opinionated, strong-willed and uncompromising in my values. Many people wouldn't like that. The Southern accent, silly facial expressions, jokes and ad libs add up to a character — a *version* of me — that's very different from who I usually am offstage but is, frankly, more lovable.

Recognizing that your offstage personality might not 'make missionaries' on stage takes some brutal self-awareness.

Maybe, but I dearly love connecting with the audience so I wanted to create a performing style to allows this to happen. I know it's heresy to magicians but I couldn't care less whether I'm doing magic or playing the violin so long as I can entertain an audience. The only thing that's important to me is having that connection.

Many magicians forget that how the audience sees you is more important than how you see the audience. And I know it may sound sophomoric, but it's not as easy as it seems. Always try to imagine yourself as an audience member. Ask yourself, "How are they perceiving what I'm doing or saying? How do they perceive my facial expressions? Am I communicating my ideas properly?"

I love people in general, and I try to view everyone equally. I don't care what your celebrity or status may be in life. I only care about what kind of person you are. I'll just as soon have a fifteen-minute conversation with a truck driver or plumber as with a politician or attorney because I find everybody's story fascinating. Yes, we need to put butts in seats, but the audience is still not just a bunch of warm bodies. Life has taught me that you can find something fascinating about anyone if you just listen. Enjoy people. Love people.

On Faith

How important is your faith as the owner and lead performer at Warren & Annabelle's?

Very important. When we first opened, my prayer was this: "Father, please bless me and let me be a blessing with this business. Let this business be a blessing to the community. And more importantly, let this business glorify you."

Before we opened, I decided that we'd be dark on Sunday, even though Sunday would be a perfect business day. Even though anyone who knows me might think of me as the biggest hypocrite in the world, it was important to me to keep Sunday the Lord's Day.

I've always tried to operate Warren & Annabelle's to glorify God. That's another reason I've chosen all of the performers at Warren & Annabelle's. I've never allowed any four-letter words on stage. I've never allowed any so-called 'adult' material. It shouldn't be necessary. It doesn't do anything to benefit society to lower ourselves to the lowest forms of language to get a laugh. My faith and values have driven how I've wanted our business to be perceived.

A Pizza Feeds a Family of Four

Do you have any favorite stories from your showroom?

One night, I asked a guy in the audience the usual questions: where was he was from and what did he do? He said he was a musician. Anytime anyone says that I use the old joke: "Hey, do you know the difference between a large pizza and a musician? A pizza can feed a family of four!"

After the audience laughed, I asked him what sort of music he played. He paused, looked pensive, and said, "Well, probably nothing you'd listen to." I acted as if I were somewhat insulted. "What do you mean by that? Do you play in a bar or something? Or do you have a band?" And he said, "Well, yeah, I have a band. I sing and play the guitar." I said, "Anybody we've ever heard of?" He paused once again and said, "Well, probably." I looked at him with a direct and challenging look and said, "So, what's the name of your band?" He paused once again and said, "Metallica?" The audience burst out laughing. At that point, the joke was on me. It was James Hetfield!

He's come to my show at least three or four times since then. And we've done the same bit for the audience every time. We've never actually set it up ahead of time but somehow it's always worked out. He's always played the perfect straight man for me.

Few magicians these days take the time in their show to have an entire conversation with someone in the audience. They just want to get on with their act.

I've had hundreds of conversations with people in the show. If something is fascinating or even entertaining about their story, or better yet, if they are funny, give them the floor! Turn the show over to them within reason. The audience loves those moments. The secret, though, is knowing when it's enough. Read and feel the situation and the audience. How long is long enough, and how long is too much? You must know the difference and move on with your show at the right time.

The Rolex Through The Phone

I know that you don't call yourself a technician or finger-flinger. But you do have an excellent watch steal story.

Years ago, I did a private show in Los Angeles. After the show, I did a few tricks for some of the guests. The last thing I did was steal a guy's watch off his wrist without him noticing. Of course, I meant to give it back to him. But the instant I stole his watch and put it in my pocket, his wife asked me the same question you asked me earlier: "Warren, how did you ever get into magic?"

Well, I got into telling the whole story. I forgot that I had the guy's watch in my pocket. I left the party and drove two hours back to my house. I got home at 1 am and unpacked my magic paraphernalia. When I started getting out of my show clothes, I reached into my pockets and saw that I still had this guy's watch!

I immediately recognized that it was a vintage Rolex. It was about 2 am when this happened. Lisa and I were getting up at 4:30 am to fly to South Carolina in order to spend Christmas with my family. I knew how to get in touch with the owner of the watch but I couldn't very well call him at 2 am. I also knew there was no way for me to get it to him before our 6:30 flight. So I ended up taking the watch with me to South Carolina.

When we arrived at my family's house, I called the guy and said, "Hey, it was great seeing you last night and I hope you enjoyed the evening. But I've got one more magic trick I'd like to do for you!" He laughed and clearly didn't believe me. I said, "No, I'm serious. I want to do one more magic trick for you. On the count of three, I will make your watch appear in my hand. One, two, three! Yep! I've got it right here. I made it travel through the phone."

He said, "Yeah, sure, Warren." And I said, "No, seriously. I'm looking at it right now. You have a vintage Rolex with a brown leather band. Where's your watch right now?" He said, "Well, I'm sure it's on my nightstand where I lay it every night when I go to bed." I said, "Go and check your nightstand."

Within a minute, he comes back and says, "Oh my gosh, my watch isn't there!" I said, "I know! I've got it in my hand!" I described his watch to him in detail, and he said, "Unbelievable! How in the world did you do that?" I said, "Well, I told you I wanted to do one more trick for you. We'll be in South Carolina for the holidays for about two weeks, so I'll ship it back to you."

I insured his watch for $30,000 and mailed it back to him. When I called him to ensure he got it back, he said, "I still can't believe you did that trick over the phone!"

I've stolen thousands of watches over the years, but that's my favorite watch-stealing story.

Looking Ahead

What's next for the Gibsons?

Good question. I don't know. But I'm sure God has a plan. I'm winding down my performing days. I've done over 10,000 shows in my theater and have had all the applause in the world I'll ever need. Will I still perform? Sure. Will it be a lot? Probably not. It's time to pass the baton to you guys.

God has a plan.

The author with Warren and Lisa Gibson

And The Curtain Comes Down...

"The purpose of a relationship is not to have another who might complete you, but to have another with whom you might share your completeness."

— *Neale Donald Walsch*

Hana Hou!

The Wizard of Waikiki

Over the years, magic has allowed me to provide for my family, pay my mortgage, travel and bring excitement and laughter to thousands of people. Magic has made me a passionate reader and writer. It's allowed me to meet fascinating people and make friends worldwide. I don't know where I'd be without magic.

But I'm no prodigy.

As you've seen, I am merely the product of extraordinary friends and mentors — most notably Curtis Kam. If I know anything about sleight of hand, performing and scripting magic, it's because of the thorough teaching that Curtis shared — and continues to share — with me. Frankly, I can't pick up a pack of cards or a silver half crown without hearing his lessons in my head.

But that's not the primary reason this project is dedicated to him.

Since 2010, Curtis has been my 'father' in magic. He bought me dinner and gave me rides all over Honolulu when I was a broke grad student. He coached and cheered me on as a budding school teacher and performer. When I landed my first job, Curtis performed for my middle school band program every year for seven years.

Curtis has given me invaluable legal advice, helped me through break-ups and provided insight when considering big career moves. He's called out my errors and mistakes when everyone else was being too nice. He was a groomsman at my wedding.

Every aspect of my magic, thinking, sense of humor, public speaking and artistic vision has been is influenced by him. His example of loyalty, kindness, and generosity has made me not just the magician but the man I am today.

Now that I think of it, that first paragraph needs a rewrite:

Over the years, ~~magic~~ Curtis Kam has allowed me to provide for my family, pay my mortgage, travel and bring excitement and laughter to thousands of people. ~~Magic~~ Curtis Kam has made me a passionate reader and writer. ~~It~~ He has allowed me to meet fascinating people and make friends worldwide. I don't know where I'd be without ~~magic~~ Curtis Kam.

Thank you, Curtis.

Ginóskó is for you.

Curtis Kam with Aileen and David on their wedding day

Thanks & Acknowledgments

This book would not have been possible without the help of several skilled magicians who also have years of writing and editing experience. In particular, Lance Pierce's insightful feedback, technical writing knowledge and meticulous editing elevated this project to a level of polish and clarity that I couldn't have achieved alone. In Google Docs, you can watch edits and recommendations in real time. It wouldn't be an exaggeration to say that Lance has checked each word of Ginóskó — all 80,000 of them — at least a dozen times.

Ian Rowland reviewed and edited the entire text, edited and tweaked many of the photos and did the page layout. He also guided me through the self-publishing process.

Jay Jayaraman helped refine the Introduction's meditation on Ginóskó.

Others who provided their valuable editing assistance and feedback include Kainoa Harbottle, Curtis Kam, Tyler Wilson and Pete McCabe.

The hand drawings were created by my lovely wife, Aileen Kuraya.

Ginóskó is the story of rich relationships in magic. I'm fortunate that not most but all of my dearest friends and mentors chose to offer their unique voices to this book. Thank you Curtis Kam, Ron Pyle, Kainoa Harbottle, Tom Dobrowolski, Jason Fleming, Nathan Coe Marsh, Tony Cabral, Lance Pierce, Jade, Jack Carpenter, John George, John Shryock, Chris Blackmore, Dana Daniels and Warren Gibson.

Special thanks to Derek Hughes, Eddy Wade, Doc Eason, Hidekazu Kimoto, George Wang, William Rader, Ian Kendall, Tomas Blomberg, Bryan So, Tom Stone, Stephen

Hobbs, Kent Gunn, Steve Ehlers, Peter Samelson, Brad Kerwin, Jason Alford, Steve Friedberg, Matthew Holtzman, William Wheeler, Richard Hucko, Michael Kekoa Erickson, Luiz De Castro, Jeremiah Zuo, Colin Robinson, Noel and Karen Kuraya, Russell and Susan Ishida, Derick Sebastian, Tessie Suyama-Nagata, Drew Carrizosa, Doyle Choi, Craig Ousterling, Paul Kozak, Danny Cole and Jay Alexander.

Photo Credits:

The portrait photo of Tony Cabral was taken by Andrew Morrell.

The John George portrait photo was taken by Andrea Domjan and the 'Make a Wish' photo was taken by Brett Padelford.

I'd like to thank all three of these photographers for their kind permission to include these photos.

To my Heavenly Father:

"Thou my best thought by day or by night,
Waking or sleeping, Thy presence my light."

— 6th century Irish hymn

www.ingramcontent.com/pod-product-compliance
Lightning Source LLC
Chambersburg PA
CBHW050125170426
43197CB00011B/1714